My First Year In Purgatory

The Real Life Adventures of an Inner City Teacher

A Memoir

Written and Illustrated by M. Clabeaux

Note To Reader

If you're looking for a typical "feel good" story about an inner city teacher who wins over the hearts of a bunch of tough kids, then this memoir isn't for you. If you want a neat, happy ending, with lots of grateful students hugging their dedicated teacher - the only teacher who really cared - you should look for fiction. This is not fiction and I'm not that hero-teacher.

On the other hand, if you are looking for a dark comedy interspersed with social commentary that, like life itself, doesn't come to a simple, neat conclusion then this is your book and my reality.

Everything I've written comes from memory or notes I frantically scrawled during my first year of teaching. I altered the sequence of some events and added a few anecdotes from later years. To protect privacy I changed the names of people, places and some physical descriptions. The conversations involving adults are what I remember, but not always word for word. I created a few composites of kids and incidents. I did not exaggerate.

You might wonder why I chose the word purgatory to describe how I earn a living instead of hell. As bad as teaching can get, I believe hell would be an overstatement. Hell is living or working in a literal war zone. For the most part, I only work in a figurative one.

"The Job hunt pays off."   Chateaux 2006.

1. Summer's Hunt

Home Alone

A hopeful spring has turned into a stifling summer with no job offer in sight. I refuse to spend another year substitute teaching. I've been home all day, mostly in my bedroom, job searching on the computer. No one's called and I've sent out tons of resumes. Public radio talks away in the background. The BBC is on. I think Julian Marshall is talking about Burundi. It's always Burundi. After awhile these arcane references get on my nerves. Interviews with people I have not heard of, all of them doing something important with their lives. Nobody interviews me, and it's starting to remind me that I am not doing anything with my life.

Evening falls. I turn off the radio. Alone in the kitchen, I pour a glass of cheap "camping" wine. That's what some younger girl I "dated" two summers ago called those economy size jugs I buy. Red wine stains the new butcher-block counter. The new counter stands in stark contrast to the dirty old linoleum floor and sagging fiberboard ceiling.

As I reach for the jug to pour another glass, the phone on the counter rings. I bought the phone partly because it was black. I always liked that color. It's the middle of 2000, and who would know that within a year black wouldn't just be for the counterculture anymore? Corporate America would soon be coloring everything black. I pick up the ringing phone.

Brandy is on the other end. She asks me if I want to go to the drive-in. Brandy likes drive-ins. Goths and other bohemians often like old-fashioned things, things that are dying out.

"No I gotta get up early and get back on this job hunt."

"Come on Matt, you're always busy. It's summer and you're not even working." She's starting to sound frustrated. Brandy has her own problems and needs some relief.

"Look man, I've got to stick to a schedule," I tell her. Now I'm getting frustrated, not with her, but with my life. Maybe it is with her. She just reminded me that I don't have a job. I'm going to turn thirty-one soon.

Thirty was my deadline for having my first "real job." So now I'm nearly a year behind schedule.

    At twenty-three, I don't know if Brandy understands this pressure.

    "OK. I got you," Brandy says, defeated.

    I finish my drink, watch an old movie, and go to sleep.

The Call

    I'm deep in a dream when the early 1980's "flesh" tone phone next to my bed rings. In the eighties, this beige fleshy color was all the rage. Phones, computers, anything plastic was that color. It looked like the color of prosthetic limbs. It was disturbing and an odd choice for a trendy color.

    That ringing. How can I sleep? It's seven AM. A job offer? Last time the phone rang this early it was for substitute teaching assignments. Who else but an employer, or a family member with an emergency, would call at this hour? It would not be for a couple more years that an early morning call would be a collections agent.

    I reach for the phone and try to sound awake. "Morning!" Whatever I was dreaming about slips away from memory and is replaced by the stranger's voice.

    "Umm yes. Is Matt Leebroon there?" The voice sounds authoritarian, but also has a grating nasal whine that gives it a cold impersonal air.

    "This is Matt speaking. Actually we pronounce the last name 'Lebrun.'"

    Silence, an intimidating silence. The sort of silent pause cops use to make suspects squirm.

    "I'm the supervisor of art for Rust Belt Public."

    This is the first time I hear the voice of the man who will become my unreliable anchor, a scowling-faced constant in a multi-year sea of changing faces and schools. His soon to be all-too-numerous observations and criticisms of my teaching will bring both the comfort of a familiar face, and the distress of constant nagging.

    "I can't promise anything yet, but your exam score put you near the top of my list for new hires. I've got a couple ahead of you but one of them took another job and the other doesn't seem to be around." Doesn't seem to be around? What's that supposed to mean? Why is he inexplicably AWOL? Is this a bad sign? I repress my doubts; not wanting to admit to myself that this opportunity might not be so golden. It's the one that doesn't seem to be around whose position I will fill.

"Wow. Being good at tests finally paid off. I feel like I won the lottery," I tell him. I really do feel like I won. My first real job could finally be at hand. I too may soon join the ranks of the Great American Middle Class. Me, middle class. I'm so used to being poor. If I get this job I could buy a new car, go out to eat, and spend money at clubs. Most important of all, if I met a woman at one of those clubs I could honestly tell her that I have a job.

"Don't get too excited. It looks good though. I'll get back to you," he replies.

I hang up the prosthetic-limb-colored phone feeling awake, excited and hopeful. Most people's reaction to this potentially good news would be to celebrate, maybe give Brandy a call for an afternoon rendezvous. Mine, on the other hand, is to get back to the job hunt with renewed vigor. The supervisor didn't actually make me a job offer; he only notified me that an offer is possible. That possibility alone proves to me that all those months of disciplined job hunting could actually result in more than a "thanks for your interest" letter.

I must maintain discipline. I wash my armpits and face, walk downstairs to the kitchen and make coffee. I sit down at Granddad's old wooden desk, turn on the computer, dial in, and start another day's slow web search. Despite the slow dial up, that AM phone call and caffeine inspire me to keep going. Key word "teaching." It's too late in the summer to find teaching vacancies in desirable locations, but I still look. After a full day of searching, typing, printing cover letters, resumes, and stuffing envelopes, I log employer addresses into the booklet the unemployment office sent me. Having to report to the Department of Labor is also quite motivating.

Like a lot of unemployed people, I take up exercise and make a second attempt at youth. (At that time, I thought thirty was old). Today, it's jogging. People often consider a man jogging shirtless in a public park to be a "cheese ball." I jog shirtless anyway. While pounding the track, I pass twin sisters I recognize from freshman year of college. My friend dated one of them, and I used to be jealous. Now, like me, they're not so young anymore. On the second pass, I stop and stretch while we talk. One gives me her phone number. I finish my jog. I never call.

The sun has nearly set by the time Brandy arrives at my door. Her bleached blond hair contrasts with her all black goth attire: skirt, corset, and combat boots. Mostly we stay on the couch. She wants to go hiking tomorrow, but again I feel compelled to job hunt. I give her that recycled speech about, "I can't commit right now, I'm in transition, and this has to be casual." It's a similar speech that I recently received from someone else. Brandy never comes over again.

Meet Your Supervisor

Seven AM. A week later. I hear that beige phone next to my bed ringing. "Do you still want the job?"

A few days after I accept, there is an early morning orientation for the new art teachers. We meet in a basement room at a public school. Eight of us wait at large cafeteria-type tables for the meeting to begin. I'm the only male other than the supervisor. He's tall, with the stout build of a chain restaurant manager, dark mustache, meticulously styled hair, and a frown that seems to be carved into his face.

My attention is drawn immediately to one of the women. Sabrina is around my age and very pretty. Her lips are thick and full. They look like implants. She wears Doc Marten boots, punky black clothes and a nose ring. She tells me she's a vegan, so lip implants don't seem likely.

Another has a drastically pockmarked face and a "feathered" hairstyle popular among rock and roller kids in the eighties; we called them "heads." Next to her is a brunette with the features of a German peasant woman, maybe in her forties, with frumpy yet bohemian hair and dress. That's Clara. I recognize her from the arts scene.

The supervisor stands. Clears his throat. The meeting starts. He's the one who hires, fires and places all art teachers in the Rust Belt Public School System. The supervisor informs us what schools he assigned us to. He turns to Clara. "You're going to Fantasy Careers High. It's in the inner city. The kids can be a little tough. The principal there did not want the last art teacher to return. He said she couldn't control the kids. You'll pick up where the last teacher left off. They have security guards, but you'll still need to lay down the law yourself." He changes his ominous tone for one of reassurance. "Really the school has an undeservedly bad reputation. You should be able to handle it."

"I'm sure I'll be fine; I taught art along the Mexican border," Clara says as evidence of her street cred.

As she says this I think, "famous last words." I subbed at that school for most of last year. Those kids can be pretty vicious. They even threw books at me once. Another time a student, while threatening to beat me up, said, "If I bust you in your mouth, there would be blood all over." When I escorted a kid to the office, his classmates sang, "We shall overcome." A brawl erupted one day and the hallways filled with kids chanting, "Attica!

8

Attica!" Study halls were nothing but rowdy social halls, as was the in-school suspension room. Attempts at discipline focused on tardiness and preventing boys from wearing hats, the easy and obvious infractions. Most substitute teachers couldn't handle Fantasy Careers, but somehow I did. I was called in to sub every day. By the end of the school year, the principal told me he wanted me back as a full-time teacher. I wouldn't have minded; at least I'd know what I was getting into, unlike now.

Did this supervisor even look at my resume? Doesn't he know that I worked there? Shouldn't I be the one placed at Fantasy? That would make more sense than placing someone who's not familiar with the situation. I raise my hand to speak, but quickly put it down. He doesn't seem like the type who likes suggestions. I better keep quiet. Besides, maybe this supervisor put me somewhere better.

"Now, you two," he says to me and the pockmarked lady, "are going into very tough situations. You'll need to be planned, directed and strict. Speak and act sternly. If the students won't listen, make a startling sound." He slams his open palm on the table. "You've got to be firm with these kids." I guess he didn't put me somewhere better.

The supervisor spends the rest of the meeting going over the state and city standards for the arts. He pulls out a "How to draw a rabbit" handout, the type that shows you how to draw step by step, by starting with a circle then adding an oval and so on. I think that's a good method and plan to use that technique. "Can you believe I actually found this on some art teacher's desk?" the Supervisor says in that mildly pissed-off nasal whine. He continues, "Everything turning out the same is not art! Children need a chance to be creative, to express ideas and moods." Looks like I won't be teaching that rabbit after all.

As we leave the meeting, packets in hand, I try to digest the supervisor's words: Don't show the kids how to draw, be mean to them, and insist they create something original. The orientation left me completely disoriented.

Meet Your Principal

School opens in less than a week, and the supervisor just gave me the OK to meet the principal and see my classroom. According to my map, my assigned school, Grand Plans Middle and Elementary, is in the heart of what locals used to call the Fruit Belt. At least that's what Grandma called that part of town. The streets there are largely named after fruits: Peach, Pear, Plum. A lot of neighborhoods in Rust Belt have thematic street names.

In my neighborhood, the theme is old-fashioned ladies' names: Gladys, Ethel, Martha. The Fruit Belt is largely owned by absentee landlords and populated by lower income African Americans. My neighborhood is owner occupied, largely black but modestly mixed. The Fruit Belt however is exclusive to its clientele.

An eight-foot fence surrounds the parking lot adjacent to the school. A newly erected sign clashes with the 1940's era gray and beige school building. The sign reads "Grand Plans Middle: planning for the success of your children." The lot across the street is unfenced. It looks like the locals park their cars there. A guy in his mid twenties washes his shiny black Ford. The windows are tinted and the car speakers blare loud gangsta rap. Profanity spews into the air, something like, "F*ck the bitch that...." A local kid, one of my future students, watches him admiringly. "What's up?" I say to the man as I pass by. We exchange nods. I was on a rap kick in my early twenties, so the music feels familiar. Later on in my teaching career, I will temporarily join the ranks of those who hate rap.

I walk up the school steps, pull the door handle, but the door is locked. I ring the buzzer. "May I help you?" asks a cold voice from the intercom above.

"I'm the new art teacher," I say, craning my neck to the intercom. Another buzz and the heavy green metal door gives way. My gut churns. I feel like I'm entering prison, unsure if I'm warden or inmate.

I navigate the dim beige corridors searching for the main office. Sparse natural light filters in from an occasional open classroom. There may as well be a thick blanket of fog hovering just above the floor. An indifferent secretary ushers me to the principal's door. The principal and I shake hands. This will be the only time she ever smiles at me. "I'm Ms. Henderson." She's a tall, thin African American woman with short-cropped hair. Short hair that later on I will realize is the result of chemo treatments. Draped over her shoulders is a multicolored African style scarf. The walls have African themed prints such as giraffes and women with baskets on their heads.

We sit. Ms. Henderson's looking down her nose at me, furrowing her eyebrows, sizing me up, while she monologues about "the children" and "the community" -words to which she gives special emphasis. "We serve a diverse population. I hope you can handle the children here. You need to engage them, meet their needs and the needs of the community." She stops speaking, and looks at me with her head slightly upturned and to the side, as if forced to look at something repulsive. Suddenly, I feel self-conscious and oafish.

10

"Oh yes. I thrive on diversity." I start to doubt myself, and am unable to make solid eye contact.

Her face lights up as she describes the other art teacher. "She does wonderful things with the children." There it is, that word, "children," emphasized that way again. It's as if Ms. Henderson thinks she herself is the only one *truly* concerned about them, and needs to protect the kids from this sketchy new teacher. "I asked her to come fulltime." Her happy expression changes and her voice trails off, "but she didn't want to have the older kids."

That's who I will be teaching, the students in grades five through eight. This can't be a good sign.

Then Henderson's voice regains vigor, "Last year we had this other temporary art teacher. The kids loved him," her voice trails again, "but I guess he wasn't certified so he couldn't come back."

Great, I think to myself sarcastically. She basically just said that she wishes someone else were teaching art here instead of me.

Ms. Henderson looks at me skeptically and concludes, "Just make sure you make art fun." OK, so now I have a supervisor telling me to be stern and strict, and a principal telling me to make it fun.

As I walk the dimly lit first floor corridor leading to my basement room, a tall amply bosomed middle-aged teacher greets me with a large warm smile. "It's so good to have another man in the building. We don't have enough!" After making some small talk, she loses her smile and warns, "Do not send kids to the office. You will get the blame. She yells at teachers right in front of students."

At the foot of the basement stairs, to my left, is the instrumental music room. Inside the room there's a short chubby man, sporting a mullet. He's arranging chairs. We greet each other.

"So you're the new art teacher? We've gone through like five in the past two years. None of them could handle it. It'd be nice to have someone who lasted until summer."

"Five?"

"The last one was out most of the year. There was a string of long-term subs. They'd last a few weeks then burn out. Keep your lessons simple. Last year's teacher had these elaborate art displays and projects, but it didn't help. The kids were running wild."

"So what should I do if kids run wild on me?"

"Whatever you do, don't send them to the office." That's twice today.

"I heard she yells at teachers in front of kids?"

"Yeah, I've seen her do it."

11

See Your New Room

My art room waits for me at the opposite end of the hallway. I pass large green lockers and enter the room through a dark green steel door. The door's window is a thin rectangular slit with metal mesh, from which passersby will be able to peer in and witness the mayhem and shouting matches to ensue.

Boxes overstuffed with yarn, felt and other odds and ends are piled everywhere, last year's papier-mâché projects are strewn about. A crudely modeled and painted figure holds what looks like a basketball. It's a nice looking project, the type of art that kids would love to make. So why was this last teacher mentally crushed?

Stacks of magazines, which will briefly serve as an adolescent and prepubescent hunting ground for nudes, are stacked high and precariously on the counter tops. Wooden surfaces are gouged and scratched with names, and the occasional profanity. The cabinets are jammed full of things. I'm not sure what they are.

The teacher's desk is large, sturdy and made of oak, but it too is damaged. It bares insults, like "fag," scratched into the wood or written in marker. On the side where people would come and talk to their teacher, is a violently smashed in area, like someone kicked it. There's a large spider-web crack in one of the basement windows to the left of the desk. A small student desk, with a chair that is pulled out from it and turned in the wrong direction, faces the cracked window, creating the appearance of a stepladder. As if someone tried to escape the room and smash their way out. There does not seem to be any safe area for a teacher in this room. Nearly every possible sanctum shows signs of attack by rebel student forces.

Strike

There isn't much time left before students return to this defiled room. I arrive early every morning, attempting to create order out of the chaos. While I sweat, pushing, pulling, and lifting boxes, piles of papers and damaged art supplies into some sort of useable arrangement, word comes around that we will go on strike. Today will be my last chance to work in this room. If I go in tomorrow I cross the picket line. A memo in my teachers' mailbox informs me that the strike is illegal. Of course, that makes me nervous. Am I going to jail? I never heard of teachers being locked up, but I'm the worrying type.

We teachers meet at seven fifty AM the next morning, the time we would normally show up for work. It might be fall but it still feels like summer. I leave my jacket in the trunk. A matronly teacher hands me a sandwich board placard which reads, "Smaller Class Size." Many of the teachers look matronly. They look like my image of teachers. The women wear pins shaped like apples with the proverbial worm eating its way out. Men wear ties with embroidered images of pencils or plus signs. They're mostly older than me, and seem a little dim. Already I'm beginning to feel like I don't fit in. Some of them remind me of teachers I had when I was a kid, ones I felt misunderstood by. Conformists who knew a little, but who felt threatened by anyone who knew a little more.

A large old beat-up American car with two women in it and some kids, who cannot go to school now because of the strike, cruises slowly by. The ladies look at me like wolves sizing up their prey. The passenger says loudly enough that I can hear, "If you're a teacher then I don't know!" What she means by this I don't know, but it adds to my growing feeling that I don't belong here.

We march in circles around the building. A big, gregarious Latino Spanish teacher spots my sign. "Smaller class size. I like that one!" he laughs. Then heartily adds, "Beh'leave me. Ju are goin' to want as few of dem as ju can have." I wonder if he ever got yelled at in front of his students?

As the day progresses, I ask everyone I can for advice on teaching. How should I conduct a lesson and run that all-important first day? The other art teacher and I leave the picket line for a bit. She's wearing a denim outfit and has long hair tied in a ponytail. We step up to the trunk of my car. I push my jacket aside and pull out the handouts that I labored over by night. "Here's a lesson on positive and negative space." She nods her head in approval, looking at my illustration of geometric shapes.

"That's a good one you drew; it's simple. They'll like it." She looks away from my drawing and takes on a stance, like she's about to rap. "These kids love to make things with their names, like 'Shaniqua is the bomb!'" she says, gesturing downward and doing a small dance step.

Back in the picket line, the band teacher with the mullet concurs with what the other art teacher said. Offering his own advice, he says, "The kids here can write their names with bubble letters. They like to do that."

A few days later, the strike is over. The students are coming tomorrow. At home, I sift through my plans and handouts and wonder if they will even work. I draw up seating charts based on the class lists I've

13

just received. For some reason, these weren't available earlier. I try to adhere to a "boy/girl" pattern, as my supervisor told us to do. I've got eight tables to work with. The last art teacher only sat kids at six. "He used the other two for elaborate displays. Which didn't seem to help any," to quote the band teacher. With more room for seating, maybe the students will be less likely to fight. After the seating charts are done, I write a script of what I will do and say, and when I will say it. Then I revise my lesson plans. The lesson plans are more to show to administrators than to help me teach. Next to me are piles of folders with handouts explaining the rules and what is expected. I also have three by five cards that students are to fill out. As I obsessively organize and reorganize, I become mentally scattered and nervous. The "fight or flight" response is setting in, a response that will set in many times throughout the years to come, but it's a response I know won't help. To quell it, I down a beer or two or three, set the alarm for six AM and sleep the restless sleep of slow-burning anxiety.

2. Show Time

The Buses Are Coming

That alarm rings. This is it.

After signing in at the office, I walk down to my basement world. En route, I pass the supply room. The door's open, someone's inside.

"Hello. Excuse me," I say. The supply room lady slowly makes her way to the door. She's a large woman with thick coke-bottle glasses. I ask, "May I see what you have in there? I really need some new supplies for the children." Notice I used the phrase "the children." I'm learning to put things into "education-speak."

She's unmoved. Her breathing is labored. "Write down exactly what you need, the supply number, put the note in my mailbox, and I'll see if we have any." The supply lady informs me that only she's allowed into that room. The problem with that is I don't know the supply numbers, and I'm not entirely sure what I'll need this year. I just want to browse and see what I can use.

Luckily, the art room seems well enough stocked and I've got it organized – compared to before. I should be able to hold out until I can decipher these numeric codes.

Back in my room, I make do with the battle-scarred supplies. I step back and survey the arrangement. How's the Feng Shui? Not quite right. Better put the handouts here, color pencils there, move this table a little to the left. This table a little . . .

Ms. Henderson's voice blares over the PA, interrupting my obsessive-compulsive behavior. "Teachers, it's seven-fifty A.M. Report to your morning posts." My duty is monitoring the basement hallway adjacent to the cafeteria and telling boys to remove their hats. "The buses are coming. The buses are coming." Her announcement has an ominous ring. Kids begin to file past me.

"Please take off your hat. You need to remove your hat. Young man . . ." Already I am expending valuable energy enforcing the "No hats on boys" policy, energy I will need to get through this day.

15

"How come the girls don't have to take off their hats?!" a boy challenges, as girls brazenly strut by, wearing the same hip-hop style caps as the boys. The young man heads up stairs, taking his hat only halfway off.

I turn to the gym teacher sharing hall duty with me this morning. He's a gray-haired man with a hollow voice. "Why do only boys have to remove their hats?" I ask.

"I guess I'm old fashioned but it shows respect. Hey! Remove your hat," he volunteers ineffectively. It's as if this gym teacher doesn't notice that the girls are wearing Chicago Bulls caps, and not their Sunday best. He's living in a by-gone era. Not that it matters. This is my first real job. I'm not going to make waves about an unjust hat policy.

The next big pre-show energy drain is getting kids to stand for the pledge.

"I bought those..." Chateaux 2006.

Let the Games Begin

"It's show time," I think as I do some relaxing breathing exercises and grip my plan book while waiting for the first class to be dropped off at my room. A scowling Ms. Bentley brings down a small troop of fifth graders. She's an African American teacher in her late twenties. Her stern demeanor works to her advantage. The students seem scared into submission. By contrast, I smile and greet the kids warmly, as I was taught to do.

After she departs, some of their fear evaporates. I line the fifth graders up along the wall, and call them to their assigned seats and tables. Kids squirm in line, try to hide, or dart out the room. One of them opens a cabinet door and uses it as a hiding place. Some grunt in protest at having to sit next to a member of the opposite sex. Others lie about their names. Low-grade defiance and antics slow down the process, but despite grunts and giggles my lesson plan is still working.

Once they're seated, I take up a position at the front of the room and begin to address the class, but half of them have their backs to me. It's because of these cafeteria-style tables. "Turn your chairs around and face the teacher." Many resist turning. Why aren't there desks in here, like we had when I was a student, all chairs pointed to the chalkboard? I guess the powers-that-be believe that art class is the time for children to learn "group socialization," but I'm finding it hard to get them all to look in the same direction. It feels like I just lost a little more control.

I get these fifth graders to fill out three-by-five cards, contact information on one side of the card, and a what-do-you-want-to-do-this-year type of thing on the other. Once they finish writing, I encourage them to make some drawings. Suspicious remarks are made, "Don't let him know your phone number." Then lots of problems I hadn't anticipated: "How do you spell my street name?" "I don't know my Mom's last name." "Our phone is disconnected."

The cards are done. Most of the kids drew a picture. We read the rules out loud. Now what? My script calls for "art room orientation." What exactly did I have in mind when I wrote that? For the first time this morning, I'm fumbling. I gesture to a print hanging on the wall and begin to explain, "I made this one when…" I'm interrupted.

"He didn't make that!" a freckle faced boy shouts.

The first class is nearly over. I'm relatively unscathed. "Time to line up," I say. The long twisting, shifting, squirming line of fifth grade bodies resembles a giant snake. Its head poking out the door and its body writhing along the sink, cupboards and all the way to my desk at the back of the room. Ms. Bentley is a couple of minutes late, so the kids are getting restless. Some try to scoot out ahead. Others shove from behind.

As the day goes on, the defiance and testing grows. Another, even rowdier class is dropped off at my door by their bearded teacher, Mr. Tussle. They're sixth graders. Two of his students draw my attention as being potential trouble - Baxter and Jordan. Baxter is chubby, four-foot something with a dark complexion. Jordan is lighter, with curly hair and a gravelly voice. Today they are content to settle for making a few fart sounds and only roll their eyes when I call them on it. Later on in the year, Baxter and Jordan will go berserk.

Next comes an eighth grade class. While not cooperative, they're relatable. The sight of a kid with dreadlocks reminds me of my own youth. Over the next few months, he and I will become friends of sorts; and really I think his popularity in this group will make this my only halfway decent eighth grade class of the year.

After that class leaves, Ms. Rosebloom's eighth grade homeroom arrives. Ms. Rosebloom is a short, very serious, very into her career, math teacher. Her kids are exceptionally big, or at least they seem that way. One, named Huey, is taller than I am. Right now he doesn't seem so bad. He turns out to be, in terms of size and persistence, literally the biggest bully I'll meet this year, bullying me and the kids, and swearing at us all with abandon.

I nickname this student Huey for a reason. Because, he looks strikingly like "Baby Huey," a cartoon character from my childhood, a giant klutzy curly haired anthropomorphic duckling. Of course, I never call him that to his face.

Years later, I'll drive by Huey at a bus stop on my way to another crap school. My middle finger will creep up. My hand will reach for the horn. Then I'll chicken out.

The seeds of Huey's hostility are planted today. He is one of those kids who has some talent in art but decides that his art teacher, me, sucks so much that after he achieves the minimum requirements for whatever project we're working on, it's time to act like an asshole. Yeah, I know. You probably blame me for this. If only I was a better teacher I could "meet his needs." I understand. Believe me, when I finally have a few classes running smoothly, I'll momentarily forget how bad it gets. I'll see flailing teachers struggle with miserable classes, and smugly shake my head, "If only they had what it takes."

As these oversized kids sit at these oversized lunchroom style tables, they do what I think they would do. They start talking as they would if they were at lunch. I reclaim their attention here and there, but really they are just here to hang out. They're only a little shorter than the teenagers, and

18

occasional twenty/twenty-one year olds, at Fantasy Careers High where I subbed last year. Ignored by the class, I'm feeling like a sub again.

Huey asks me "What are we going to do this year?" Really, I don't exactly know; but I give him what I think sounds like a good answer, "Well, I'm glad you asked that. We are going to learn how to create depth in art, use different line quality to express mood in our work, and draw influence from other cultures." As I am saying this, I can see a look of disapproval cross his face. This answer might have been good for my supervisor, but not for Huey.

Lesson learned, but I already lost the class. "Come on guys, how's those cards coming?" It's impossible to quiet the group down. I am reduced to frenetically visiting each table, trying to coax them along. Largely I'm just ignored by these eighth graders who, by my standards, are hitting adolescence a little too early and acting like I'm interrupting their social hour.

Someone is shouting at someone. They might fight. A girl is dancing in the aisle. A hand slaps at her rear. Kids are getting up without permission and doing whatever they want. I'm only nominally in charge. For the first time today, I raise my voice. No effect. I raise it louder. I'm yelling. Blood rushes to my head. My heart pumps faster. My shouting at them just pours gasoline on the fire, but I believe that's what my supervisor wants –"make a startling sound."

In the chaos, they've gotten hold of the color pencils. Since the class is so off task now, and we can't read over the rules, or talk about anything; I decide that if letting them take the color pencils keeps them busy, go with it. This is a mistake. Those color pencils that I went out and bought with my own money are being "pencil popped." That's what the kids call it. Huey sits facing another boy, Buster. Huey holds a pencil stretched out across both hands. Buster takes another pencil and keeps banging it across the outstretched one until the pencil breaks. The next step in this process is to throw bits of the pencil at other kids in the room. The room is filled with Hueys and Busters breaking and throwing my pencils.

"Hey, what are you doing?"

"What man?! We're pencil popping!" a pencil popping kid shouts at me with indignant rage. They don't stop no matter what I say. I try to take the pencils. They get angrier. One of the boys says, "That's my pencil!" It isn't, but he says it anyway.

Another one of them tells me, "Last year was great, man. Kids were fighting every day in here."

"Well that's not going to happen this year." I say sternly and resolutely.

After they leave, I think that's how I will make it through this year: with a survival mentality. A bitter determination rises in me: "*This is my room. I will not be driven out of it.*" I pace up and down the room trying to emotionally reclaim it and recover from this deep sense of impotence that last group left me with. I've got two more groups to go, but already I feel like a chameleon with its tail cut off. I feel like I've been wounded and the sharks can smell the blood.

Lady's Lunch

During my lunch break, there are only women in the teacher's lounge. Four of them create the main clique. All late middle age. Two white. Two black. "Pookie," as she likes to be called, is a heavyset African American woman with what look like false teeth. She warns me: "Honey, any time a man comes to this lunch they can't take it because we are a bunch of…." I forgot what she really says next, but what she meant was "lonely middle-aged horny women who are going to sexually harass you."

"I'm a good sport," I say.

Pookie gets up and sits on my lap. Everyone laughs. I laugh too. Laura has dyed fiery red hair, and wears tight fitting clothes. She tells me about her late night adventures. Her son is away at college. She has a pool, and likes to swim in the nude. I can come over. Mrs. K is married, but she isn't getting along with her husband. She misses her son. He's in his twenties. I think these women think I'm in my twenties.

"How old are you?" Laura asks. They all look at me.

"I don't want to say."

"There's nothing wrong with being young," she tells me. Mabel, the other black lady, just chuckles at it all.

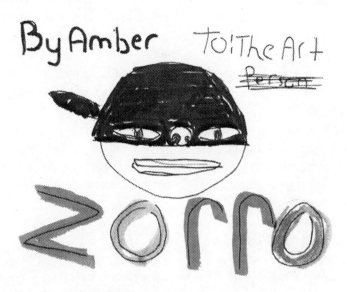

Inspiration from a Kid's Art

My lunch break is over. Is it time to ride out another storm of angry kids?

The stoic mantra "this is my room" won't be enough to get me through this year. I need to feel like I'm doing some good here. Another class comes. An aide accompanies them. Mr. Beanbag. He seems like a friendly character. With big smiles, he waves goodbye and leaves me alone with the kids.

There's a skinny quiet girl named Amber. She turns out to be a very creative artist and an interesting kid. She's a bright spot in a troubling year. Her hair is braided and her complexion is light, like one of her parents is white and one black.

Amber comes up and hands me a piece of paper. It's a simple child's drawing, rendered in strong marker lines and colors. At the top it says "By Amber" in bold black. Across from her name she wrote "To: the art person," but scribbled out "person," leaving just "the art." Under that is a large circle forming a face with a combination bandana and eye mask drawn in the same confident black marker as her name. The almond eyes, pig nose, and unsmiling lips form a determined look. Below this stoic portrait, in large multicolored marker she wrote "Zorro."

Flashbacks of black and white Zorro reruns play through my head. I must have been six the last time I saw one.

"Is this a gift for me?"

"Yes," she says. As the class leaves I sit recuperating and look at the picture. Why did she cross out the word "person" and call me just "the art?" I guess her ten-year-old brain decided the "art person" didn't sound quite right, and not sure what to call me settled for "the art." It endears her to me; thinking of the mental debate she had as to what to call me, and how she, like me, is wrought with internal debates. She finalizes her decisions and makes some bold decisive moves. The drawing is strong.

Why did she give me a masked hero? It's a message, a sign of hope. It's telling me to keep up the fight. It's a way for her to say, "I'm on your side. You're helping out kids like me. You're a hero." Or maybe, "You need a hero." I tape it up on the cabinet behind my desk, and look at it for inspiration, knowing "someone has my back."

Vice Principal Mr. First Visits

I anxiously pace the room waiting for my next class. Vice Principal Mr. First walks in. "How's it going?" he asks, making piercing eye contact.

"It was going pretty well up until Ms. Rosebloom's eighth graders came. They treated me like a sub."

"They what?" he says with a sharp expression and tone, appearing to suppress real anger.

It feels like his sharp cut is aimed at me as much as at them. Sensing this was not the right thing to say, I try to use education speak. I say, "It seemed like I had some trouble *engaging* them."

His look changes and he seems sympathetic. "You got a tough group there. Call their parents."

"Really, I can call their parents?"

"Yep, they act out, call their homes." I never heard of doing this in student teaching or anywhere. The thought of calling homes and complaining about the children living there is not very appealing.

He leaves the room in time for me to face down my last group of the day. They are only in sixth grade but it's like they've been empowered by that eighth grade class. Empowered to act out and disrupt.

Bus Duty

After my first day is done, but before bus duty, I sift through note cards the students filled out earlier, trying to locate useful phone numbers and relevant ideas. In response to my "What would you like to do or make in art" question, I read things like: "I have no idea." One kid wrote, "I do not like to draw balloons or tropical fish." Smugly, I think how much better my lessons will be than these other art teachers who stoop to tropical fish and balloons.

On my way to bus duty, I stop by an English teacher's room. Like the supply room lady, he wears thick coke bottle glasses, making his eyes look disproportionately large and alert. "This was a tough first day," I tell him, "one group started breaking all my pencils."

"What I say to them is, 'Sure we all pencil popped when we were kids....'" As he's saying this I think, "We all pencil popped? I don't remember pencil popping, never even heard of it until today." I don't question him. It's time for dismissal.

I descend the stairs and exit the large metal doors, followed by a horde of kids leaving for the day. Their feet pound like a marauding army on my heels.

Fresh air. Green trees are splashed with brown and gold. Summer recedes. Fall advances. I see the vice principal again and take up a position near him. Those marauders, some wearing Oakland Raiders caps and jackets, who saw me earlier today look and point at me, but standing with the vice principal gives me immunity from verbal assaults.

"What did you do before this?" I ask.

"I used to farm and teach, but then I had to give up the farming." He breaks to shout at a kid. "This is a hard way to earn a living."

"Eh, every way to earn a living is hard."

"Not like this."

At this time, I don't realize just how much he really means that last remark. I will later.

3. First Casualty and Life after Work

After a few weeks at Grand Plans, I've survived children pounding their fists in unison on the tables, chanting, "New art teacher! New art teacher!" I've watched girls rise from their seats in the middle of class to practice "drill routines" - a rhythmic stomping and clapping. And I've listened to students shouting, "Jerry! Jerry!" like we were on the set of the Jerry Springer show. The first time I heard "Jerry! Jerry!" I realized a fight was erupting. After preventing the brawl by banishing the potential combatants to timeout, the chants for "New art teacher" broke out. With steel in my voice I told the class: "It's not going to be like last year. This time there *isn't* going to be a new art teacher."

Repressed Memories

I've kept the ceaseless onslaughts in check, in large part by following Vice Principal First's advice: call the homes. Teaching each class has been like trying to steer a ship through a stormy sea. White knuckled, I cling fast to the wheel, desperately trying to ride waves of disruption and keep the sails aloft through pounding rains of disrespect; trying to bring my entire mutinous crew to calm waters.

The student behaviors put me in a state of semi-shock and disbelief. I block out the bad memories. Stress causes people to become forgetful. Crime victims often forget the details of their trauma. When the time comes to make the calls, I can't remember the day's encounters.

To help me recall, I bought a notebook and christened it my "battle notes." I scrawl on its pages during the heat of the moment. My handwriting is frantic, fearful, hurried and often illegible. During break time, or at home, I try to decipher my notes. Next, I call the parents or guardians. Usually I can only recall an isolated fragment in time. The parent or guardian gets only the tip of the iceberg. And that's all anyone who reads this memoir will get, just the tip of the iceberg. As bad as this year may seem, in reality it's much worse.

Illustration of a student's copy of the rules.

Spanish Teacher

Not all my colleagues manage to keep the flood waters at bay. Over these same first few weeks of school, rumors went around that the big, gregarious Latino Spanish teacher was getting "run down" by students. That's what kids, and some adults, call it when students are taking over the classroom. Other rumors had it that the principal was giving him a hard time for being too harsh with the kids. Something about him "grabbing" them. "Grabbing" a student might not seem like a big deal if you grew up like many of us did, but I will find out that around these parts, the kids know they can get a teacher fired over it. Alternatively, you may be thinking, "How could anyone grab a child?" If you are, you should know how it can get in here, when kids are flying around the room and you feel yourself sinking into a shark-filled sea of student chaos.

I wasn't taking these rumors too seriously until, at the end of a long day, he stopped by my room for the last time. The Spanish teacher seemed like he was acting a little funny, but I was so caught up with my own troubles I didn't see his distress immediately. In fact, I just assumed I was the only one these students *wouldn't* listen to. He was flicking through architectural magazines left behind by the other art teacher. Magazines left for me in a great heap of random publications, which I organized into categories. Art, architecture, National Geographic, pop culture, etc.

"Hey Matt, can I take some of these home? I'm working on my house."

"Aw come on man, I might need them. I got to keep the kids busy every second or they'll eat me up."

"Ha! These kids won't appreciate this stuff."

"Yeah. I don't know."

He left looking lonely and confused. He took my hording of these magazines pretty hard, I thought at the time. I noticed he wasn't in the next day or the next. He was the first teacher to disappear that year. It took a while until anyone gave me clues as to what might have happened to him, something about the principal wanting him out. I'd learn that when teachers disappear, no one seems to know anything. It's like a wall of silence.

After bus duty, I begin to form an after-school routine: sort the day's wreckage, re-order supplies, work on lesson plans, hit the gym to let off steam, check email for date ad stuff, then "down-time" - put in a movie, (more "Dune" tonight. It seems like the author based a lot of his sci-fi on the Middle East and Islam.) During the video, I begin drinking a little. Sleep restlessly. Wake at two AM in a panic. Drink more. Sleep again. Drive in to work with knots in my stomach.

On weekends, go to coffee houses, bars, or see if I can find art openings.

Gray

Since I've found the section in the paper that lists art openings, I seem to be able to find one almost every weekend. Here's one: "Paintings and pottery from Chicago-based artist, at Le Gray Gallery." Should I go to this, or happy hour? Doesn't sound that great, but I should stick to my plan of getting involved in the arts. Maybe attending these openings will help me figure out how I'm going to get out of this job. Maybe I'll see someone I know. An art prof I had once said, "People may go to galleries to see art, but they go to openings to see people." This seems pretty true. I know where Le Gray is well enough. It's at my old undergrad campus.

Walking in, I survey the crowd. Mostly older than me. The youngsters are really young, teen kids escorted by their parents. I spot the curator. She and I were in "Child Book Illustration" together. She stayed focused on art and now her career is here, running a gallery. It looks like heaven compared to my purgatory as a teacher. She's got a snobbish look about her. Dyed black hair and a black gown. If she recognizes me, she pretends not to.

I head over to the snacks and drinks. One good thing about this, over happy hour, is the fact that there is free wine as well as free food. The art openings attended by a younger crowd seem to charge for alcohol, but not these gray-haired functions. I pour one glass, stand back, watch the crowd, drink it, then pour another. I'm buzzed and feeling isolated. I walk around a little and look at the art; then head back to the table. Finally, someone else I know. Maybe I'll have someone to talk to.

She's an older single art teacher who works in a wealthy suburb. She looks "ex-hippie" with her long graying hair. I subbed for her last year. At the time, I felt a little jealous of her, and thought the lessons she was having me teach were a waste. One was "Make an Egyptian style picture of yourself doing something you want to do in the future." When one of her students asked me how to draw something I asked her "Didn't your art teacher show you how to use guidelines?" Then I acted shocked when the answer was "No." Pretty petty of me, looking back on it. Now I realize that if it keeps them busy, it's a good lesson. Half of the students don't give a crap about guidelines and just expect fun. I'm just happy to see a familiar face, and one that's also alone like I am. Only she's older than me. Now, instead of feeling so out of place, I feel solidarity with someone here.

"Hey good to see you. I subbed for you remember?"

"Oh yeah! What are you up to?"

"I'm a teacher now."

"Great. Congratulations. How's that going?"

"To be honest . . ." I fill her in on some of my horror stories.

She looks at me sympathetically, but tells me that there's a trade off between the lamented disorder of the inner city and the seeming orderliness of the wealthy burbs. She lowers her voice and looks around conspiratorially. "At my school the kids have a lot of power. They think they're better than the teachers because their parents are rich. I overheard some students sitting around plotting how they were going to get rid of a new math teacher they didn't like, making up nasty stories to tell their parents. Then their parents started complaining to the principal. The teacher got fired."

After she leaves, I have a few more free drinks and drive home.

Back home, I turn on the computer. No one new has answered my date ad. I drink some more, and settle for watching more Dune. Something about "Fremens" living on a desert planet, trying to drive out the foreign invaders. I stumble up to bed.

4. First Showdown

Creative Thinking

My weekend reprieve is over. Ms. Wispy's sixth grade group is here. Ms. Wispy is a thin chain-smoking teacher, with short hair, a raspy voice and a husband who doesn't like her serving leftovers.

It's still early in the year, and I'm trying to teach a lesson on "creative thinking." It's pretty elaborate. I put a lot of time into it, making a handout with directions and an illustration. By now I've learned I cannot count on having the chance to explain things. I naively thought the lesson was one kids would like.

The illustration I drew at the top of the handout shows a scene with animals and plants with parts that don't belong, like a duck with a smiling human head wearing a hat, a flower with feet and a face, and some other crazy but cute stuff. The directions explain: "Creativity involves combining things in new ways. Try it!"

By now they know their assigned seats, but the game of switching chairs, and arguments over who sits where starts again.

"Creativity is basically combining things you've already seen in new ways," I announce showing the handout like some sort of talisman.

For an instant it grabs their attention.

Then the conversations and jokes begin. I am losing the crowd fast. I try to draw for them on the board. At this point I'm not skilled at on the spot, under pressure drawing. For a moment I regain their attention, but I'm trying to show them how to sketch, so the chalkboard renderings have a very rough look. Cries of "Ha, he can't draw!" can be heard. I start to protest, "Well *I* drew this handout . . ."

I realize that I must try not to react. I forge ahead with the lesson, and hope that choosing helpers to get out the supplies will get the class working. I pick only children that are cooperative. Resentment swells among the bullies. Bullies are used to being kept busy by teachers. That's been the norm since I was a kid. Better to reward a "troublemaker" (sorry for not being PC) than have him make more trouble. Without being fully conscious of it, I'm breaking the unspoken contract between the authority figure and the squeaky wheel. "How dare this art teacher not call on us!" they must be thinking. Most teachers learn to play the game of greasing the wheel. Successful teachers learn to play a game of divide and conquer, holding out rewards to some disruptors, while "timeouting" others. For the moment, I'm not one of those teachers. Now, Amber's Zorro drawing, which is taped up behind me, is whispering in my ear that justice will prevail, telling me to reward only the truly deserving. My chosen helpers attempt to distribute handouts and drawing paper. The disruptive and disenfranchised, secretly seething with jealousy, grab at them as they pass, attempting to pull paper from their hands. I jump to the rescue and join the push to get out the supplies. After these initial disruptions all the students now have a copy of my illustrated handout, and a piece of drawing paper.

The kids look at the illustration up close with genuine curiosity. The class seems content to have paper, drawing supplies, and an interesting picture to look at. For a moment the room is quiet. But that moment doesn't last long, because most students don't know what to do next. Few heard my directions, and the same kids who prevented me from teaching orally are now preventing the others from reading the instructions.

If I harbor any thoughts that children are "naturally" open minded and creative it starts dying now. Over the next six years of teaching my artwork will generally be liked by kids. They will often steal it.

But today, a girl rejects my art. She looks at the handout, crinkles her nose, and says, "This is weird." She says it with scorn in her voice and disgust on her little face. It was like some twisted art teacher was handing out satanic drawings to a pristine church-going little angel.

I speed along to each table. "Try it out, just draw something you already know how to draw, and combine it with something else you already know how to make, to make something new!" I'm trying to be friendly and encouraging. "Come on Davantah, let's see some cool drawing on this page," I say to this kid in baggy clothes with cornrow hair.

He slouches way back in his little seat, raises his hand parallel with his face and shakes it at me hip hop style, while he says "Naw, I ain't feelin ya. I ain't feelin ya," and resumes pencil popping with another kid at the table. Later I find out he's been angry at me for a while because I was calling him Davantah, instead of the way he pronounces it "Davantay."

I look around the room and see kids tracing the "duck man" instead of trying to draw anything original. Edges of my handout are being torn for spitballs, kids are laughing or angry, and the volume level is turning louder and louder. Eventually I learn that some of the most "successful" art

29

teachers in the city are those that give lessons showing exactly what to make and everything comes out roughly the same, just what I was taught not to do.

It's becoming harder and harder for those who are trying to try; so I use a stern voice and say, "OK. I want to see everybody with their knees under their desks, chairs pulled up, and working."

Then Cody, a spiky-haired white kid stands up. He takes on a stance from professional wrestling, crosses his arms down and in front of him, and says, "Mr. L, suck it!" The world stops for me at this point and a hush overtakes the room. I can almost feel the class wondering, "What is the teacher going to do?"

CREATIVE THINKING EXERCISE #1

Creativity can be as simple as taking familiar objects and combining them into something new. Look at the above drawing and notice all the combined objects and designs.

Instructional handout. Made by teacher.

Walking the halls, I see Vice Principal Mr. First. "Uh, excuse me." In a way I don't want to tell him because it makes me look bad, but I've got to do something. "Cody from Ms. Wispy's room told me to 'Suck it,' really loudly."

"He what?"

"Yeah, he told me to suck it."

"Where is he now?

"I think he's in the cafeteria."

30

"Come on. Lets get 'em." We descend the stairs, two white guys in dress shirts, looking like used car salesmen.

"Watch him cough up his lunch," he says.

"What do you mean?"

"He'll be sweating."

The clamorous cafeteria quiets down. Kids' heads turn to look at me and the vice principal. It's as if they're wondering, "Who are they after?" Cody freezes when he sees me from across the room. We make eye contact. I bet he's thinking, "They're after me." He tries to play it cool at first but I can see his fear building. We walk in silence to Vice Principal First's office. The silent walk. The one I've had bosses do to me when I was younger and working crap jobs.

Mr. First snaps into action, "What do you think you're doing? You're treating this man like a dog, worse than a dog." He leans towards Cody, his voice is sharp and mean. He's on the attack.

Cody launches in on a hard to follow defense, about someone doing something. He's hanging himself. I jump in. "Cody, you went way too far when you said that." I accidentally give him a chance to switch his line of attack. It happens so fast I won't catch it until later.

"No. No. I didn't say *that*," he says with earnestness. After being lied to with passion at Fantasy Careers High, I shouldn't have let this throw me off.

"What did you say to him then?" Mr. First snaps. A second ago he was excusing why he told me to suck it. Now he's denying he said it at all. The switch was imperceptible at the time.

"I didn't say 'Suck it.' I said '*Wait a minute.*'" He says it slowly and choppily to make "wait a minute" sound as much like "suck it" as possible. The vice principal looks at me. I begin to second-guess my memory.

"I don't know, memory isn't perfect and there was a lot of noise."

I'm having flashbacks to all those reports I've seen on PBS about how eyewitnesses get it wrong most of the time. Reports about DNA tests proving the guy on death row was innocent, even though someone thinks they saw him do it.

I momentarily forget the obvious facts. Cody just went from blaming other kids for him saying, "Suck it," to denying he said it at all. When he said it, he crossed his arms in front of his crotch, like that one professional wrestler - whose name escapes me - does when he shouts "Suck it!" It's a semi famous thing. I forget the fact that "suck it" has only two syllables and "wait a minute" has four.

31

Mr. First didn't second-guess. He looks annoyed and ignores my comment. "What do you want me to do to him, suspend him, call his mom, detain him? Just say it and I'll do it."

This was the last moment of total backup I will ever experience from any administrator in four years of teaching. (During my fifth year I would get some sporadic support). Instead of taking him up on it I say: "OK Cody, we will let you go this time," I think I added on a few other impotent, but what I thought were magnanimous comments.

"MAYBE I SHOULD TELL THE PRINCIPAL?"

In my imagination I'm being noble, generous and forgiving. According to my delusion this great moment of understanding will be rewarded. Students will say, "He's an honest and just teacher." They will cooperate out of loyalty to such a fair man.

You can see the relief on Cody's face. He's holding back a grin. If I were omniscient I could see the word about my "mercy" spread around that class and that school. "Mr. L is soft!" A comment I will really hear. "Get ready to rumble!" A comment I imagine them making.

32

While eventually I get Cody to cool down with enough well placed phone calls to his mom, other more sinister agents watch and learn. Those who would figure out that if their parents couldn't stop them from giving me a hard time, no one could. What can this guy do? The office won't do anything. He can call my home and ask me to go to timeout. Big deal.

Art Ed Magazine

Pulling in my driveway I can see that the mailbox on the front door is full and has a couple of magazines in it. It's an unusual front door on a 1940's built house. The front door is green and round at the top reminding me of something from a children's book. The only drawback is I wanted to get decoratively barred screen doors. But I can't, at least not cheaply. I park in the garage, which is cluttered with my Granddad's and Dad's old junk. So even this two-car garage feels small. After closing the garage I make my way to the mailbox.

Along with the so-called "free" adult magazine in the box, is my latest subscription to an art ed magazine. Yeah free. Don't sign up for this stuff. What they do, is just start billing you for it after you get your free sample. The supervisor suggested we get it, so I did. Not the porno but the art ed magazine.

The cover article is on Japanese style manga comics. The article laments how there is a type of kid who draws manga style art all period and refuses to do the art teachers' assignments. It offers an idea about how kids can develop their own heroes. Really what's interesting here is how art is being taught. We didn't do much drawing when I was a kid in art class, and I don't see a lot of other art teachers doing much either. We spent a couple classes putting masking tape on a bottle, then shellacking it. I remember that. Add on to that the bias art education seems to have against cartoons. At least they do in 2000. I've heard a lot of people say "cartoons are not art," and the flyer I got for admitting kids into the arts academy said "No cartoons in the portfolio."

So really I sympathize with the kids who prefer drawing their action heroes to making turkeys using felt and pinecones.

I don't get it. They could learn everything they need from "cartooning." Shading, lighting, all the "principals and elements of design" could be worked in. It's my first year so I don't want to rock the boat too hard. What I do instead is try to make it clear that they can draw this stuff as long as they meet the assignment. But this message never was understood very well.

Chalkboard art lesson.

Wispy Lady and the Iron Triangle.

It's time to see Ms. Wispy's students again. I've completed a lesson on mosaics, and made a pissed off looking self-portrait to use as the example. As usual it's impossible to talk, which makes for a lot of kids not knowing what to do.

Cody has subsided into the background of "high needs" students, and been replaced by an iron triangle of disruption and defiance composed of Sade, Curtis, and Levi. Curtis is the tallest, with a long thin head, followed by Sade (pronounced Sharday) in height. Levi, despite his loud bravado, is short for his age, with a large round face and big front teeth.

I like that name, Levi, once it dawns on me that it's from a book in the Old Testament. Many people believe, secretly perhaps, that inventing names is a common activity among black people. Actually some of those names at least, are from sources forgotten by the general population. Last year, when I substitute taught, I had a student named Lavenia. It took me a while to realize that comes from Shakespeare.

Out of the general interruptions, like angry demands to go to the bathroom during directions, these three students emerge with more bizarre and aggressive tactics. Tactics intended to prevent me from speaking at all.

Sade plays patty cake. Curtis sings a repetitive song about jellybeans. Levi starts singing a rhythm and blues sounding tune, and does a little dance. Now Sade is angry and shouting at me for asking her to be quiet. I'm trying to get at least one of them into a timeout and do a written assignment, so they face some consequence, and I don't have to call all their homes.

"Sit down Levi!"

Levi informs me, "I don't like you! Man, the art teacher we had last year, when we saw him and he saw us we just liked each other right away. But you, you're something else." This gives me some confidence because I think, "Which one of the many art teachers who were driven out of here are you talking about?" Sade grabs my attention again.

"Sade you need to copy these rules."

"I ain't copying these rules."

Before I can address this, Curtis is running around the room. He grabs a girl by the neck. She repels him, and he knocks a chair down.

"Curtis!"

He runs out of the room. I walk slowly towards the door. He comes back and flicks the lights on and off a few times and runs out again.

"Get in this room and sit down!" My voice echoes through the hall.

Curtis re-enters and is acting tough.

"You're soft!" He shouts at me.

"You need to sit…"

"You'll get dropped!" At some point he tells me his dad will punch me out. When I foolishly ask him, "Why are you behaving like this?" He replies, "To tell you the truth, because you're ugly."

"Sit!" I say sternly. He does.

Levi shouts out "You're talking to us like we're dogs! We ain't dogs!"

Sade is sprawled out, lying across the chairs. Now she's sitting up again but shouting at me "You get on my nerves!" She rises from her chair and does a drill routine.

"What about those rules Sade?" I remind her.

She slams her books on the table, "Here go you stupid rules," and then finally sits to copy them.

Today the trouble stays mainly contained to these hardcore "high needs" kids. The others are working on their collages. It's getting late. "Get your things organized and ready for helpers!" Kids delay as long as they can. It's hard to get them started, and then it's just as hard to get them stopped. Finally helpers are collecting supplies, while Levi, Curtis and Sade add some final bouts of chaos.

After they leave I review my "battle notes." This stuff is so surreal that without these notes I'd forget it all in seconds. They don't help much though. Problem is I had just enough time to jot down some illegible scrawl, before the next incident occurred.

Phone Calls from Battle Notes

I head to the downstairs faculty lounge, the one in the basement across from my room. I take out my notebook and phone lists. The pages are filled with quickly jotted names and scrawled infractions next to them. They often start legibly then trail into illegibility. "Nate –rowdy all..." The kid's names are followed by squiggles, lines and arrows pointing to more illegible notes. Looking at my frantic handwriting I can see the stress I just went through. I look for often-repeated names, circle them in black, repeating the circles over and over, still feeling the stress. I call Curtis's dad.

"Hi, this is Curtis's art teacher from Grand Plans Middle. Is this his parent or guardian?"

"Yes, this is his dad." The voice sounds older than I expected.

"I think he has some real potential in art class and a good imagination, but unfortunately he is really focusing on acting out."

The Dad promises to take action. I mark Dad in large black ink over Curtis's name. This way I remember who I talked to if I call again. At Levi's, I get an answering machine. I think Levi's dad is burned out with me at this point. Next I call Sade's, and talk to her brother. I pause and look for other circled names from other classes and take out other phone lists. Mostly I get hold of moms, some grandmas and a few aunts. The women generally sound shocked and in a state of disbelief. They say they will take care of it. That's an often-repeated phrase: "take care of it." Sometimes they really do, and the next time I see the kid he'll bring in an apology note, and behave well for a while. I'm surprised how many parents are nice to me when I call, since so many other teachers have said, "The parents are terrible."

"You really call all these parents?" An unfamiliar voice snaps me out of my musing.

"Huh?"

"Why bother? I don't." He starts unpacking his lunch. "Who are you?" He's a six-foot, heavy set, Nordic looking guy, with curly blond hair and a ruddy face. If this man were older he'd make a perfect Kris Cringle, only a bit of an intimidating Kris Cringle.

36

"I'm Ryan. I just started teaching Spanish here." So this is the guy who replaced that Latino Spanish teacher. He looks about my age.

"Dude, if you don't call the parents it gets worse."

"The parents don't do shit."

He's sitting with two other new teachers, both mid-twenties females, both rubenesque and buxom. "These kids suck," says the younger and fatter of the two, after chomping into a sandwich. "I can't friggin' get them to do anything."

"Oh yeah, I've seen you. You replaced that African American lady didn't you? Is it cool if I join you guys?" I say to the younger female.

The female who complained about the students is Tina. I've witnessed her group's discipline deteriorate after that sternly demeanored woman, Ms. Bentley, left. The other one says some negative stuff too, but she doesn't seem to mean it as much. You can tell because her kids don't give her such a hard time like Tina's do. The calmer one is Christine.

The four of us let off some steam for a while. It's a real relief, because lunch with those women upstairs is kind of fun, but not like this. Their sexual innuendos are a release from stress in a way, but this is direct. We say things about students that could get teachers fired, and it feels good.

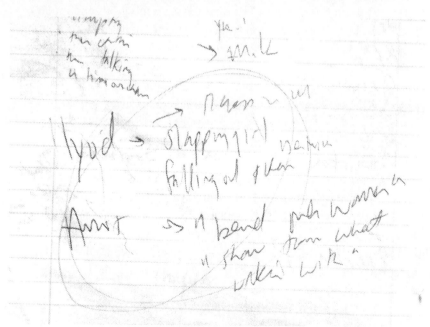

Excerpt from Battle Notes.

Coffee house

It's Saturday. While very little green is left on the trees, fall is indecisive. Yesterday the heat and humidity were stifling. Today the cool air is refreshing. When I was a child Rust Belt had four definite seasons. Now, as global warming changes the weather, the seasons bleed into each other.

I try to make bringing work home somewhat enjoyable, so I pack my bag and head down to a coffee house. It has a long bench with a bunch of tables stuck together in front of it and chairs on the opposite side. It's much easier to meet someone new when you're sitting at this bench than it is when your sitting alone at one of the small tables, trying to strike up a conversation by shouting across to another small table. I take off my jacket, unpack my bag and take out the plan book and sketchpad and sit on the bench.

I start to revise a handout on value and shading. I need something that can explain itself, since I won't have a chance to. The handout must be understandable within the time it takes to dodge a flying crayon. I take breaks to people watch.

For meeting women, this is a far cry from subbing. I look professional. Better yet I can say I actually have a job. My good mood is broken when I see Yuri pull up in front of the café in his rusted out white car. As he enters surveying the scene he sees me. There will be no meeting women now.

Yuri was briefly an adjunct professor at my college. He looks in his early sixties, kind of swarthy, slouchy, chain smokes, uses a lot of profanity, is single, and talks a lot about younger women.

"Hey Matt! How's teaching going?"

"Pretty rough."

"I'm surprised you've lasted this long." He was an art teacher at Fantasy Career's high for a while. Eventually he quit because of his students' bad behavior. "I would send a kid to the office and he would come back with this big grin on his face because the principal didn't do shit to him. He'd come back smiling because he won and now I couldn't do a fucking thing," he says.

"I'm just working on this lesson on shading here."

"Oh. OK, I'll let you get to work." He seems pretty down on his luck and I don't want to give him the cold shoulder, but I may as well get something accomplished this afternoon.

I sketch out a multi-layered value scale with different shading techniques they can copy, and write out the instructions. "Create your own version of this chart and then draw *any picture* you want and shade it using one of the techniques." Then I write down page numbers from the book kids can draw from if they finish quickly. This way I'm hoping I can win over those who like to draw cartoon style stuff because they *can*.

Yuri takes a seat nearby and is blocking my access to these twenty-something girls who are acting like they are studying.

"How long do you think you're going to last at this?" he asks, after getting brushed off by the twenty-somethings – women that I could have realistically tried for if he weren't blocking my access. I'm not as aggravated by older guys going for younger girls like I was when I was really young. In high school, a bunch of us were in the bleachers watching the girls' swim meet. There was this older guy sitting behind us, alone. He was in the army and going out with one of the swimmers. We all hated him for this. We looked back towards him making quiet comments, but not loudly since he was in the army and none of us were that tough. I'm not hostile anymore towards older guys trying to take out younger women, but Yuri's eliminating my chances right now. Not because he might succeed, but because he won't. I shrug off my aggravation.

"What else am I going to do man?"

"You're young, college educated and you know how to talk to people. Your skills would be useful in a lot of places."

"Thanks" I say, but actually wondering, "Why have I only had crap paying jobs before teaching; and where are these 'lots of places' that would value me?"

"I'd like to last at least five years. I hear that's how long it takes to have your pension vested. I don't think it would be much of a pension but something's better than nothing."

"When I was in the system it took ten years. I didn't know. No one fucking told me. I made it nine years. Nine years, then I quit. I couldn't fucking take it anymore. If I knew I only had one more year to go."

"Yeah, I mean I don't really want to come away from this with nothing at all," I say.

He lowers his voice and says: "You don't want to wind up like me. No fucking money. You've got to have money." I feel some spit hit my face.

Now I'm comparing myself with him. I'm sizing up my chances of winding up this way. I think a lot of us make ourselves feel better by comparing ourselves with someone doing worse; someone making decisions we don't think we would make. Then laughing to ourselves: "Ha, I'm not like that guy. I'd never be like that guy." A lot of us know this isn't a nice thing to do, but in someway it's what our market system promotes. Fear of ending up sleeping under a bridge is a powerful motivator.

What are my odds of winding up like this? Well, I had the wherewithal to look into things like pensions vesting. So that's a good sign. He didn't do that. I feel safer.

"Not so fast" a conflicting thought says, "he lasted nine years. You haven't even lasted one yet." My confidence slips as quickly as it came.

"All right Yuri, I'll catch up with you in a bit. I have to jog out of here now."

He wishes me, "Good luck".

"Thanks. Same to you." I leave him alone, nursing his one-dollar cup of coffee, and me without a new phone number. All I've accomplished this Saturday afternoon is another art lesson that is destined to be condemned by those harshest of critics: my students.

Levi as Jackass

Sometimes I feel like a fraud. Maybe these lessons do suck. Kids demanded Halloween projects. I didn't deliver. Thanksgiving isn't far off and my supervisor doesn't seem into holiday art; actually I'm not too into it either. The children will be disappointed again. Maybe I'm no good at teaching art. No. I work too hard. My evaluations are all basically good. Ms. Henderson was just in here, and even that evaluation was pretty OK.

As if sensing my insecurity Levi says, "You're not a real art teacher." I'll hear this comment often. "You're somethin else." He laughs and shakes his head, as if I'm pitiable, contemptible and amusing. I'm trying to get him into timeout. "Say please. Say please," he says. It's a set-up. He sounds phony. Not wanting to admit this is all real, I kid myself into thinking he's sincere.

"OK. *Please* go to timeout," I say.

"Ha! Ha! Ha! He said please!" Levi is pointing at me laughing. He's beaming with pride. He's slapping his thigh. His head is nodding back and forth, and I can see his front teeth. They're adult front teeth. They must have come in already. They look so big on him. The way he's nodding his head with those big teeth, and laughing that way, it's reminding me of something. His laugh sounds more like "Haw. Haw!" It sounds like something I've heard somewhere. What? Not a child. I've got it. It's like he's a braying donkey. Yes, that's it. He looks like an obnoxious cartoon animal! Fury rises in me. "Be quiet! You Jacka…" I catch my self, just in time.

40

His eyes light up. He sits up. He's excited. He's got one over on me. It wasn't just in time. It was almost just in time. I caught myself too late. He shouts out: "He was going to call me a jackass. You heard that didn't you! You heard that right!" He says to whoever will listen. He's confident. I'm nervous. What if he uses this against me? He stands pointing at me, about to say some more.

I tell him to sit. "Sit!" I say sharply.

"We're not dogs. I'm not a dog!" he says.

I feel like I've calmed down. I've composed myself; but something in me still is upset. Calmly and coolly I say, "Yes you are."

He gets excited and stands again, "What?!"

Now I'm jaded. Just as calmly and coolly I reply, "I didn't mean it that way."

Levi's Dad

His Dad is coming in to meet me. It's the second time that he's come. I'm in the middle of cafeteria duty, feeling like a lunatic trying to run the asylum. I can see him standing across the room. He's around my height, a few years older than me at most, with his head shaved, and wearing silver hoop earrings. He's lean and looks strong. It's a look I'd like to have. We shake hands and step into the hall near my room. He works for the state. Something about this adult contact makes me feel like a normal person for a second. Normal. As opposed to freak of nature who gets picked on by kids all day.

During our last conversation he said, "I can come down to the school anytime," since he's out on workers' comp. He doesn't seem injured. The thought of him coming down "anytime," is not exactly comforting. I tell him what Levi has been doing. He maintains his poker face. Was Levi successful in turning him against me? I explain that my reaction to his son is probably exaggerated due to the stress Levi's buddy, Curtis, is putting me through. He gets a serious look. I tell him about Curtis's insults, "He tells me I'm ugly, threatens to jaw me."

He interrupts. The pitch of his voice rises a little. "Does Levi ever go off on you like that?" He looks angry. Not angry at me, but angry at the kids putting me through this. I don't know why, but I lie. "No. No. Not like that." I say reassuringly. Maybe I just wanted to pretend I was normal for a while longer.

Nothing changes with Levi. His dad stops coming into the school for a while. When he finally does come in one last time, he's apologetic but hopeless. He explains he's been raising Levi alone. No Mom. This explains Levi's behavior. Every hostile person has a history that nurtured his or her hostility. Don't think I don't sympathize. I do. But a school system that lets disturbed youth break rules, and blames teachers is not doing these kids any favors. It will just set them up for bigger trouble later.

Levi's dad says, "I don't know what else I can do. I've grounded him. Made him stay in his room. I've taken his toys away, his TV away. Everything." My head is filled with an image of little Levi, sitting in a stark, dark room. I imagine him shouting out from his room, for his Dad to hear: "Keep me in here all you want. I'm not gonna be good! I hate that art teacher!" I give up on calling the dad. Later in the year I repeatedly write Curtis and him up, and give the write-ups to the administration, which, as far as I know, does nothing. Ms. Wispy, his homeroom teacher, devises a punitive system to manage her students' behavior. If they receive too many warnings they can't go on the field trip. Once Levi gets too many warnings, he's merciless.

"AFTER SCHOOL DETENTION"

5. Crayon War and Travel Abroad.

Build up to Crayon War

On the drive into work today I'm extra stressed because I've got to see that really wild eighth grade group. Not only that but my supervisor, while giving me a positive evaluation overall, told me his usual "You've got to be tough and firm with these kids. You're in a difficult situation but I want you to keep laying down the law." What exactly does this mean? If I shout it just seems to make things worse, but I've got my orders. I see Vice Principal First as I head to my room.

"How do you think I'm doing here?"

"Don't worry. I know you're still green. I told your supervisor that too. We understand."

"He told me to get tougher with them. What do you think?"

"If your supervisor tells you to sharpen pencils upside down, you sharpen them upside down."

"Yeah, I know. I'm pretty cooperative."

"Just keep hanging in there and keep tightening the screws on them."

More of the same: more of these vague commands like "tighten the screws." Both of them are telling me to get harsher. I see Tina's kids, then Christine's. With both groups I bark like a drill sergeant to appease my supervisor. Once I turn on that voice, it's hard to turn it off, and I fear that it is resonating through the heating ducts. I wonder who else can hear me. I'm barking things like: "Heads down! I said heads down and I mean heads down! OK, then get in timeout. Don't make me call your dad! Oh sorry, I didn't know you don't have a dad."

I go to the upstairs lounge where the ladies usually hang out because it's too early for my three new pal's lunch. I heat up one of the frozen fish dinners Leroy the janitor has been hooking me up with, since he knows I don't have or like spending money. He's a good guy, and likes to help me out. I don't know where he gets these frozen meals from. They look old.

They're packaged in aluminum trays with white cardboard covers. As I warm it up, one of the white teachers complains about the smell. So I leave and find another microwave to heat it in, in another more isolated lounge. Man, some of these people are uptight. I come back in time to eat with the ladies. Pookie tells me, "You know people can hear you shouting. Ms. Henderson is going to get on you about this. I'm warning you." Mabel, another matronly African American woman interjects on my behalf, "He's a lot more organized than that art teacher last year. That teacher was chasing kids up the stairs." At least I know I have last year's performance beat, but now I've got cross commands again.

That really rough group is on its way, Ms. Rosebloom's eighth grade. The students meet me at the stairs descending to my room, already a little disorderly. "Stop," I command. Huey boos me, others laugh. "Enter in silence." Instead they enter, and take their seats noisily. At least they're seated. I work through the lesson. The crayons are out at each table. The last time the class painted they threw water around, so today I decided, just crayons. Huey is shoving his table into another group's table. Two short, blond, spikey haired boys are seated there. They laugh, and begin to throw paper balls. As the mayhem escalates, I get nervous and "revert" to street lingo.

"All ya'll need to stop your mouths and get to work. Yo, Huey! Sit yourself down," I say.

"Shut the fuck up," is Huey's response.

"Get in that timeout."

"No way, gay ball." He was calling me cue ball for a while, making reference to my *nearly* shaved head, but recently it's evolved into gay ball.

"Don't make me call your home."

"Go ahead asshole." Huey rests for a second. Now, one of the two blond boys is crawling on the floor, the other is standing on a chair.

"Get back in your seats right now," I say sternly. The blonder of the two says, "You're just yelling at us because you're afraid of them," gesturing to a wide swath of the room filled with mainly African American kids who are larger than they are, and not behaving either. So now if I chastise whites I'm a reverse racist. It's a no-win. I can be labeled either prejudiced or a guilt ridden white liberal, depending on which side of the melanin-divide I aim my chastisement.

Peace Corps.

During my prep period I take my "Battle Notes" and phone lists into the lounge. Huey's phone number is wrong. I go to the office. Get the new number. Try it. It's wrong too. Hike up the stairs to Ms. Rosebloom's room. She has the same phone number the office has. My whole prep period is wasted. Time to join Ryan, the new Spanish teacher, and the two new female teachers for lunch.

Ryan teasingly asks Tina, "How's your new boyfriend?"

"Shut up" she says looking down and turning red. It's friendly banter but Ryan is touching a sore spot.

"What? What is it?" I ask, turning to her and smiling, trying to coax it out of her.

"Boy, he's a real winner this one!" Ryan says further egging her on.

"Come on, everybody else knows. What is it?" I say leaning back in my chair to give her a little space.

"He's in jail. He got arrested," she answers, sounding exasperated with life. "I know. Pretty ridiculous. I find a boyfriend finally, then he gets arrested."

Ryan laughs. Christine chides him, like she's keeping an obnoxious husband on his leash. Ryan says first to us, but mostly to Tina: "What a loser!" Then laughingly to everyone, but mostly to me: "Her boyfriend doesn't even have money for bail. He wants Tina to bail him out."

Christine changes the topic. "So Matt, what about you? How's your girlfriend doing?"

"I don't have one right now," I say looking down ashamedly.

"A nice guy like you?"

I look up again. "I've got a lot of complicated criteria. A part of me was thinking I wanted some sort of cross cultural or international relationship." Thinking this sounds strange, I avoid eye contact with her while saying it. People often think that if one avoids eye contact it indicates lying. I avoid eye contact when I think the person just won't understand what I'm talking about, which seems to happen often this lifetime. Those Koreans I knew told me that it's considered rude to look someone in the eyes if that someone is older than you are. In fact Kwon (that was one of the Koreans) told me, "We think people who look you in the eye all the time are retarded." He seemed to try do the American thing and look me in the eyes, but instead he seemed to always focus just above on my thinning hairline. That was three years ago, just when my balding was "starting to become noticeable" – as they say in the "cure" for baldness ads aired on late night

TV. When it was still ambiguous if I was balding or just having a bad hair day, people would stare at my head trying to decide if I really was balding. During that time I was trying the "leave it a little longer on top, than the sides, to make you look less bald" trick.

Ryan says, "Trust me dude, you don't want that. You don't want a 'cross cultural'" - he does the finger quotes thing, and puts special emphasis on the phrase "cross cultural," to mock my politically correct way of putting it – "relationship."

"Ryan's got an international wife," Christine says with a wry smile.

"You do?" I ask.

"You don't want it. I regret it," he says. I'm not too dissuaded by his warning. Ryan's the type to make outrageous statements to be entertaining.

"I don't know, Ryan, she's pretty cute," Christine says with that same knowing smile.

"You guys all met?" I ask, feeling a bit left out. It seems like a lot goes on with these three when I'm not here.

"Yeah we get together sometimes, the four of us, with my husband. We're trying to get them to come over and use our hot tub," Christine says.

I'm not sure if I should ask about the hot tub or Ryan's wife next. "You've got a hot tub? I love those." It turns out his wife is from the Philippines. So I know there really is a wife since Christine met her, and this lends credibility to Ryan's travel stories. I think I know bullshitters and I don't think Ryan is one.

"How did you two meet?" I ask. People usually ask that question of interracial couples. Most people like to say they are color blind, but it looks to me like most people stick to people who look like they do. So it seems unusual, even though people wouldn't admit it, to most of us when two people from two different "parts of town" are coupled. Maybe in a big city where everyone is mixed together it seems normal, but not in most of middle America, not in 2000.

"We met in the Philippines," Ryan answers.

"You were there? When?" By now nothing really surprises me about this guy.

"Yeah, when I was in the Peace Corps."

"That's awesome. I always wanted to do something like that. I got some brochures after undergrad but that was about as far as I went. How did you wind up getting married?"

"My time in the Corps was up, and she couldn't come with me unless we got married."

"That's cool I think, you get to broaden your horizons. You can learn a new language, you've got another country to go and visit. It sounds like a good deal." I say.

"It sucks. The cultural barriers are a pain in the ass. We've got totally different interests."

"Like what?"

"She doesn't like to go flying. She gets motion sickness." Should I ask about flying, or point out that motion sickness wouldn't qualify as a cultural difference?

"How often do you fly anyway?" I say, thinking it can't be that often.

"I'm working on getting a pilot's license. So I fly a lot."

"You're gonna fly a jet?"

"No, I want to get a license to fly cargo planes in Africa when I go back there."

"What would your wife do?"

"She's a nurse. Probably stay here and work."

Christine chimes in "She's a hotty. You better watch out." He ignores this comment.

"What more could you want?" I ask. "She can work and support your lazy rear (I try not to swear these days because I'm worried I'll slip in front of the students) while you go on your adventures." Ryan doesn't say anything and goes back to eating. "Do you have pictures from overseas?" He invites me over for beers and a viewing on Friday.

After leaving the lounge, and a few more classes down, it's time for bus duty. I shoo kids away from school, "Head home!" On their way, the "walkers" traipse through yellow and brown fallen leaves, shoving each other as they go. I tell Vice Principal Mr. First, "I can't get a hold of Huey's home." He explains: "It's no use, even if you could. Good luck trying. Huey's mom's a dyke." Later on in the year I will talk to her. She sounds young for having such a big kid. She sounds white.

Crayon War

There's a moment of calm with Ms. Rosebloom's class, before the next storm. We're doing a lesson on "radiating lines." Basically it's drawing some shapes, then making ripples around them. The ripples crash into each other, so the students have some artistic challenges. The examples I've drawn involve simple designs, like my initials or geometric shapes. The

47

instructions explain to use my illustration for ideas. I try to demo it on the board, but hoots and hollers prevent that. As usual I walk the room, prodding kids on, and explaining the lesson to each table individually, while I simultaneously watch for trouble. It's a simple repetitive project that kids seem to like once they start it. Many of them are just copying my initials, which I find odd, but I am happy to see them working.

On Mr. First's advice, I ease up on the seating and it seems to work. "Don't go crazy worrying about where everybody is sitting," he told me. "Go back to your own seat," I say calmly to one of the kids wandering the room. When I'm ignored, I just move on. "Ok, you can stay where you are if you're working." This saves a lot of energy I was burning up on the seat battle; but still a part of me thinks if I give in on the seats there's going to be trouble.

After locking the door at the end of class I cross the hall to the Home and Careers teacher's room (Home Ec. to the people my age). Home and Careers is taught by a woman old enough to be my mom. Like my mother, she wears her hair in a typical late middle-aged mom fashion: sensibly short, parted to the side, and dyed back to a pre-gray color. Whenever I stop by her room she always has time to talk to me and offer some friendly encouragement, and, if I ask for some, advice.

"It seems that with Ms. Rosebloom's group it's better off not to battle them on the seats, but let them just sit where they want," I say.

She agrees, "Yeah I think that with that class, you need to give them some space."

They come again. And again I give them some space. I start a new assignment fearing they will be getting bored with the old one. Yet about half of them go back to the old one, disobeying me and getting up without permission, going to their folders and getting out the rippling lines project. I don't bother to object, and it works. Some are doing one thing and others doing another. They are helping themselves, and they are running the class, but it's running well. They've self segregated into girl groups, boy groups, black and white groups, and it's going much more smoothly than my cross-gender cross-racial seating arrangements were, at least for the time being. The Home and Careers teacher walks by and looks in, she smiles and nods approvingly at me. The kids are all working. No shouting, no shoving, just working, like you'd dream it would be.

Still I feel nervous as I watch them do as they please. When I chide, "Get permission before you get up," I'm blown off. How can the students governing themselves go on well forever?

The Home and Careers teacher comes to see me after class. "Hey, I saw Ms. R's group all working. Most people couldn't get them to work like that." She says, beaming with pride in me.

"Thanks. I'm not really sure why they are behaving, though."

"Oh come on; you're just being modest. You got through to them!"

The third time my luck runs out. Alexis passes out the table folders and Jerome passes out plastic buckets with crayons in them, while Jasmine passes out plastic baggies filled with pencils. After giving up on instructing the whole class at the same time, I start to visit individual tables instead. Kids are sitting where they want. But unlike last time when they were working, now they are just playing around. They are too bored and distracted to listen to me explain the new assignment and no one seems interested in doing the old one anymore.

Bending over a table filled with boys I say, "OK, let's get working here guys. All you have to do is…"

"I just got hit with a crayon," Jerome shouts out.

"There is no throwing things at all," I say to the room sternly, looking around like a secret service agent. Then I move on to a table filled with rowdy girls. "Now you just need to finish coloring in this part."

"I don't feel like it." Another crayon flies. The victim laughs, like victims of bullying often do hoping that humor will defuse it. I look up. My gaze is getting even more serious. I see that a kid has his books erected like a little hunting blind he can duck his head behind. He's squirming around behind it holding back laughter, as his victim looks around to see who threw something at him.

"Put your books down so I can see your face."

"I just have these books up so I can…" A crayon flies at him.

I turn my head, "Hey!" Suddenly more kids have books erected like shields.

"Ow, what the fuck is you doin'?" says a girl who just got hit in the face, as she whips a crayon hard at the alleged perpetrator.

"OK, everybody stop working and heads down." I'm ignored. I shut the lights off. "Heads down!" Having the lights off only increases the throwing. Now it's dark and the crayons are flying harder. I run up to a kid, "Give me those crayons."

"No." He hurls them while I am talking, like I'm not even there.

"Ok Alexis, collect all the crayons." Instead she just throws them with gusto.

I start to grab the buckets of crayons and remove them from the tables, but it's too late. While I grab one and put it aside someone runs over and grabs a handful from it. Kids have crayons hidden in their hands and in their pockets. I turn the lights back on. It feels like gym class in here. People are standing and throwing, hiding under tables, behind book shields. "Get up and out from under that table!" To another I shout, "Put that book down!"

"What, you want me to get hit? No way!" The logic is irrefutable. It's like depriving him of his shield in this mini arms race.

It reminds me of a game of dodge ball, a game now prohibited. When I was in high school two teams of us would throw inflated rubber balls across a divide at each other as hard as we could, until only one was left standing on the losing side, usually it was Phil. He was the type to get picked on. All of us on the sidelines would rhythmically chant his name, "Phil! Phil! Phil!" which had the paradoxical effect of mocking him and inflating his ego.

Only this game of dodge ball is being played with crayons, which are harder and more dangerous than large inflatable rubber balls. I pick up the phone, and dial 1000, for the office. "I need an administrator down here!"

"Who is this?" The confused secretary says.

"This is the art teacher. I've got Ms. Rosebloom's class. Send someone down here."

As I scurry about shouting and taking crayons, I get hit. "OK Matt, you better change tactics fast before you wind up like that other art teacher," a voice in my head says.

I decide I'd better take one position where I can see everything, watch and shout rather than move at all. I stand near the door and lean up against the sink so I can save some strength, but they can see I'm watching, and still standing, so some semblance of adult authority is maintained.

Looking across the room seeing the anger and excitement, I shout sternly and repeatedly, using my vocal chords as a natural bullhorn, "Stop throwing the crayons!" Then, watching the crayons continue to fly and feeling the futility and ineffectiveness of my admonitions, I start laughing.

My laughter snaps Jerome out of his frenzy. He looks at me curiously and says, "He's laughing." Another student also momentarily stops, and says, "Why are you laughing?" Things quiet down for a minute, and those who see me laughing seem embarrassed and angry. In my fantasy I start to point at them and laugh and laugh, the way Levi laughed at me that time. Doing that would sabotage this brief truce. My laughter disoriented them. If I keep it up, I risk their shame transforming into genuine embarrassment, which could blow up in my face. For all their tough talk, these kids have very fragile egos. Feeling insulted they might turn brazenly hostile.

Instead I answer truthfully, "Because my life has become such a joke that I may as well laugh about it." I shake my head looking down for a second, laughing, and muttering, "What a joke." Then I bite my tongue to hold back any more amusement and resume saying, "Put down the crayons!" and I wait for some kind of backup to arrive.

Within a few seconds Ms. Rosebloom walks in, apparently summoned from her prep by the office. "Thank God she didn't see me laughing," I think. She puts her hands on her hips and shouts at them. They quiet down. "Line up immediately!" She says, her voice quavering with anger. They do. Standing in line, with the adrenaline cooling down, kids begin to notice where they were hit. "My eye," one of them says. She sends that one to the nurse. "Not a sound" she commands. "To the top of the staircase." They file out of the room sullen but silent.

Still leaning, immobilized with stress against the sink, I see a room torn apart. Tables are scattered around at odd angles and broken crayons lie all over the place; chairs are knocked down, and magazines are thrown on the floor. With shaking hands I begin to clean up.

Later that day Ms. Rosebloom and I bump into each other in the hall. "Buster won't be back," she says. Buster is one of the white kids in the room. He's an average size eighth grader, but tough and unruly.

"Well that's good, but I don't think he's the worst one in there. What happened?"

"I was making them march the halls in silence because of what they did in your class. Buster started punching a locker and said 'Fuck you Ms. Rosebloom, you fucking bitch.' Threatening me like that."

"That is ridiculous. He should be sent somewhere else for threatening you," thinking nothing ever happens to anyone who threatens me. "Thanks a lot for backing me up like that and making them walk."

Then we work on a new seating chart for them. During my prep, back in my room, I write each kid's name on a small square of paper with their new table assignment. During my lunch I go back to Ms. Rosebloom's room. "Excuse me Ms. R. May I give the kids their new seats?"

"Go ahead."

"Why do we need new seats?" one interrupts.

"Because that last outburst was too much." I rattle off each name and give them the square of paper. "This way there will not be any excuse for you to claim you don't know where you are supposed to sit," I tell the class. "I hope this helps," I tell myself.

Mr. First comes to my room next time I have that class. He barks at the kids: "What do you people think he thinks of you, when he goes back to where he lives?!" He's promoting the myth that white teachers like me fly away from the ghetto in our gold plated UFOs, off to our happy dreamland suburbs. I don't know if this is helping me any. It's Friday anyway. Time to go see Ryan's Peace Corps pictures.

Ryan's

First I stop off at the corner store. I shouldn't just go to Ryan's place empty handed. The Vietnamese workers stand behind the counter on a platform, which makes them appear taller than me. I set down a twelve pack of the most economical, but OK tasting beer I can find. I ask, "Which are your cheapest cigarettes?" pointing to the smokes. They don't seem to understand me, so I repeat the word "Cheapest." The lady hands me a pack while the guy rings me out. They both look only a couple of years older than me and I wonder if they're the owners. Really they could be my age or even younger. I'm probably just used to looking at a more youthful face in the mirror. I've been looking at a twenty something version of me, for many more years than I've been looking at this thirty something year old I am today.

It's always my habit to go for the least expensive but still palatable thing I can buy. This neighborhood is a good place for that. The people are blue collar or no collar, but either way they're not in the habit of overpaying. I spot my neighbor, a retired African American autoworker, in the store buying lottery tickets. Recently I started buying lotto tickets myself here. When I was younger, more hopeful and more idealistic, I vowed I would never play lotto. I considered it a back door tax on the down and out. I even thought of a slogan I was going to have printed on T-shirts "Don't revolt! Play lotto!" I still consider it a back door tax on those who need hope, but now I need hope.

After greeting my neighbor, a couple of kids who look like they could be my students come to the counter, holding chips, candy and bags of those salted unshelled sun flower seeds that are all the rage now among urban youth. Starting in 1999, when I was subbing at Fantasy Career's High, I noticed the kids at that school were crazy about these seeds and were happily devouring them during class, in the halls and anywhere else you shouldn't be eating. On the one hand eating these seeds is impressive

52

because it takes some skill to crack the shells with your teeth and then suck the seeds out. On the other hand I'd find piles of broken shells hidden inside, under or on top of desks, chairs, and the floor. The kids were either too cavalier to put them in the garbage, or not wanting me to know they were eating them in the first place, decided it was better just to hide the evidence.

I feel nervous for a second seeing these young guys, instinctively flashing back to children at school giving me shit. But then remember that I'm not teaching now, I'm on a beer run, and I don't have to ask anybody to be quiet and sit down. You could say that I am beginning to develop a sensitivity to people four foot something. Whenever I see someone this height I think about the trouble they might start, and wonder if I will be able to stop it.

I thank the clerk in Vietnamese, which gets a surprised smile, exit and head off to Ryan's.

He lives near me, in an adjoining suburb, the same burb I grew up in. It's not a place I thought anybody would choose to find an apartment in. To me it's a place to leave. A sterile, close-minded place; where my misfitted adolescence was squandered. The neighborhood quickly goes from black to mostly white, with houses a little farther apart. When he tells me what a bargain the rent is, I can see why he'd want to live there.

Ryan and his wife live upstairs in a cheap looking double. He invites me in and we set up in the kitchen with beer, chips and photo albums of his travels. We flip through the photos, filled with exotic foliage, huts and people of all complexions. After a while his wife comes in from the living room to introduce herself. She's a short, stout woman, with a brown complexion and medium length black hair. We talk about where she came from, nursing and what a portable career it is. It's portable unlike my career, I think, feeling tied down.

Ryan informs me of his plan to relocate out west, after he gets his pilot's license and comes back from Africa. "She can be a nurse in California as easily as here," he says. It all sounds complicated and tentative. I try to advise him that he should stay here, be a teacher and save money; but he's set on more adventure. I don't think I can afford to leave Rust Belt right now, but I need some adventure of my own.

On the drive home I think I need something or someone new and foreign in my life to break the grind of dealing with tough inner city culture and youthful bravado, day after day. I log on line to see if anyone new has responded to my Internet date ad. Here it is, my prayer answered -maybe. "Hi. My name is Marisol. I am a thirty-one year old girl from Indonesia. I

53

am working and living in Rust Belt." She sent a picture. It doesn't look bad, although she's wearing sunglasses and is standing far away, so it's hard to tell. We exchange a few emails talking about our lives and hopes, and her home country, Indonesia. After a few of these exchanges I offer my phone number first to show her I am entrusting her with it. Then she offers hers. In Internet dating I found it works best to simultaneously ask for hers and give yours. Thus showing you don't expect the girl to call you, but are open to the possibility. We talk on the phone a few times before we finally set a date.

6. Justice or Survival?

Bringer Of Justice

While I'm frying an egg, hot oil spatters onto the stove. As I hastily prepare breakfast I have an inner debate. I've read in the teaching literature that you should give disruptive students small jobs to keep them busy. "No. I won't give in to this," I think, remembering what it was like when I was in school. Select bullies got to help the teacher out, and seemed to be able to get away with stuff I couldn't do, especially if those bullies were on the football team. I can't bring myself to empower them, while the quiet kids get ignored. The "squeaky wheel" won't get greased on my watch. This is my stand, for now anyway.

"Those kids that act out are high needs. They act out because they need your attention. The well behaved ones don't," a colleague recently told me. He was explaining how giving the bulk of our attention to those kids is the right thing to do. This didn't sound right to me, but I needed time to think it over.

By the time I arrive at work I feel like talking about the "high needs" issue with a real person. I have a way of finding people that are good-natured and fairly quiet, then engaging them in sometimes twenty minute monologues where I verbally work out some idea or other. Looking for someone, I cross the hall from my room to the Home and Careers teacher's. She's bent over, rummaging around in a cardboard box.

"Hey there!" After recounting the conversation I start my rant: "What about the quiet kids whose names we can never remember? I don't know the studies on it, but I wouldn't be surprised if suicide rates are higher among the introverted students, the ones who don't bother other kids. While all us teachers, guidance counselors, and administrators do is lavish attention on the loud kids who disrupt class and harass their peers."

"You're probably right about that. It's sad we always know who the loud ones are and forget the others," she said.

"I've been seeing myself as a righteous sword." She laughs as I hold up an imaginary sword. "I only reward the cooperative and never give in to a corrupt system that grants special privileges to bullies."

I start to remember my own youth. Back when I was in middle school I thought, "Why do teachers look the other way while Mary gets called 'frog eyes' and is goaded to tears on a daily basis?" Mary was thin, bordering on skinny, and a very "plain" looking girl. She wore thick glasses, and clothes that seemed like they might have been her grandmother's. Mary was driven right out of our school.

When I was a teenager in high school I wondered, why do teachers act like they don't see this football player bullying a kid half his size? How come guys like him can break the rules and I can't? How come no teachers see that Charlie, this tiny crazy acting kid, who wears floods (pants that are too short) and has a short "Davy and Goliath" hair style – at a time when we all had to have hair parted down the middle, feathered back and covering our ears – is routinely harassed? Why can't they see it but we kids can? Charlie would get his "nerd style" pile of books that he always carried around kicked out of his hands and strewn across the floor. Then kids would kick his books down the hallway. His ears were "twanged" until they turned red. When the bullies went on attack some kids joined in, others, like myself offered the picked on an occasional sympathetic word. I expected a teacher would defend the victims. But the adults were like mannequins, without reaction.

The bullying was sometimes racial. A black girl named Phyllis walked into the cafeteria, and these guys we called "heads" started rhythmically pounding on the tables. Heads were heavy metal, pot-smoking motorcycle gang style teens. They occupied their own part of the lunchroom, and they resembled motley Viking marauders. Phyllis was one of only a few black females at our school. She didn't behave strangely, like Charlie, but she was the quiet type. The heads were white. Their pounding was accompanied with chanting, "Ace of spades! Ace of Spades!" The lunch lady walked up and swooshed at them with her fat hand. But that was it.

Back then, in the eighties, we called them "lunch ladies." This one was quintessential: tall, matronly, garbed in polyester, and beehive hair. She'd wander the cafeteria while taking french-fries from our lunch trays.

Blake, the only black male in my graduating class, didn't get picked on when he came to lunch. Blake was on the football team. He was big, and had a lot of football friends. Phyllis left the school. Blake stayed. Due to bias harassment laws, blatant racial bullying might not go on as much these days. But bullying still does. Couldn't racism be, in part at least, a form of bullying? "You don't belong here," means "You don't have friends to defend you," and that means: you are an easy target.

As a kid I was nice to the "meek." Mary got a crush on me because of it. Charlie asked me to carry his books.

"Charlie. If I did this for you, it would only make you look weaker." Actually I was just scared that the other kids would come after me. I started lifting weights at the time, but I was no hero.

Isn't this how it always is? People are just frightened so they pretend they agree with the belligerent, leaders who call for war, or whoever is dominant in their group. As a middle school student, being nice was as far as I would go. As a middle school teacher I thought I could go farther.

I tell the Home and Careers teacher about Charlie and Mary. "Now that I am the authority, I see why teachers let some kids get away with breaking rules, and turn a blind eye while the weak get picked on. In a way, school is governed by the consent of the governed. It's like society. It follows its own pecking order. Being the teacher who always sides with the meek eventually turns that teacher into one of the bullied."

"Yes, that's a good point," she agrees.

"Time to go and defend the meek again."

Back in my room I prepare to ride out the next storm of rowdy students. It's time for a moment of quiet. I sit at my desk, close my eyes, and think good thoughts.

When Good Kids Go Bad.

"My eyes are open and I am wide awake, in perfect health and feeling better than before." These are the words I use to end my brief meditation. My head bows and my hands fold in prayer: "Bring me peace." I sign the cross, forehead to chest, and shoulder to shoulder. Standing, I take a deep breath and exhale, then walk to the door, stand firmly, feet planted, knees slightly bent and hands clasped behind my back just in time to see the column of fifth graders descend the stairs at the far end of the hall.

Alongside of them, and gesturing in the direction of my room is Ms. Wispy. Earlier that day in the upstairs faculty lounge, she insulted me. We were debating something; it seemed congenial, until she bellowed, "Because you're an idiot!"

"I've got to deal with insults from students all day. I'm not going to sit here and deal with them from teachers as well." I walked out. It was one

58

of my rare moments of having a good comeback. Granted, I was the one to leave, not her.

As the column draws closer, Ms. Wispy, in her chain smoking rasp tells them to "Behave." Levi bounces out of line. With a big grin on his tiny face he taunts her, "You sound like a man!" Apparently it's not just me he harasses, so I feel relieved at this. But this can't be a good sign.

Pointing to the chalkboard illustrations of "positive and negative space" I drew, I hurriedly explain the concept then try to get helpers to pass out supplies. This time, even the kids at a usually well-behaved and hard working table refuse to help.

My vision of myself as "bringer of justice" is crumbling as the meek, who I saw myself as here to uplift, are turning against my authority. Levi sits window side, at the front of the room next to the mentally challenged kid. Levi's bouncing in his chair. I sat him there hoping to isolate him from Curtis, who sits across the aisle. Now the challenged kid is an easy victim next to him, or an easy convert.

Levi is half chanting, half singing: "You's a ho-ohhh. You's a ho-ohhh." He's singing it loudly enough that I'm not sure who it's aimed at. I need to get this class rolling, before others get bored and join in.

"OK!" I say. You know a teacher is half lost when he starts his sentence with "OK." "I like how Sade and Davantah are quiet." They're not really, but I am stuck for helpers, and I decide to give "empowering the disruptive" a chance.

They pass out supplies with bravado, hitting kids, and slamming boxed markers down on the table. Obviously I made a tactical error.

Sade, angry at me for taking her off the job, sits at my desk and starts rummaging around. Another student is rolling on the floor. Curtis is doing a dance. As I begin to bark at the class Davantah starts tossing markers at kids. Then Davantah shouts out at me, "You're so weak dude!" He sits back momentarily shaking his head, laughing to himself. "You're so weak."

Trying to get the class working, I wander the room briefly pausing and chanting at each table: "Read the handout, answer the questions, then begin your drawing."

I come back to my formerly best-behaved table. Looking back on the previous months I can see the mistakes I've made. I praised this group publicly for good behavior. Praising alone isn't bad. But you need more than one good group out of eight to praise. Praising only them might work if they were the "cool kids," but they are not. So, praising only them turns from a badge of honor to a mark of shame.

Instead of being a model group, they are making a mess and laughing about it. The boys at this table are into skater – punker stuff. Last week I tried to bond with them by showing them pictures from my punk rock youth. Now they've turned on me. When I say something, one of the girls imitates me, then concludes with: "Whatever dude!"

I'm losing even the good kids? Is this some kind of joke? I reached out my hand to them and they bit it. These ungrateful little....

I know there are no good kids or bad kids - they're all just wonderful children. Ok I'm being sarcastic, but only a little actually. I'm trying hard to believe in what Martin Luther King said about not hating the evildoer, but only the evil he does. However at the moment it's very difficult to *not* hate these evildoers.

In addition to knowing that I should adhere to MLK's noble principles, I also know that I should not take these children's bad behavior personally. But, under the strain of wanting this job to work out, and feeling like it isn't, I give in to the emotion. "Tyler!" I snap at one of the ex-good kids. With the same chastising tone my grandmother uses, I add, "After all I've done for you, showing you those pictures from my youth, and this is the thanks I get!" Tyler straightens up. Guilt works.

"Whatever" girl is un-phased. She acts guilt free, and like she's on a sugar high. I try to win her back: "I count on you in this classroom and I need your cooperation."

She goes on imitating me: "I count on you..." The sugar synergizes with the thrill of rebellion. I'm feeling egged on, backed into a corner. While stress is causing me to forget a lot of exactly what these kids are doing to egg me on, guilt will help me remember what I do next.

What I do next isn't really that terrible, it's more whom I do it to; whom I choose to take my stand against, that leaves me with moderate pangs of guilt. I will choose to mock a generally well-behaved child, and not a Levi.

I begin to descend to "whatever girl's" eleven-year-old level; morphing into an uber eleven-year-old, larger and savvier than other eleven-year olds, willing and able to use eleven-year-olds' ways like a master, as only someone who's old enough to have been an eleven-year-old nearly three times can.

"Yeah-ha!" I say with a mocking surfer-stoner drawl, doing a little bounce-dance and giving the thumbs up. "Yeah-haaa! You've joined the cool kids!" She tries a lame come back: "That's right! I'm cool." She still looks confidently defiant, so I make a second attempt:

60

"Allriiii-hiiiight! You're one of the cool kids now. You are sooo cool. Sooo cool!" Other kids laugh. This time she looks really caught off guard, with a shocked expression that I haven't seen before.

Maybe you think this little brat had that coming, or maybe you think I just acted like a jerk. Not that this girl is a saint, but my singling her out of an entire class to pick on whisks me back to my own childhood. In those days, when a usually well-behaved child like I was decided to go on bender – like I did on occasion – the teacher meted out swift and immediate justice. Contrarily, if someone like Levi acted out, he would be typically treated with kid gloves; given ample warnings, maybe even smiled at and chastised in a loving tone: "now, now Levi." As a kid, this state of affairs struck me as blatantly unfair. As a teacher, my motto is "fairness." Yet here I am, like a teacher from my youth, incensed and unnerved at losing a "good kid." While I feel a little guilty, I understand how those unfair teachers must have felt: losing the good kids is an ominous harbinger of worse times ahead; it's the kiss of death.

And here comes death, or near death anyway, in the form of Ed.

Et tu, Edward?

Down the aisle from the "good table," sitting next to Levi, is Ed. Ed's mentally challenged. And was, up until this moment, shy and good-natured, definitely one of the meek I saw myself as defending. He's freckled and roly-poly, with sandy-brown hair, cut into an uneven flattop. Did a barber cut his hair, or his mom? His mom dresses him in what look like hand-me-down plaid shirts. The overall impression he makes is that of likeable, slow kid from the 1950's. The type of kid who could have played the role of sidekick to Beaver on "Leave it to Beaver."

Today Ed is playing the role of sidekick to Levi. His new role might be amusing if I were watching this in a film, like a teacher version of "Clerks." It's not in real life.

Ed's taking on a "If you can't beat 'em join 'em" philosophy. A giddy look of mischief crosses his pudgy face. He's a willing disciple of Levi. The same Levi who just last class was mocking and grabbing Ed by the neck. Levi loudly commands Ed: "Throw this at Mr. L." Curtis joins in from across the room: "Yeah, throw it at him. Throw it at him!" Ed cranks his hand back to hurl a broken crayon at me. He looks me dead in the eyes with that giddy grin. His eyes twinkle. He's thrilled. He's *almost* been accepted. His acceptance is conditional however; all he has to do is throw a crayon at this beta teacher. This teacher who "you don't have to listen to."

"Edward!" I march towards him. The education literature says, "Don't be stationary. Wander the room. Use your physical proximity to calm students." (Quell would be more accurate). I will eventually find that my wandering the room seems to agitate students. It could be they're self-consciousness about being seen making art. I'm not sure. Over time I will spend more time stationary and less wandering - unless an administrator is watching me.

As I near him he puts down the offending crayon and playfully runs around to the other side of his table, hoping to engage me in a game of chase.

"Get back to your seat. Same rules for everyone."

"No! I don't have to listen to youuuu," he says, dragging out each word, in his trouble-making-kid-from-the-nineteen-fifties accent. Ed is happy. He's no longer a lonely boy who draws dark brown circles all period, while chaos whirls around him. Ed's a mover, a shaker, and a chaos maker. He's laughing and invigorated by his newfound power, and the newfound approval of his former tormentors.

I could try to subdue Ed with mockery, like I did to Whatever-Girl, but I think if I did that a part of my soul would die.

This is a pretty rough moment, losing this formerly good-natured fat kid with a mental handicap. In his plaid second hand clothes, and "kid from the fifties" accent he's a pitiable character.

No one ever told me what his handicap was. I noticed that he used to come to class accompanied by a middle aged white lady. She was a teacher's aide. She had bleach blond hair, cigarette-stained teeth, and looked sleep deprived. She would sit next to him and help him with the assignments. It was good for both Ed and me, having her there. The additional adult set of eyes seemed to quiet the room down a bit, and help Ed stay involved. Then the aide stopped coming, and left Ed on his own. It seems aides accompany "inclusion" kids everywhere except art and music.

After the aide stopped coming, Ed started to make drawings with what looked like a little sad person in the corner surrounded and being closed in by swirling black and brown crayon. Then he stopped doing anything. Now here we are.

Ed tries to run past me out the door, changing my name into "Mr. LeBone! Mr. Bone!" and repeating it in sing song fashion. He brushes into me. "You touched me! I'm gonna get you fired!" He's picked up on the text of the defiant kids. But his voice lends it an almost tragic sound.

"Edward, go back to your seat now." I follow him at a distance.

"Ryan's your boyfriend," he must have seen me and Ryan talking in the hall, "he's your boyfriend! Ha Ha!" Then Ed runs to a different part of the room ducking behind a chair, still trying to get me to play chase.

In a last desperate measure to regain control, I take on the "Sergeant" persona. "Not another sound from anyone!" This produces limited success. Some of the kids get back to work. I pace the aisle like a prison warden.

Feeling this role a little too much, I mutter out loud but to myself, "My next career is going to be a cop." I fantasize catching some of them in future criminal activity, and when I do…

Perhaps inspired by Popeye, I took up muttering at an early age. Really, I come from a long line of mutterers.

A white girl, the daughter of a teacher's aide, gives me a funny look and she does that twirling motion with her finger at her head, implying my mental instability. This moment will come back to haunt me.

In the lounge I phone Ed's mom. "Oh yeah. Well he never acts this way for anyone else," she says. Ryan laughs when I hang up the phone in defeat. "See I'm telling you. It's a waste of time calling their homes." It's the first time a parent has turned on me. She's white. Now I'm nervous calling whites. No black parents have openly turned on me yet, so I don't hesitate to call them. Since now it's mostly black homes I'm calling, their kids start saying I'm racist. I've gone from white kid's shouting, "You're afraid of them!" to black kid's yelling, "How come you only call our parents?"

Inspiration From A Movie

At home, I've finished work on another lesson plan. I sit on the couch and stare at the curtains, thinking about my life and this miserable job. It's a no win situation. I can't do this anymore. I can't go back into that prison.

Up until now, I went in imagining I was defender of the meek, but now the meek have turned against me. Hatred for me is nearly universal. My days boil down to screaming kids, a snobbish principal, and a scowling supervisor. Who am I going into work for? Who am I supposed to be now?

While feeling too depressed to even get off the couch and drown my sorrows, some part of my brain is sifting through ideas and memories to find the answer, to find a reason to get up tomorrow. Through a depressed haze hope emerges. I begin to remember a foreign film I saw one lonely Friday night. A local art house theater was showing a Polish movie with English subtitles. Was it called "Blue?"

The theater was in a historic building from a bygone era, it's domed ceiling covered in faded paintings, its ornate trappings cracked and peeling. It was an ideal place for a date, but I was dateless, sitting alone among mainly gray haired patrons - the elderly were the main appreciators of the arts in mid nineteen-nineties Rust Belt. After the lights dimmed the middle-aged Polish male lead emerged on screen.

As foggy (possibly revisionist) memories of the film actor's struggle stream into my consciousness, I can see that his struggle is my struggle. (Or at least bears some similarities.) Blue is my ray of hope, a dark, cynical ray of hope. The lead character was nearly penniless in post-Soviet Poland. But he worked out a scheme to get rich. He went to buy some land from an old farmer, knowing the land was far more valuable than the paltry sum he was offering. The old farmer looked wearily at the offered money. He never needed, or even saw money during the communist era. What would he do with it now? He paused. Thought it over. Then nodded his old wrinkled head, and declared: "Yes, I could bury this money somewhere. That would be nice. I could bury it." The audience chuckled at that comment.

Organized crime grew out of communisms' collapse. The Eastern European movie gangsters were big guys with slicked back hair and shiny black leather jackets. They too wanted the farmer's land, so they were out to steal the deed from the middle-aged hero. The star hid the land deed safely away. The Polish mafia came after him. He gambled that they wouldn't kill him since if he died, the deed would be lost forever and then nobody would make money. (At least this is how I remember it). They broke into his house, choked him, dragged him across the floor, and held his head underwater until he nearly drowned. They didn't kill the star. He won his gamble and got rich.

As I remember the saga, I imagine a split screen movie. On one side is the Polish film and on the other, my own life plays. He was penniless in post Soviet Poland; I was penniless in post graduate-school Rust Belt. He had a scheme to get rich; I have a scheme to get... well, just middle class actually. He cons a farmer; Vice Principal First was a farmer - that last analogy doesn't hold up too well. How about this analogy: I con the school system by showing up for a job I secretly can't stand? The lead actor is strangled by gangsters; I get heckled by students as I stand at the chalkboard. He gets dragged across his living room, and thrown into furniture; I get told to "Suck it" and "Shut the fuck up, gay ball." He's being

64

held under water; I feel like I'm drowning, as I try vainly to stop students from destroying my room.

The movie is like a lot of mid-late nineties art films I've been watching. A hero or anti-hero having a miserable life concocts a semi-criminal scheme, succeeds, and then is lounging on a yacht sipping fine wine or otherwise enjoying the good life. The characters don't crumble: they scam, come near death, and win.

These art crime films are like my life, and a lot of people's lives. People go to the factory, or work for some miserable boss, secretly hating what they do, but that check keeps coming. My students are hostile, some parents are hostile, some other teachers and administrators are hostile. But they probably won't kill me, and if I endure the mental beatings I will make money, and like the movie hero, I too can make an escape from my miserable present – somehow. Maybe I won't make enough for a great escape, but at least I won't go back to being broke.

I'm inspired. I scrawl on a yellow post-it, "Tough it out and get your money." On another post it I write, "Take the money and run." I have the strength to get off the couch and drown my sorrows. Proceeding from couch to kitchen I tape my notes to the fridge, and pour a glass of "camping" wine. I raise the glass, toast the hero of the movie, and say out loud, "To getting paid."

7. Culture Gap and the First Date

Slapping Festival

The wind rattled my windows all last night. This morning frost covered the ground, yet two facts make me feel warmer today: it's payday and I'm finally going to meet that Indonesian woman from the Internet. Before I can get paid and start my weekend adventure, I need to suffer through one more day at school.

Ms. Rosebloom's eighth graders parade through the door displaying the current inner city fashions. The boys are *still* all wearing the baggy pants and big loose fitting t-shirts draping past their elbows and rears; but the girls are post hip–hop and have caught on to the tight fitting craze, especially where the pants are concerned. It's almost like the fashions have inverted.

At the turn of the 20th century women were expected to dress modestly, but guys could show their forms. Now, in the year 2000 in the urban teen crowd, and among these eighth graders, it's the men who dress modestly, wearing loose clothes that reveal nothing.

This trend is mirrored in the adult world at hip-hop dance clubs I go to. I wonder what the contrast between scantily-clad women and fully-cloaked men is doing for male-female relations. While the chicks dance provocatively with each other, the guys kind of hang back waiting for an in to join the bump and grind.

The newly assigned seats are ignored. I try to stay the course, "Jasmine, get back to your assigned seat." Physically, she's very mature for an eighth grader. She ignores me as she wanders over to a boy's table. Jasmine playfully grabs at him. He gives her a flirtatious slap. "Jasmine get back to your seat now!" Another kid is out of his seat and starting to play around with Alexis. Another ass is slapped. "Go back to your assigned table now or I will call your home!" Soon boys and girls are all over the place. Asses are being slapped left and right. It's not long before Jasmine takes off her belt and tries to use it as a whip.

"Regain control, but act calm and confident," I tell myself. "Jasmine, you've been asked many times now to go…"

66

"I don't haaave to listen to you!"

I confiscate the belt and do the drill sergeant voice. It's having little effect. I start to fill out write-ups and threaten students with being sent to the office. Write-ups only provoke them: "What the fuck is you writing me up for?! That's complete bunk!"

Finally I go to the phone to ring the office, even though I know I will get the blame if the principal gets involved. The room quiets down as I lift the receiver.

"Yes"

"This is Mr. L"

The noise and shouting begin anew.

"Who? I really can't hear you."

They switch to the PA system.

"Yes?"

"This is Mr. L. I need an administrator here."

"I really can't hear you."

Then the PA is dead.

I pick up the phone.

"Hello? Hello?"

Dead.

The kids look at me with a sympathy that says, "Poor guy, even the office won't listen to him."

The Phone Call Culture Gulf

Later that day, I head into the lounge and begin my phone calls. "Hi, this is Jasmine's art teacher. Is her parent or guardian home?"

"This is her Grandma," a women's voice replies, sounding resolute, suspicious and younger than I remember grandma's being. I speak rapidly, trying to get as much in before she has a chance to disapprove of me.

"I am very sorry to bother you, but she was out of her seat without permission, and this has been going on for a while, and now it's graduated to profane language, her slapping kids in the rear and her getting her rear slapped…"

"She whaaat?!" her grandma says indignantly. It's impossible to know if this grandma is angry at me, or the kid. I imagine her standing sternly in the kitchen, her free hand resting on her hip. She's silent for a bit, as if wanting me to sweat for a while, and I can't tell if that "she whaaat" is telling me "Jasmine never does anything like this" or is saying: "She is in a lot of trouble when she gets home."

67

As the silence lingers, I nervously fill in the gap, prattling off a list of smaller infractions and compliments, "She is a gifted artist, but she needs to work on not interrupting me when I am trying to instruct. You know I am a believer that the big problems start with the little ones…"

She cuts me off, and gruffly says: "You should have called a lot sooner."

"Yes ma'am, I know, I know. Sorry. It's just I hate to bother parents. I know how busy you are and sometimes you never know what reaction you'll get." I try to convey apology, and briefly defend myself at the same time.

I hear her voice soften towards me, "Mmm, mmm," and imagine her hand moving from hip to chin, then back to hip as she draws her conclusion: "Well, she is gonna get a real whooppin when she gets home, believe me."

"Thank you very much."

I hang up the phone, and pause to take some breaths, looking at the gray tiled wall in front of me. It looks like this parent is on my side. But how many more of these parents do I have to call? One of them is bound to turn against me sometime (besides Ed's mom). It often goes this way with calling parents, especially the ones who live in the Fruit Belt. I get that tone, that indignant "he whaaat" that puts me on guard because this wasn't like anything I heard growing up and I can't tell how to take it at first.

People think that cultural differences are the big noticeable things like spicy food or different clothing styles. In part they are, but the real differences lie in the little things like the way people say and do things and especially what they mean by it. This is where the confusion really comes in. There was this tall Sicilian guy in undergrad school, and his sense of space was very different than the Anglo-Afro American culture I grew up in, where we don't stand "too close." This guy and other southern Italians I met get right up to you when they talk and put their arm around you. In spite of what people often say, even the sense of personal space is cultural. I will learn this the hard way later in the year.

Getting back to the "indignant 'he whaaat?' thing," I think it's saying "My kid is gonna be in trouble when he gets home, and not saying…" Ryan comes in and interrupts my whole thought process: "It's Friiidaaay!" "Yes. Thanks for reminding me," I say smiling.

Marisol

Last week, when we set up tonight's first date I said, "Should we take separate cars or do you want me to come and pick you up?" You see

68

the strategy here? This way I showed her I was not trying to get her in my car, just offering it as an option. She could still feel free to come and go as she pleased. "Why don't we take your car?" she countered. (See I told you ;)). I don't shave like my brother would before going on a date. We disagree on this point. I always find I get more female attention with a little stubble, although it can scratch faces if it comes down to making out. But he thinks it makes you look sketchy.

As I get ready to meet her, my emotions are a mixed bag of giddy anticipation, nervousness, and a dash of creepiness. When I'm meeting a blind date for the first time it feels like opening a Christmas present - although it usually turns out to be a present I don't want. And partly, blind dates just feel weird and awkward: I'm meeting a total stranger. What do I say? How do I act? Who is this stranger?

Marisol's house is on a busy street only ten minutes from mine, but in the opposite direction from Ryan's and in a more expensive white-collar suburb. It's dark and I find it hard to read the addresses, as I drive by at thirty-five miles an hour with these f-ing cars riding my rear trying to push me to forty. I try not to even think in swear words, in case I slip in front of the kids. Not that some of them would mind, but then they'd have one over on me. Shit, I missed the house again. I'm a little nervous and part of me is hoping I can say "Awh man I couldn't find your place!" There it is, 345 Sun Baked Boulevard. I turn in the drive and pull in the back parking lot. I've got another minute to myself in my car with the ignition off, before meeting her. I take a couple of breaths and admonish myself to act normal. Don't act like a weirdo or something, I tell myself. She lives in the lower apartment.

I ascend the steps wondering who I'll be meeting and what I'll be getting. A five foot two, brown complexioned Asian woman, a little darker than Ryan's wife, and with a more 80's styled hair, comes to the door. "Hiiiii" she says very girlishly with a wide smile as she offers me a warm hug. She's acting like she hasn't seen me in awhile, not like she's never seen me before. The warm welcome puts me at ease. I take my shoes off, as is the custom in most Asian households. To my left is an upholstered brown and beige 80's style couch. Across the small living-dinning room in front of me on the wall, below a framed picture from her home country, is a big picture of Tweety Bird. Not initially what I'd expect to see here. "I love Tweety," she sweetly tells me.

I've been seeing Tweeties everywhere this year, on girl students' backpacks, notebooks, shirts, and even on the tire covers that go on the back of jeeps. A lot of my girl students work drawings of Tweety into their artwork. So do some of the younger boys who haven't been made aware by more "sophisticated" kids that "Tweety is for girls." I've seen Tweety drawn by the Egyptian Pyramids, Tweety worked into Greek style vases, and standing in a still life. If it weren't for what I perceive to be my supervisor's anti-cartoon and pro "original work" bias, I would just give the kids what they want and teach them how to draw Tweety, but since I do perceive this bias, I don't give the kids what they want.

Then I see a fish tank filled with tropical fish, and think it's a sign of loneliness, not as strong of a sign as a cat would be, but a sign. She chain-smokes thin long filtered cigarettes. We get along well, but after a while I don't think she's the one I've been waiting for.

Maybe out of loneliness or just the pleasure of being around someone nice and warm, instead of some of these hardened and mean acting kids, we go out a few more times. I make it clear that "we are just friends" but still I have to resist. We're both at lonely points and both feeling unappreciated. I asked her how she wound up in America. She met an American musician back home. He was working and bumming around there, and wound up bringing her back here. The musician was quite a bit older than Marisol, and started becoming physically abusive.

It would be easy to treat this relationship like one of those flings I've had, that I took no more seriously than warm cognac on a cold night. The problem with that is, one of us in these flings always seems to have expectations. My guilt over disappointing someone increases with the older the lady is; her biological clock is "ticking." Marisol is thirty-one, already divorced and has no kids yet. She probably has been disappointed enough.

Even if you know someone isn't for you, it's so easy to get to that "why not" stage. I hear younger people are doing that all the time now, and have something called "hook ups," and "friends with benefits" which means you can have sex but not be in a relationship. A lot of friends my age have already been married, and some are divorced. I grew up in a dating culture where it's all or nothing. Either we are boyfriend and girlfriend committed and giving it a real try, or we don't even talk. I know some guys my age are better at the "let's just be friends" thing after a few go-rounds. Not me though. After we've gotten close, and it doesn't work out, that's pretty much the last I hear from them. I like this Marisol. I value her friendship. I value the window she gives me into another culture, so I try to resist making a move.

We set up another date for next week as "just friends."

8. Battling music teachers and the Mountain

Mr. Cantwell

At the foot of the stairs, just across the hall from my basement art room is the music room. The teacher inhabiting it is a toweringly tall, strong looking, black man: Mr. Cantwell. He dresses in fancy, flowing silk shirts and matching pants. Some of his garb is embroidered with musical notations, and other designs. I would describe his style as "Liberace Lite."

Mr. Mullet, the band teacher said of him: "They say he's an ace choral music director. But every time I go by his room he's just showing videos."

Inside his music room, Mr. Cantwell has hung all sorts of Bible related illustrations. They're laminated and show scenes like Moses holding the Ten Commandments. "Can he really do this?" I wonder. Religion plays a big role in the black community, and doesn't seem to hold the controversy it does among whites.

He has a firm handshake. But the look in his eyes is a little crazy. He's new here too. Not a new teacher though. He transferred from another school. Is that good or bad? I figure he should have it easy. He's seasoned and been through it all before. What I can't see now is that he's burning out with "going through it all." Unlike me, I'm still "ready to serve," to quote losing presidential candidate John Kerry.

You might be thinking that because he's black he'll be getting more respect down here in our basement world than I am. As it turns out, being black hasn't helped his cause. Students display their disenchantment with Mr. Cantwell as freely as they do with me.

The two of us are commiserating about our lousy jobs. Voice steeled with determination, he says, "I am not putting up with garbage. I marched a whole seventh grade class to Ms. Henderson's office." I nod my head, impressed, but inside I'm shocked. Other teachers warned me, "Never send kids to the office." He just did it. Should I do it too, and really show the kids, "I'm not playing around"?

71

A few days later he tells me: "Matt, I just took this seventh grader to Ms. Henderson's office. You know what she did?" He sounds paranoid, like he's being conspired against.

"No."

"After I told her what this kid was doing, she said 'what's his last name?' You know what Matt? I couldn't remember."

"Oh no."

"She said 'You don't even know this child's last name?!'" He mimics her voice, making her sound accusing.

"Was the student there?"

"She said it right in front him."

"That's terrible," I say, while thinking thank God I heeded the warnings.

CD Design
1. Think of a real or imaginary music group.
2. Lightly sketch a cover for a CD.
3. Use lines and colors that match the mood.
4. Give your work a title and put your name on it.

Illustrated handout.

Mullet Attacked

Mr. Jason Mullet and I are in the first floor lounge –AKA the "ladies lounge." He's the instrumental music teacher with the mullet. I'm eating one of those frozen fish dinners Leroy the maintenance guy gives me. Leroy knows it's my first "real" job and I need to save every penny I can. He calls me "frugal Matt," which sounds a little like "fruity Matt;" but since he's giving me free food, I don't complain.

I've always had luck with people giving me free food or libations. When I was eighteen and going door to door to raise money for an environmental group, a housewife gave me fresh fish that her husband caught. Another person gave me a glass of wine, which really loosened me up when asking for money.

Mr. Cantwell, the other music teacher, enters. He's dressed in one of his fancy silk shirts.

"Hey Matt!" he says, happy to see me. Jason Mullet starts to give him a hard time.

"You must dress in the most expensive outfits of any teacher I have ever seen." Mullet says, looking at him sidewise and chuckling.

Mr. Cantwell stammers for a comeback: "This doesn't cost much." Jason chuckles some more, "Yeah right."

I can't stand seeing him suffer like this, thinking a couple of white guys are ganging up on him. I know the feeling of being caught off guard by unexpected attacks myself, so I come to his defense. Jason drops it.

Other teachers join us for lunch. A kid knocks on the door and pries it open a little. The teachers give him a harsh look. They make the kid wait a while before anyone addresses him. "You can't come in here!" At first I'm confused. Aren't we here to help kids? This kid seems to need help. Over time I get it. Most faculty lounges I will go to keep the doors closed, and have an unofficial "no kids allowed" policy. It's a safe haven from the battles of the classroom. But now it's time to leave my safe haven, and return to the front.

Ms. Rosebloom's kids are the current occupying army of my room, a force I am trying to both reign in and placate. A lot of them are absent so the room feels airier. Even so, it's mainly the more sociopathic ones today, a small but power-packed bunch. Sometimes I think the kids with the best attendance are the ones whose parents want them at home the least.

Mullet walks by hearing the clamor. He steps into the doorway and gives the kids "The Look." For a second it works. I'm happy for the backup, but I'm also embarrassed that they quiet down for him and not me. My embarrassment dissolves as Huey shouts out "Nice mullet!" Others laugh.

The authoritarian teacher-look washes off his face. It's replaced by a look of confusion. "What?" he says, but his "what" sounds like a regular guy honestly asking "what," and not like a teacher's "What did you say? Oh I didn't think so," type of "what."

"Yeah. Nice Mullet. That's real eighties there, Rod Stewart!" Huey again says with confidence. Another kid chimes in, "Get out of here, mullet." Jason stands there another few seconds, weakly giving the class "The Look" again, but this time without any subduing effect.

He quickly withdraws looking genuinely embarrassed. I'm shocked, relieved, and disappointed. I'm disappointed that his backup didn't help any. Relieved because it confirms that I'm not the only person they feel they can humiliate. Shocked at his reaction. I assumed he knew his hairdo was very "eighties Rod Stewart" and just had the self-confidence to do it anyway. Instead it's looking like he actually thinks his mullet *is* cool. (Maybe a few years from now this look will make a bit of a comeback, but it hasn't yet).

Retro

On the drive home I tune into "Alternative Edge Rock." It used to be a "classic hard rock" station, but then morphed into an "Alternative Rock" station, and now "Edge Rock." Eventually it will start reverting back to its original hard rock format.

A new genre of music, which sounds to me like punk rock, rap and metal mixed into one, is popular now. In the early eighties I tried being a "metal head" but was too nerdy. Then in the mid eighties I discovered punk and stayed with it into the early nineties. In the early and mid nineties I half-heartedly got into rap. By then I didn't feel young enough to go all the way and be one of those baggy "pants'd," big clock, backwards-baseball-cap-wearing guys, but I had my subtle influences. And I can remember trying to "jump" when that "House of Pain" song's chorus told everyone on the dance floor to.

Usually my jumps seemed to be out of step with everybody else's; the crowd would be up and I'd be down. I'd try to smile with everyone else jumping up and down in unison and remain cool. Then I would exit the floor, waiting for a less challenging song to come on.

Now here it is, I've just passed the thirty-one year mark, am taking a second stab at youth and that second stab is facilitated by the fact that every music that reflected my teens is now rolled into one. In some ways I feel good about this because I can still relate to youth culture unlike people a bit older who won't see their stuff come back for a few more years.

None of the subculture "hardcore" stuff I used to listen to is underground anymore. Now it's popular and mainstream. Ads for football

74

are accompanied by punk-metal sound tracks. In some ways it's disturbing, that such an angry sound, once reserved for a few self-selected and actual misfits, is now the norm. To us, or me anyway, mosh pits (we called them slam pits in my day) and the rhythmic growl of hard core were a catharsis from mainstream culture. I can't figure out who the mainstream is "catharting" against. Is it even catharsis or just stirring up anger?

A Limp Bizkit song pounds through my car speakers. The vocals are a familiar melodic growl, only raspier and "rappier" than the hardcore music I grew up with. The singer chants something about "taking a chainsaw" and something about "I'm gonna"…semi audible but sounds like "cut your face raw." I'm used to groups with this much anger being something only some of "us kids" knew about. All my friends knew the band "Suicidal Tendencies" and their subculture hit about "seeing your mommy dead," but no one else at school did. Now all the kids would be humming along with it. Is this stuff really healthy for kids like Huey?

It's time to forget Huey for a while. At home I phone Marisol to confirm our next "just friends" date. I've got something to look forward to.

Roller Rink

Back at work I spend half the day chaperoning seventh and eighth graders at a roller rink field trip. During the daytime the outside of the rink looks pretty tame compared to nighttime. At night I've seen large crowds being dispersed by police. "Come on and skate!" staff and students encourage. But I don't. I never learned how. I missed the whole "tween" eighties roller-skating thing somehow.

Instead of skating, I sit on the sidelines with the mostly boy students who don't know how to skate either and have a hard time relating to girls. After "supervising" a couple of boys playing a violent video game, I do a French fry run for the kids.

Huey is at the fry hungry table. He's showing off his CD's. Limp Bizkit is in his collection, the band that sings about chainsaws. I lamely try to make some small talk with him about it, to show "we're not so different after all," but I just come across like a nerdy teacher.

Huey is a living example of why I find it unsettling that the disturbing music from my youth has become so mainstream. He's what you get when you take a child from a dysfunctional home, feed him lots of donuts, and pump his head full of violent music and video games. You get a big kid like him who, in the middle of class, tells a teacher like me, he'll put his foot up my ass.

75

Even though I can't skate, and my attempts at bonding with the kids are only weakly successful, this morning's outing is great because it gives me a break from having to maintain an authoritarian façade - telling children to "be quiet" and "take those headphones off."

The buses pull into Burger Time for lunch but then someone decides the kids are too rowdy to actually go inside. We pull out again with busloads of hungry, angry kids. After we get the students fed back at school, I go up to the second floor lounge and eat my brown-bag lunch. The tables are crowded with teachers talking about the day trip to the rink.

Mullet Be Gone

Mr. Mullet walks in shortly after me. He looks different. "Did you do something different Jason?" Someone says. Right away, I can see his mullet is gone. His hair is cut short. I can't believe it; this guy seemed like he always had that mullet.

The women ask him "What happened to your long hair?" He answers in a slang dialect typical of "the cool" kids who were older than me in high school, "My old lady kept raggin on me about it. So I cut it to get her off my back." People offer their condolences. The word "raggin," I haven't heard that in a long time. He actually said, "raggin." If you're too young to know what it means, it means something like "she's on the rag - having her period - and is in a bad mood."

His reverting to cool-kid slang of his generation seems like obvious cover for the real reason he cut his hair. I contemplate saying, "Bull, Jason! Huey made fun of your mullet yesterday and you cut if off man! You're embarrassed by what young people think. Your wife had nothing to do with the loss of your mullet." Instead I let it be. Ryan, I can make fun of. We're the same age and are sort of friends. Jason, I'd better not.

Hike

On our second date, Marisol and I are going for a hike in the mountains. We drive past huge antique shops, and through an Indian Reservation famous for tax-free gas and cigarettes. After one wrong turn, we're at the state park. It's an unusually warm day for this time of year, but only a few brave leaves cling to the barren trees. The peak of the fall colors has passed. It's too early to ski. In the off-season we're pretty much alone on the mountain walk. We stop frequently and stand close, but I resist.

That evening we take in a Bjork movie called "Dark Dancer" or something like that. It's an arty, depressing, tragic musical. The theater is almost empty as it usually is here in Rust Belt at art films.

After the show, we're at my house sitting on the same couch I was on with Brandy. As if we can both feel the spirit of this couch, we begin. We're nearly going all the way, but I know that will kill it. I can never hope to "just be friends" if we consummate this. "OK, we better stop. This is too fast and it could damage our friendship," I say. The stereotype is that it's the woman who makes these levelheaded remarks in the heat of the moment. Not here, not in my life. When I was more active and I brought up the condom issue I'd usually hear, "Don't worry, I'm on the pill." Willpower wins this time however. We leave the couch. We leave my house. After a last sobering stop at a coffee house, I drop her off at home and cool the evening down with a hug, but that's all. It will be the last warm night for a while.

As the days wear on and no one new turns up in life or on the Internet, I keep thinking about Marisol and that time on the couch. Winter begins its push against fall early this year. My cold house and this monastic lifestyle are starting to bother me. I pick up the phone and begin to dial her. If I see her now my "why not have fun" drive will easily defeat my "no it will ruin any friendship," sensibility. I hang up after dialing half the number.

It's a similar "should I call or shouldn't I call," pick up the phone, put down the phone, kind of agonizing I do when I want to call in sick to work. I want to call, I want to stay home but I don't want these kids to think they've won. I don't want the principal to think I'm running scared.

Weeks pass and Marisol calls me. "Hey Matt. How's it goin?"

"Same old," I tell her. "You want to come to a party?" What kind of party I ask. "They'll be a lot of Indonesians there." Did my will power pay off? Can I go there with her "just as friends" and actually meet a new woman while the two of us are out together?

"Sure I'll go."

Observation – still not tough enough

After Rosebloom's students stomp mob-like into the room, a much taller figure than any of these already big seventh grader's follows in behind them. It's the supervisor. He's wearing a black leather trench coat and his scowl. "To your assigned seats. Everybody at their assigned seats!" I say sternly to show that I am "laying down the law." When they don't, I pretend they are. The last thing I need is for him to see me in a losing showdown.

"Quiet!" I rapidly and nervously go over the directions trying to squeeze it all in before I lose my audience more than I already have. "You will complete your... Huey! Stop that!...illustration of a Chinese character using either a warm...Alexis!... or cool color scheme."

The helpers dole out tempera paints and pass the students' art back to them. It's noisy and rowdy, but it's all getting done. But my supervisor's scowl remains. Still I am relieved, because I've been threatened by kids in here, had near brawls break out, ass slapping, crayon wars, uncontrolled swearing; and here nothing big is going wrong and they are working.

After they leave, it's just me and him. He sits writing, leaving us both in silence, looks up and in his stern and whiny voice says, "Mr. Lebrun, you still need to clamp down and be firmer. The discipline needs a lot of work." I've gone along with him at every observation, but now I'm feeling exacerbated.

"Dr. Supervisor, I've been clamping down on them, but it just makes matters worse. Look I..." He cuts me off.

"You cooperate," he says, looking me dead on until I look away nervously. It's a good tactic. He's reminding me that I am cooperative as I begin stepping down the path of defiance. "The art teacher here before you, he didn't cooperate. He was always arguing with us. He thought we were picking on him. We are trying to help." I'm not sure who the "we" is he's talking about.

"That other teacher was in a lot of different situations, and it never worked out. The discipline was always a disaster." "Different situations" is education speak for different schools. His stern tone is a warning to me, a warning to not defy my superiors as many do under this stress. Now his voice takes on a slight sing-song, like he's talking to a child, "But you are working out because you cooperate and know we're trying to help you."

I compose myself by recalling a scene from The Matrix. The scene where the little boy who looks like a tiny Buddhist monk, bends a spoon with his mind. Keanu asks the boy how he does that. The tiny monk says the secret is to realize there is no spoon; everything in the matrix is an illusion. With this knowledge Keanu can defeat the matrix. In a similar vein, I half jokingly tell myself "There is no intimidating supervisor, there are no defiant students. This school is an illusion. With this knowledge I can survive until summer."

"Yes, thank you Dr. Supervisor," I say, regaining my agreeable meekness that he's accustomed to.

78

Now he reverts to his stern tone, "Your directions were a little vague and hard to follow."

I think, "Of course they are. I've only got a minute to explain everything, before my students get bored and boo me off the stage."

He returns to his reassuring voice: "But that's OK. That will come with time. Really this takes about five years until it's easy." Damn, five years. I could have picked a lot of careers that take five years to get good at it. (Actually when I do finally start my fifth year this job is still rough.)

"Thank you for the encouragement."

We look down at his notes, and he goes over what he's written on my evaluation. I say many "Thank yous," shaking his hand for a final round of gratitude. He leaves. It could have gone either way, but I know I've just reached another small milestone.

When I see that class again, one of the girls asks me about the visitor. "Was that your supervisor?"

"Yeah."

"What did he think?" I can tell she thought the class did pretty well. That's what I thought.

I tell her the truth. She gets a little mad, "He had that look on his face," and scrunches up her face like he did. It's one of those rare moments of solidarity that I imagined would have been commonplace with me and the kids.

9. Sci-Fi Becomes Real and A Teacher Gets Accused.

Dark Day in the Basement

The problem with this whole "cracking down" thing is that the stress of persistent chaos while trying to be firm wears one down. Sterness transforms into real anger.

The mood has been really bad here in the basement all day. Earlier today, the kids were hooting and hollering more than ever at Mr. Cantwell and me. Now he's late coming back from break to meet his next music class. His seventh graders are milling around getting rowdy. He must be avoiding the class. It's the usual catch twenty-two. The worse the kids are, the worse you perform for them. The worse you perform for them, the worse they get. But the worse they are, the more they need a tightly organized lesson.

I'm trying to keep an eye on his students. "Just wait along the wall. He's on his way."

My eighth grade group comes pouring down the stairs. I try to herd them into the room but instead they join the crowd of seventh graders. It's getting chaotic.

Mr. Cantwell finally shows up. No one wants to go in the rooms. We both resort to yelling to corral the kids. Once his kids are inside their room, he tries to help me out. But my students offer him fresh resistance. One girl is hiding in a locker, laughing. It might be cute if these groups weren't so prone to complete tumult.

He shouts, "Get your rear out a that locker and into your room." I've seen African-American teachers use this informal way of talking to their advantage with kids. But for Mr. Cantwell it backfires. She gets out and her anger boils over.

"Shut the fuck up! Who is you? You're not even my teacher right now."

He's losing his cool now too.

I join in: "Hey, he's just trying to help."

"You're not even a real teacher anyway. You're the art teacher!" She says to me.

Mr. Cantwell is feeling the sting. "What did you just say to me?!" he shouts.

"You heard me. I told you to get the fuck out of my way." She defiantly attempts to storm past him.

Then the two get physical. I can't believe what's going on. Did he just shove her? I blank it out of my memory.

My students, mostly in the room by now, are rushing to the door trying to get out again and see the show.

"Get back in the room now! Into your seats!" I say as I am blocking the door with my outstretched arms. A wave of kids pushes me. I hold firm.

The anger leaves my voice but the volume remains. I've got to stay calm but firm. This could get really ugly. I keep chanting: "Get back to your seats now. Get back to your seats now." All the while I maintain a vantage point from the door where I can see the whole room. I briefly turn my head to look down the hall for the girl who was in the locker, but the hallway is empty. I can't chase her down now; I've got to stay focused on the class. My rhythmic chanting is working somewhat. Students have retreated from the door and are near tables. A few are sitting. I direct one of them to pass out artwork. It's cooling down. I walk around the room saying, "Let's get to work." Shaniqua, the girl from the locker, returns. She looks sullen but others prod her for a story. As she recounts her tale her sullen mood passes. Now she's smacking her fist into her palm.

Before I can walk over to calm her down, I hear commotion coming from the hall again. Mr. Cantwell and one of his students are shouting. This time he's arguing with a boy. Then there's a thud. It sounds like a fight. Again my students run to the door. Again I block the door with my body. "In the room and back to your seats!" I say for the second time this period.

Loud noises come from his room. It sounds like the kids are urging on a brawl. As I crane my neck to look, while still watching my own class, I see Mr. Cantwell storm back into his room. His music room is set up like a mini amphitheater, so I can see multi-leveled, bi-racial rows of seventh graders shouting and jeering at him. They look like rows of pirates, or mutineers.

After our classes leave we meet in the hall and talk in hushed voices. "That was pretty bad. Thanks for helping me out earlier," I say, even though if he wasn't late none of this might have happened. "What happened after that 'thing' with my student and you? I heard that second showdown and then all your kids shouting at you," I ask.

81

He explains to me the hard time one of his kids was giving him in the hallway. The kid was the last one to refuse to go in the room and was making a big show about it.

"Matt man, I'm from the projects. So when Terrelle was acting like such a punk and swearing at me, how he's gonna kick my ass, it was like it was just me and him, in the projects and on the street. I thought, 'Your ass is mine!'"

"Yeah, I mean I'm not from the street or anything, but I know what you mean. These little teenagers would be nothing against a grown man. These kids are getting away with way too much," I say, only half knowing what he means.

"You know what?" He adds, standing taller and acting more indignant than conspiratorial.

"No. What?" I say, genuinely wondering what he's going to tell me next.

"Those little brats. They all wrote letters saying I hit Terrelle, and said they are going to give them to principal."

"Thank God she's not here now," I conclude.

It's a few periods later in the day. I've weathered a couple more storms, and I'm doing my usual organizing of the wreckage, when Vice Principal First comes in. "What happened down here?" He says in a sharper tone than usual.

"Huh?" I'm used to him being the "I'm on the teacher's side" type.

"I've got a bunch of letters from his class saying Mr. Cantwell hit Terrelle during music; and your student, Latrice, is in the office saying he shoved her too." He looks pissed and I realize this could all go either way. I recap the events, and he looks a little more satisfied. I stay as vague as I can without lying.

"You might have to testify about this. So you didn't see what happened with him and Terrelle?"

"No, I was in my room. I mean I heard some noise, but not really." I almost start to get Mr. Cantwell in trouble, but then catch myself.

"Probably just as well you didn't. I'll tell you, he is lucky Ms. Henderson isn't here," Mr. First says. My thoughts exactly. She hasn't been here for a while. I guess she's having issues with her recurring cancer.

Two days pass since Cantwell was accused. No one's asked me to "testify." The issue must be dead.

"Mr. L, report to the main office *immediately*." The announcement jars me. Nervously I head up there. The secretary ushers me into the principal's back office. I'm relieved to see she isn't there, but not relieved by how serious and angry the air feels in here. Latrice and her mom are sitting to my right, looking straight ahead with clenched jaws and squinty gunslinger eyes. Her mom has a similar build and height to her daughter. (We're talking D cups here). The music teacher stares at the wall behind his accusers with a similar look of defiance. From behind the principal's desk, Mr. First swivels his chair slightly towards me. He too looks stern and unfriendly. "What happened here Mr. Lebrun?"

"Well." That's as much as I can say for what seems like a long time, but is probably just a few seconds. I remain standing, shifting my weight from one foot to the other. Thinking about what I will say next. My "peace maker" nature kicks in. "Latrice, what's going on here? Such a good artist and here you are in the office?" I say to diffuse the mood a little.

"He shoved me," she says.

"Come on now. It wasn't quite like that. You were hiding in the locker, and you did swear at Mr. Cantwell." I say in a sort of singsong like voice, not wanting to antagonize her or her irate mom. "I know you didn't like him yelling at you like that, but it was starting to get out of control in that hall, and we needed you back in the room." This builds some understanding on the mom's part and puts some blame on the music teacher. "You did swear at him," I say smiling a little here and there, while keeping a tone of chastisement towards her.

"Yeah I did," she admits. Good. This is working.

"Then you tried to just barge right past him. He put his arms out, but you just barged right into him." My tone seems to work. She's admitting some guilt and everybody seems in a better mood. I'm excused to leave.

Later on Mr. First finds me. "You did well. That was good." Mr. Cantwell made it out unscathed.

Cookie Crumbles

The next week, I go into Mr. Cantwell's music room and ask: "What happened to your Bible pictures?"

"Ms. Henderson made me take them down," he says dejectedly. She's returned, lowering our morale. "Matt, there has got to be a better way." He's losing hope fast, "I've been calling and telling my supervisor 'You've got to get me out of here!' But he doesn't return my calls." Of course he doesn't, I think to myself.

A few classes down and Mr. Cantwell and I are eating lunch in the upstairs teacher's lounge. This "school employee," Young Mr. Nosey, walks in wearing a collarless flowing shirt. It looks African. He looks familiar. I

83

recognize him from undergrad, probably student government beer drinking venues. Young Nosey works here, but I can't quite figure out what he does. He always struck me as a fake.

Mr. Cantwell looks at him with a broad grin and shouts "Nelson! How you doin' Nelson?" It's a voice that sounds similar to Ryan's, when he's being obnoxious. I'm not sure how to react. At first I don't get the joke, so I laugh. Then I do get it. He's calling him "Nelson Mandela," the former President of South Africa, making fun of his African style shirt. They're both black guys, so it's hard for me to decipher all this. I stop laughing, feeling kind of bad about the whole thing. It reminds me of the time Mullet was picking on Mr. Cantwell, only now Mr. Cantwell is doing the picking.

Then I feel like laughing again, because I remember that I resent Nosey. Not deep resentment, just a little. I can't tell what he does here other than act like some sort of supervisor. He seems to wander the halls watching us. When he isn't doing that, he's in a large room, behind his desk, with only one or two students at a time in there with him. There're what look like games in the room, and I can't tell what they are supposed to be doing. The Home and Careers teacher told me he taught science here once. Then he got a "promotion." It looks very low stress, and he gets to act judgmental all the time. It's like he's a spy for the principal.

After lunch, when I'm walking by Mr. Cantwell's music room, I notice the kids are well behaved and cooperative. I'm happy for him. Later in the hallway I say, "Congratulations, those kids were really well behaved. What did you do?"

"I told them that if they are quiet while they complete this writing, they can have a cookie."

"It works?"

"Yeah it works until they get the cookie, then they're terrible again."

"Oh man."

We both laugh.

Maybe I should just fall.

A couple of the maintenance guys join our conversation. Leroy isn't there. These are less familiar ones. I'm the only white guy out of the four. Mr. Cantwell starts telling them about how terrible these kids are and how he can't take it.

"Come on, don't let them get to you." The taller maintenance guy advises.

"I don't know. Sometimes I think I'm just going to fall." Wow I can't believe what Mr. Cantwell just said. It sounds like he wants to have a convenient accident so he doesn't have to work.

"Then you're letting them win," the shorter maintenance guy says.

"Yeah. Come on. We need you here!" I say.

I really think we do. I think it's good for the kids to see a black male in a position of authority, a role model if you will. It's good for me, too. We've been together struggling through purgatory down here in this basement for months now. I feel a sense of camaraderie with him and the other embattled teachers here, like we're comrades in arms. The thought of him bailing out is disconcerting.

Despite my hopes that he stays on board, Cantwell has been absent more and more, letting his music classes sink into the deeper level of chaos found when subs are in charge.

He came to school today, but he's regretting it. His seventh grade class is due to arrive anytime now. Nosey comes down the hall, and tells him "Hey man. I got bad news for you. We just got a call from your cousin. Your house got robbed."

I back away a bit, but stay within earshot. "Oh my God," Cantwell says with what seems like overacting. "You've got to get someone to cover my classes!"

"Yeah, don't worry man. You need to get home and take care of your stuff." Nosey sounds like he believes Cantwell's house actually did get robbed. Like he doesn't suspect this is just a time-buying tactic to get away from his hellish seventh grade. Someone comes to cover for Cantwell.

Post Thanksgiving Party

"Hang in till the next holiday," every one says. A freak snowstorm starts that holiday early. Snow blasts the school. I'm surprised at how a nurturing instinct kicks in. I stay late and help carry the scared kindergarten kids on to the bus. Traffic is nearly impossible. I leave work at three and don't arrive home until two AM. But I get a few days to myself.

Saturday and it's time to pick up Marisol for the "Post Thanksgiving" party she invited me to. The streets are plowed and the driving ban is lifted. I'll see how this "just friends" thing works out tonight. We take the local roads across the city. The neighborhood goes from her safe clean well-lit part of town, to where the party is: a dilapidated neighborhood with boarded-up houses and guys with baggy pants and hoods wandering around. We drive up to the house and walk through a cheap wooden door to enter the apartment. You can always tell a neglectful landlord when they have a door more suited to a closet on an apartments' entrance. The walls are covered in old dirty beige paint. The furnishings look equally old and second-hand. Sheets serve as curtains. But the place is clean, aside from years of neglect to the building's exterior and interior. It's typical low-income immigrant household, besides the couple of white Americans living with them. There's a toothless old white man in flannel and work boots, one of the only people wearing shoes inside. If you haven't been to a lot of Asian immigrant households, then you may not know that they don't wear shoes inside their homes. Actually the toothless man lives upstairs for free and is related to the landlord. He tells me he keeps an eye on the place. Then there is a middle-aged Caucasian lady, Debbie, who's married to one of the Asian guys. She's heavy-set with short hair, and after talking with her I notice she has a facial twitch. Between the two of them, I can't see them having more than five bucks to their names. She seems a little crazy. Debbie's lived all over the US and done some serious "partying" in her day. She's married to a fairly handsome middle-aged Indonesian guy named Bruce. He seems normal and fairly intelligent. They seem like a real mismatched couple.

There are other Indonesians here as well. Among them are two attractive, and apparently single Asian women. One has a light beige complexion, paler than my own; the other is dark. The paler one's name is Lisa. She's here with her parents. She falls into an ambiguous age bracket of sixteen to twenty two. That bracket makes her either way too, or a little too young. The other, Lela, looks closer to me in age – maybe a possible prospect.

The three other Indonesian guys at the party besides Bruce, are twenty-somethings, sporting spikey hairdos and large chain necklaces. They're more outgoing than the two women, at first. We smoke and drink beers. I throw out a few Indonesian words Marisol taught me, and a few Arabic-Muslim phrases I picked up elsewhere. It turns out they're mostly Muslim here, except Marisol and the whites. But it doesn't seem the Indonesian Muslims I'm meeting here worry too much about the Koran's prohibition on alcohol.

A table in the middle of the living room is set with an assortment of traditional American and Indonesian dishes. I try to impress everyone with my ability to eat the spiciest foods. Prior to the mid-nineties it was fairly easy to impress people with this ability. Somewhere around then, the American taste palate became more and more open to hot foods, and I suddenly found myself one of many who could handle hot dishes.

As the party wears on and people, mainly Debbie, become drunker, she begins to yell at Bruce, her Indonesian husband, about some petty matter in front of the guests. I really can't believe these two belong together. Did he do it for the visa? Even if he did, why doesn't he get away from this woman? This is still before 9/11, so the government isn't looking for Asian illegal aliens all that hard, even if they are Muslim.

I sneak off to a side room where one of the twenty something year old guys, Lisa and Lela are playing monopoly. My attempts at small talk go well with Lisa - she lacks an accent and is knowledgeable about pop culture and punk rock bands. Next, I try to strike up conversation with Lela. But I'm mostly limited to broken English and questions about her home country, which only succeed in eliciting short one-word answers. After talking with Lisa, I realize she's definitely too young, and Lela doesn't seem to have any chemistry with me. I chalk up the evening as a good adventure and nothing more.

The party was a good escape from my daily grind, better than watching Dune. Funny, come to think of it. In a way I've gone from watching sci-fi to living the unspoken inspiration for much of it: foreign culture. The author of Dune based his ideas on a mishmash of Islamic, Eastern Spiritual, and Medieval European influences.

Marisol and I leave after people fail to calm down an ever-angrier Debbie. We drive through the poorly lit streets of Rust Belt. When we come to a stop at a red light, my eyes scan for potential trouble. Marisol asks me, "So what did you think about Lela?" Her voice has a giddy schoolgirl edge. I can tell where she's going with this, but I'm surprised. I didn't think we had much in common. "So what do you think?" she asks again. "She's pretty cute. Seems like a nice person," I say, which are both relatively honest remarks.

Falling

School's re-opened. In the morning I see the music teacher, Mr. Cantwell. "How's it going?" he asks me.

"Good, actually. It looks like I might have a new girlfriend. She's pretty cute." I tell him about Lela. My life seems like it's falling in place a little. "Ooooh! A cutie patootie!" He says with exaggerated exuberance.

Sometime later and I'm back in the upstairs lounge with those older female teachers. "Mr. Cantwell got hurt," Pookie tells me.

"What happened?"

87

"Water got in his room from a leak in the Home and Careers room's washing machine. He slipped and fell. Injured his back in the same spot where he just had surgery."

I go downstairs to confirm this. His music room is dark and the door locked. The Home and Careers teacher tells me, "Yep, he fell on some water that leaked from my machine and injured his back in the same place he just had an operation. He could be out for a while."

That's it. He's gone. I won't ever hear a thing more about him from anyone other than that same accident report repeated: "He fell and injured his back on the spot where he just had surgery."

"Hey, I hear you're retiring?" I ask the Home and Careers teacher.

"Two more weeks."

"Wow. You didn't tell the kids huh?"

"No I don't want them getting all worked up about it." I'm not exactly sure what she means. But in all the retirements I will come to see over the next few years they never seem to tell the kids they're leaving.

"Congratulations. That's awesome."

"I can't wait."

"It'll be a long time until I can get out of here."

"Wouldn't it be nice to have a career you loved and would want to keep doing until you just can't do it anymore?"

As she says that, I just look at her blankly. Does she mean "you" as in "me" or does she mean "you" in some general sense? You as in "one" before everybody decided "one" sounded too pretentious? Is she telling me I should get out of this? Is she asking me to explain what *I* am still doing here? Since she is eager to get out of here herself, and has often related to me how: "Teaching isn't the same as it used to be," and how each year "things get a little worse," I decide she means "one." I feel more at ease. I don't have to explain why I am still here. Even so, I feel hit between the eyes with a rock.

"SCHOOL 63"   Clowx 2004

10. After Tragedy Focus on the Positive

The Tape

Outside, at bus duty, I'm urging: "Get on your bus! Drop the snowball. Stop playing around and get on your bus!" As I survey the swirling mass of students, Jaylen (the kid with the dreadlocks) comes up to me with a slight smile on his face.

"What up Dawg?" he says. We do a short multi-phase handshake, going from a raised palm grasp, to finger lock to finger snap, in rapid succession. The shake hasn't changed much from when I picked it up during undergrad. It came back naturally.

"Just doin' the after school duty, cousin." I use rap style talk with the kids I get respect from, and sometimes with the ones who I don't as a way to defuse a bad situation.

"Here's the tape." He hands me a rap compilation tape he, or maybe an older friend, put together to give to me. For a second he hesitates and looks around nervously, "Don't tell anybody you got this from me."

"No, of course not man." It's given in confidence. It feels good not to always be the one kids hate, but to be the "cool teacher" for a change.

Once I get safely out of the school's neighborhood, I pop in the tape. Some pretty serious "gangsta rap" and adult themes, flood through my car on the ride home. "How you like me now? Gold teeth when I smile. You can me take out the ghetto. But I'm still buck wild…" a rhythmic militant voice chants out to a heavy mechanical drum beat. This is the tamest part of the rap and having grown up on punk rock and what we called "hard core" music, its militant beat feels natural to me. In some ways so does its theme.

These gangsta rap tunes remind me of numerous artsy crime movies I've seen, like that one with the Polish actor. The lead character creates some elaborate scam, beats the odds, then rides off into the sunset with loads of cash. The criminal's success isn't based on being appreciated for a job well done. It's based on getting something, and being able to flaunt that success. "How you like me now? Gold teeth when I smile..." Granted I wouldn't want gold teeth, but I am happy to get a paycheck and be able to afford going out to bars and restaurants.

I pause the tape and rewind it, committing just those lyrics to memory. The rest of the words are too vulgar for what I have in mind. Maybe I can use this as a classroom tool, something the more rule breaking prone students could relate to? One white inner city teacher lost his job for teaching math by putting equations into drug dealing terms. And then there was a white female teacher who used some book about nappy hair in class, thinking she was being PC, and got into some sort of controversy; so I'll have to be careful.

Eventually I work up the nerve to try it out on a class. I start with the older kids. A lot of these students are always rapping all the time anyway, pounding out beats on the tables with their fists, and interrupting me. Let's see how they'd react to me pounding out a beat.

James, one of my students, is in the middle of standing over another student and shouting. Slyly I walk up to him, "If you get back to your seat and get to work I'll do a rap."

"Get out a here!" He doesn't believe me.

"For real James."

"For real?"

"Go sit down man." We walk back to his chair. "All right, get to work."

"When are you gonna rap!?"

"After you're working." I walk away.

He shouts out "I'm working!" Once I'm back at his table I lean down, puff my arms out and rhythmically rock my head from side to side rapping: "How you like me now? Gold teeth when I smile. You can take me out the ghetto. But I'm still buck wild!" He cringes back laughing like he's being tickled. Being tickled is both a painful and an enjoyable experience. James must be feeling some pain as he watches me rap.

"Do the rest of it!" He knows the tune.

"No that's it. That's all I can do." The rest of it gets a bit gruesome.

"Go get in Dorian's face and do your rap! Hey Dorian, you gotta hear Mr. L rap!" A general excitement begins to break out.

"All right. Quiet down. I will only rap again if everyone is behaving." They behave and I do it again and the same uproarious laughter breaks out. I can sense an adult passing in the halls shocked at the fact that happy sounds are actually coming from my room. "OK, OK, calm down or I can't do it anymore."

Word spreads around the school fast and tons of kids are asking me to rap. I'm grateful for these moments of levity, even though I can't be a hundred percent certain what exactly the kids are laughing at. I assume the students are more laughing at me than they are laughing with me. Although I'd like to believe that at least a fraction of their laughter is surprise; surprise that this teacher they assumed was a complete square knows a thing or two, and actually isn't a half-bad rapper. I never ask. Whatever the case, I never really minded making a fool out of myself if it's for a good cause.

When I try rapping for my fifth and sixth graders, it backfires; instead of quieting down to hear me rap more, they go into hysterics. I continue to rap for the bigger kids, but occasionally students finish the rap for me, venturing into the more vulgar parts - which puts me in an awkward situation. Later on in my teaching career I give up this method of trying to sound cool, or be funny, to win the youth over. It will usually cause more problems than it solves. But to survive this year, I need to lighten the tension in my room anyway I can. And if being a rapping art teacher is what it takes then being a rapping art teacher is what I'll be.

Hoboes

It's cold but sunny today. Even though it's only two thirty five in the afternoon, the shadows are long. The trees across the street are bare. A light dusting of snow wafts across the sidewalks and swirls around students' ankles as they board the buses.

I look around for Vice Principal First, to see what he thinks about Mr. Cantwell's disappearance. No sign of him. How about any friendly students like Jaylen? None.

Laquita is walking past me. She's a thin, angry eighth grader, who speaks in a low growl. I've been trying the tactic of talking to students one on one about their class behavior. I was just going to let what she did today go, since eighth grade is on the way out. Soon the semester will end. When the new semester begins, my eighth graders will be leaving for music, and I'll be getting the seventh graders. But she's right here. I can't seem apathetic. Really it was kind of funny what she did. Normally she's just hostile.

Just when I had our class quieted down Laquita made her move. Everyone was looking up towards me as I stood at the chalkboard in front of the room. Using a long pointer I directed their attention to my diagram. "So today..." She was standing near me, off to the side of the tables, near the door-side wall. "Look! Look!" Laquita shouted, gesturing towards the chain-link covered window at the back. My room is in the basement, half below ground, half above, with very tall windows, so you can see people walking by. I don't want everyone seeing in, but I also want some natural light. So I close the blinds two thirds of the way. She craned her neck down, as if she were straining to see out the one third of the window that was open. "A crackhead! There's a crackhead out there!" she joyously shouted. Even I turned my head, imagining some poor wretch in tattered clothes falling down to the sidewalk, dropping his glass pipe.

Remembering her outburst, I call to her: "Laquita, we need to talk." She shouts insults and obscenities in reply, shakes her head like I am a real nuisance, and continues walking past me. As she passes, she puts her open hand up so her palm is at my eye level, and close enough that it blocks my view of her. She keeps her head facing forward, so as not to even waste time looking at me. Laquita emphatically growls (what was a popular late nineties brush off): "Talk to the hand! Because the face ain't talking!"

I'm ready to shrug it off, but now this portly teacher's aide starts acting shocked and indignant. "Who was that girl? I can't believe how rude she was," the aide says, dragging out the "ooh" in rude.

When Vice Principal First shows up she insists on *me* telling him about it. He acts more agitated than he normally would, and has a faraway look in his eyes. "Did you write it up?!" he snaps at us. She scurries away, and leaves me on my own with this angry guy.

"No. I've got it under control," I say to cool him down, "Sorry for bothering you. It was that aide."

"It's not you. I just can't stand it when people keep throwing things my way without even trying deal with it themselves."

He sounds unusually stressed, maybe a little disturbed. His face is red. He stops speaking. He seems like his mind is somewhere else. Is he OK?

"Mr. First?" I get his attention, so he must be OK.

He says nothing for a moment, which makes me nervous. He breaks the silence and explains that Laquita has been in a series of foster homes. Now she's in the process of getting kicked out of the one she's in. This is why she's so hostile.

I feel for Laquita, but why am I the teacher she apparently takes most of her hostility out on?

We go back to watching the kids leave. His head turns slightly side-to-side following individual students. Still watching them and not me, Vice Principal First begins counseling me. With a "resigned to purgatory voice" he says: "You're dealing with the worst of the worst here."

"What do you mean?"

"These are the children of tramps, hoboes and vagabonds. They've got nothing and they respect nothing." He sounds both fatherly and aggravated.

"Vagabonds and tramps?" I think. These words ring back to the 1950's. Is it natural for him to talk this way? I wonder why he's reverting to terms from his youth? His face still looks a little red.

His fatherly tone reminds me of a scene in a movie, one of those movies where a caring adult and a scared dependant child are lost in the wilderness. The adult knows he won't live much longer; so he teaches the child, who is soon to be on his own, everything he knows about how to survive in the wilderness.

"See ya tomorrow kid," he concludes. I wander across the street to my car, scrape off the ice. Pop in the rap tape Jaylen gave me. This time the lyrics are about clubbing while trippin' on X.

Back at school the next day Vice Principal First and I are walking up the basement stairs. We pass a noisy group of students. Their cheerful, rowdy taunts and laughter stop abruptly when they set eyes on Mr. First. He looks upon them sternly; then lets off a short crazy laugh, "Ha, I should just post pictures of me throughout the school." He's been yelling a lot this year. He seems to have brought order, but at what cost to him?

It's a couple days later and I don't see Mr. First. I hate it when he's not here. No backup. Even if he doesn't actually do much of anything for me, I feel like he's on my side and understands what I'm going through, unlike Principal Henderson, young Mr. Nosey, and some of these other people, who just wander around here watching things. You feel judged by them, like you're some kind of creep.

After a few rough classes I head up to the ladies' faculty room. The women are crying. Pookie tells me, "Mr. First had a massive heart attack." They are making plans to visit him in the hospital. From what it sounds like he is probably not going to fully recover. One moment and his life is permanently changed.

While these women cry, my first reaction is a mix of anger at the children who won't behave – I blame them for his heart attack, and self-centered anxiety. Don't get me wrong; of course I'm worried about his wellbeing. But I'm also worried about mine. Mr. First leaving school doesn't bode well. Mr. Cantwell is gone, the first Spanish teacher is gone, the Home and Careers teacher is leaving, and now Mr. First. I'm gradually being left on my own down here in this basement purgatory. Wisely, I keep those thoughts to myself and just act bereaved. I never do make it to the hospital.

Thank God Ryan is still here, and Tina is hanging in. When I finally see Ryan and tell him the news, I vent my outrage: "He nearly died trying to get these kids to behave. This is what it takes? He was a cool guy. I wonder what it's going to be like here now? It's probably going to get worse."

After work I hit the gym pretty hard. I need to feel fit for those new seventh graders coming soon. Without Mr. First I'm more vulnerable to be attacked by hostile forces –child and administrative. I better put up a new art-display to ward off my adversaries.

Buffalo Display

I've noticed a growing trend in cities recently in 2000. It's to create some sort of prefab public art sculpture and have artists paint on them and display the sculptures conspicuously around town. In Big City, Canada I've seen moose, and in my city it's buffalo. All over Rust Belt are life size painted up buffalos. Maybe this could be a lesson kids will get into, and my supervisor will think seems educational?

As I leave work on Friday the cleaning lady says to me, "Have a good weekend." She's a heavy-set African American lady old enough to have an eighteen-year old daughter.

"Yeah, weekend - right." I say with some sarcasm. She looks at me funny.

We always get along well and I make some small talk with her every time I see her. Last time I saw her, she was beaming with pride telling me about her daughter who is going to start college.

What I'm thinking about now is the rough day I've had, the parents I've called, how most of my lessons are burned through with little appreciation or care, and how I have to take this job home with me and do stuff on Saturday, how I take it home every evening, how it never ends, and how there's no break from it. Judging by her look I realize she's confused, maybe even hurt or offended by my sarcastic tone.

"Thanks, you have a good weekend too, I'm just coming down with a bit of cold." Really, I am too. "You should get some good bed rest," she says. Bed rest. That sounds like how my Grandma would have said it. She loads up the bag of trash she just swept off the floor.

I'm feeling sorry for me, but she's probably thinking about having to go to her night job after her shift here is done. She works two jobs just to come near what I'm making at one, probably. Mine is tough but so is hers, a different kind of tough. Hers is a repetitive motion, back injury, tough. Mine is only emotional, for this year at least.

It doesn't seem right for our society to have all this advanced-labor-saving technology, and still have created a rat race where people are insecure. Insecure as to how they will make ends meet, like the cleaning lady probably is. If they are making ends meet, like I am as of now, then they are insecure about how long it can last. How long until a job is lost, or health is lost, and any safety net is spent, and any savings was in vain. People created this rat race. It isn't a force of nature. It's a choice of politics. After she leaves the room, I go back to thinking about the lesson.

The old art teacher had a bunch of tag-board stored up on top of the shelves. I pull a bunch down and take it home with the intention of creating buffalo stencils that the kids can use to create their own "public works of art."

Jaylen's mix tape fills the car on the way home. This time the rapper is rapping some thing like "Wu Tang killer bees on attack…" It sounds a lot cooler in the car.

At home, after hours of cutting tag-board stencils, I find online pictures and make print outs of other painted up buffalos that I can let them look at for inspiration.

Come Monday, It's a success. The buffalo lesson is a hit. First I try it out with an eighth grade that I get along with, Jaylen's class. I try to have them do my new lessons first since they cooperate the most, so I can see how kids will respond. After a couple of disruptions, and once those stencils are out, everyone is momentarily into it. Then the "I'm dones" start to set in. I prod them along to completion. One kid is making this really cool one - I think it is anyway. It has a zoo drawn in the buffalo. I tell him, "Why don't you also draw a zoo in the background." He likes the idea: a drawing of a zoo, on a statue of a zoo animal, set in a zoo. Then minutes later I see him going to tear up his work.

"No! What are you doing?" I say.

"This sucks," he replies.

"Students, please do not destroy your art. I tore up stuff when I was a kid, stuff that looking back on it the grown-ups really would have liked." The destruction of work and supplies is minor in this group compared to others. You should see it, how they crumble and tear things up with zeal.

The second time Jaylen's class comes I try to have an "art show." This is the only class and time this year I will attempt to have students take turns talking about their art. (I won't try it again until a few years later and at a different school.) This particular class is unusually accepting of me, and would give a group discussion a chance. It goes OK for a while. Then a girl, wearing a tight shirt says, "My buffalo is black and ugly like me."

"Whoa" I say. Stretching my arms out like a referee. "Nobody is saying that." I don't know how to react. I can't tell her, "Hey, I think black girls are cute."

That group leaves and another one comes. It's a fifth grade and they are walked in by this fiftyish, "but still has it," redheaded teacher, with long legs, black nylons and a short skirt. She sees the art hanging up and says, "These are hot."

"Thanks!" Finally I've got something. I know I need to hang some of the buffalos around school to prove "I really do care about the kids."

Her students depart. I'm alone. I stand precariously on the tables, remove artwork from the bulletin boards, lay it out, and decide which ones to hang in the school's main hall. I notice one of the ones I've chosen has what looks like a huge fart blasting out of the buffalo's ass. It's a multi colored jet stream, possibly ruining an otherwise strong piece of work. The art is well planned, colored and eye catching. I step back from the Buffaloes I've selected. Looking at them again, it seems the fart blast is relatively camouflaged into the work.

I think of all the subtleties people miss in life as they go through the day with glazed over eyes, focused on "what's coming next." Maybe nobody will notice the fart. I want to reward the students in Jaylen's class; they are my most cooperative group. Plus I need another display. Walking back to the tables I stack them up, thinking: "What would my students do?"

The answer is "Go for it and see what happens," or, "What can you do to me?" Thinking in these terms I realize I could always deny I noticed. Borrowing a ladder from the head maintenance guy, I begin to hang them.

The man who *seems* like Vice Principal First's replacement slowly strolls by: Dr. Iman. He's wearing one of his characteristic suits, afro-centric scarf, and a wise man look on his face. Dr. Iman may carry himself like he is the new vice principal, but he isn't. Ryan and I never figure out what his job title really is.

The new vice principal is actually Dr. Airington. She's blond, and struts around with a reserved waspish air of authority. Only she doesn't seem too effective. Mr. First, with his sharp looks and harsh speech could keep the school in line. Shortly after Dr. Airington started, someone put Dr. Iman on the payroll. I assume he gets paid.

He seems more helpful than Airington. He'll actually stop and talk to me. Dr. Airington by contrast, is always in a hurry, on her way to do something "important." Ms. Henderson is simply off limits.

When I've asked for Iman's help here's how it goes: he'll slowly walk up to the recalcitrant student. His pace conveys confidence, and the student feels as if someone important is approaching him. He lectures them in a perfect, wise, caring, yet scolding elder voice. The type of voice only an older black male can effectively use on a black child. The kid usually becomes silent, looks down and nods. "Yes. No. I shouldn't have done that." Then Dr. Iman says, "Don't you have something to say to this man?" "Sorry," the momentarily shamed student answers. Then Iman walks away. The kid will be well behaved for the next ten minutes or so.

I wonder if Dr. Iman will notice the fart blast? "Dr. Iman, take a look at the art." He stops.

The two of us stand side-by-side taking in the artwork. He nods approvingly. "Do you see anything *unusual* in any of these or do they all look fine to you?" I ask. He agrees they look fine. "How about that one?" I say pointing to the offending piece. He nods, it looks good too. I lower my voice, lean into him and ask: "So you don't notice that fart blast coming out?" We both laugh and decide no one notices.

Killing the Goose

When I return to work the next day I get a couple of compliments on the display, but this cold is getting worse. I can hardly talk; my throat is so sore. "Don't call in sick your first year. Especially don't call Ms. Henderson," everyone says. After organizing my room, I cross the hall to consult my trusted confidant: the Home and Careers teacher.

"Maybe I should just call in?" I ask her.

She tells me, "You're doing the right thing coming in. Ms. Henderson even mentioned to me that you are never out."

Tina, one of the other new teachers, on the other hand has already used up all of her sick days. That's what Ryan told me. She does seem to be out all the time. Come to think of it I never see either of those two at any of the many after school functions I drag myself to. At least once a week after school, it seems like there's a small party in the library because someone's having a birthday, a baby, or getting married. Because of these gatherings, at least once a week I've prolonged my after-school-getting-prepared-for-the-next-day-routine, to show that I'm a team player, and have a slice of cake on a paper plate.

I ask Tina about calling in. "How do you have the courage to call in sick to Ms. Henderson?

"Yeah, everyone says 'don't call her.' But whenever I call she just says 'OK.'" I think it over. Maybe I should make the call. Then Tina tells me what happened yesterday, when she was out sick. "An aide told me that Ms. Henderson came into the room when the sub was there, and warned the kids that they'd better behave. Then she suspended one who didn't. Can you believe it? She backs up a sub but not me!" I decide to keep coming in.

Even while teaching through the haze of sickness, that buffalo stencil idea really works. Every class gets into it, for a while at least. It's great for kids who won't listen to directions. Grabbing a stencil and tracing it gives everyone an immediate sense of satisfaction. "Look what I made!" Feeling in an OK mood, enough of them are willing to glance at the instructional handout and photos I passed around. Now they feel accomplished and inspired enough to "get creative" and "express themselves."

While the lesson is a success, Ms. Rosebloom's class won't let me savor my one and only victory without creating a new set of challenges. As a favor to me, and to chastise her students, Ms. Rosebloom has temporarily banned her class from my room. "You can't come to the art room until you learn how to behave!" she admonished them. Instead I am going to go to her room to teach art; the theory being that this will punish them for acting out in my class. Her favor has created a new challenge: the large buffalo stencils I've so painstakingly cut out won't fit on the standard classroom-size desks which fill Ms. R's room. So now I'm stuck cutting thirty new desk-size stencils. I wonder who is really punished, me or the students?

Aside from that glitch, I've created the perfect lesson. So perfect I think of a variation of it called "Tree of my life." It's another stencil idea. This idea I got from noticing the kids clothing styles. There's a brand with a jagged tree logo that they all love, Timberland.

In the evening at home I'm using a razor to cut enough tag board trees for forty kids. I figure some will get destroyed. I sketch and type out an instruction sheet.

They love the trees. It reminds them of the clothing line. "Whoa! This looks like a Timberland!" They run with it. Another hit, except for one stoned-looking eighth grader who says, "Why do we have to do all these gay art lessons like 'tree of my life?'"

At least it was a hit until my supervisor walks in. "I could hire a teacher's aide to pass out stencils," he says. I mount a brief defense: "The stencil is just the starting point for a lesson on self-expression. It's no different than an unusually shaped canvas."

He didn't acknowledge what I said. He just repeated the idea that he doesn't "need to hire an art teacher to pass out stencils." No more buffalos. No more trees.

There are few points of irony. Later on in my career, I'll see art teachers using these pre-formed masks that kids can papier-mâché over and paint on. So why can't they use a pre-cut buffalo, trace it, and paint on that? Even worse, when I find the school system's official calendar in my mailbox, the student art on the cover is what sure looks like a stenciled buffalo randomly splattered with white paint.

I'm not tenured. I'm not going to argue. My cold medicine is wearing off.

Each morning I'm sick, I wake up before the alarm and pick up the phone. Look at Ms. Henderson's number. Rehearse what I will say. Start to dial. Then put the phone down. Pace. Repeat the process a couple more times. Give up. Then try to sleep again, waiting for the alarm to sound.

Sick and at work, another eighth grader sees how pale and red nosed I look. He's chubby with a shirt stained from dropping food on his bulging belly. "Mr. Lebrun are you feeling OK?" He normally acts so badly all the time too, but sounds sincere now. "Thanks for your concern," I say.

At the end of the day the cleaning lady sees me. I feel sticky and weak. "You really need to stay home and get some good bed rest," she says. I go to the doctor's. It's a managed care facility so I see a physician's assistant. The PA is around my age. She takes a throat culture. Listens to my breathing. "Lie down." She lifts up the paper gown and sees my hairy chest and stomach. "Whoa," she says. "What?" I say. "Oh. No. I…" she says something vague and evasive. I've heard that "whoa" before when I take my shirt off around women for the first time. The cold turned into a lung infection. I'm put on an antibiotic and told I had better stay home. I practice sounding ill, making sure my voice is as scratchy as possible. Then make the phone call to the principal: "I'm sick."

11. Romance and New Hope

Seventh Grade – Another visit

I finally get some rest. Marisol phones me with Lela's number. Lela and I talk in broken English for a while. She's sorry I'm not feeling well. I try to pin her down for a dinner date. But she has to work all week at night. "What about Saturday?"

"That's Debbie's birthday." She invites me to come over. Not as private as I was hoping, but still a good sign.

I pop in some more Dune, take some Nyquil and sleep. The lung infection is nearly cleared up, and soon I'll have my first date in a long while.

When I make it back to work the room is in pretty bad shape. I get it straightened up in time to see my first class.

My supervisor's dark shadow slips into the room just as I'm settling the class in. How many times is this supervisor going to come in here? Is he making sure I'm not using stencils? What does he do, besides make me nervous, and tell me to "clamp down" more?

At the end of this evaluation, he leans back in his chair and says "Your eighth graders will be leaving soon, and going to music for the rest of the year, right?" "Yes," I agree. "So you'll be getting a new crop of kids, with the seventh graders finished with music and coming to you. You'll have a fresh start. You'll have another chance to be strict," he says placing both hands on the table with a slight thud, to add emphasis, as he rises to get up, and concludes "Good then."

We shake hands and he leaves, leaving me thinking "Famous last words." I'm sure by now the whole school already thinks of me as the teacher you don't have to listen to, "Woo! We're goin to Mr. Lebrun's class. It's gonna be great!" My rep must be well established. I don't see any fresh start coming.

I mentally flash to scenes of the seventh graders screaming, shouting, and trying to overthrow the now-on-sick-leave music teacher. The music room is only across the hall from me. I can hear the furor, even now as I sit at my wooden desk: shouting, screaming, laughing, and arguing, while the Arabic immigrant substitute teacher shouts at them in accented English. It's even worse in there than before.

As I follow my supervisor out the door, a stream of noisy students is leaving the music room. Boys imitate the sub's Arabic accent. He stands around five four, hands on his hips, resolute, stoic, and looks upon the students with contempt. He shakes his head and mutters disparagements as they pass. I too pose with hands on my hips, to offer solidarity. A white boy steps out of the line, looks at me, points to the music sub, and in pubescent indignation says, "He just called me stupid!" I really don't know why this student is expecting sympathy from me.

As he speaks, I imagine one of those cartoon "thought bubbles" appearing above me. In the bubble I see this seventh grader scratching his head and drooling. "No. He probably just said you're *acting* stupid, not that you *are* stupid. Yes that's it. Just that you're acting stupid," I reassure him. "Now better get going." I wave my arm, and gesture for him to get back in line.

After the kids leave I ask, "So how's it going teaching music?"

In a heavy accent that I just heard the students imitate, he says, "I don't know why they have me doing this. I told them, I told Ms. Henderson, 'I don't know anything about music. I know math.' I am an engineer back home. I know math, but they keep me down here."

"Probably because they can't find anybody else who can handle the job. Keeping you here means the principal believes in you," I offer. Prior to him, I saw a slew of substitutes come for a day or two, never to return. They were music teachers who didn't have a full time job yet. They tried to actually teach. This one, the new sub, doesn't. He remains. They didn't.

"What country do you come from anyway? Just curious."

"Algeria."

"North Africa. Right?" I say inanely trying to build some common ground.

In my head I'm seeing him in a small village with buildings made from sandy colored material, populated with children who listen to and respect adults.

"This must be a real shock for you, how these kids act," I add.

"I never would have believed it," he says shaking his head.

Not really gaining any insight as to how to handle these seventh graders, I decide to go upstairs to heat up one of those fish dinners for lunch, and leave the immigrant standing, arms folded, waiting for his next class. A seventh grader, with a large birthmark near his eye, stops me as we pass each other in the hall. "I hear you call people's parents for just getting out your seat?" he asks. "Yep, that's where all the trouble starts. I want everyone safe in my room," I reply. He looks at me without speaking, so I add: "You better get to your class now. Nice talking with you." Then I smugly think, "Hmmm, maybe I was wrong. Maybe I was too pessimistic. Maybe I've got a tougher reputation than I realize. Yes, the music teacher, Mr. Cantwell, couldn't handle them because he just didn't have the right touch. He didn't have good classroom management strategies like I do. Me, I will win them over. I will succeed where he failed." Momentarily I am again imagining that I have what it takes, whereas it's those other teachers who can't handle this, not me. Momentarily I forget all the hell I've been through.

New Hope

The day to meet the seventh grade arrives. My room is packed with an almost fifty-fifty split of white and black seventh graders. I've got them seated as racially and gender integrated as I can. In this class alone, the whites seem to slightly outnumber the blacks, especially in terms of boys.

Jimmy, a plainly dressed white kid, with short sandy brown hair combed neatly to the side, a pug nose, and large almost pretty eyes on a round obnoxious face, raises his hand. Most of the white kids at Grand Plans are bused in from a white urban enclave, separated from the black neighborhood where the school is located. The enclave's borders are demarcated by vacant buildings and little used railroad tracks, earning it the nickname "Iron Island." When I was ten, I remember seeing one of those railroad bridges painted with the slogan, "Entering Iron Island. N...rs Keep Out!" The neighborhood is heavily Irish, and its residents have a patriotic zeal for it. They often sport shirts and adorn their cars with stickers that say, "I love the Old First Ward." They actually refer to their neighborhood as a "ward," conjuring images of fat Tammany Hall "ward bosses" smoking cigars in back rooms and running corrupt political machines in the 1930's. That time was the heyday of ethnic industrial working class neighborhoods. Somehow this memory lingers on in their collective unconscious.

The kids from the Iron Island mostly dress in a plain or mildly rap-influenced fashions. (This will change a few years later) I'm shocked - how just having subbed in the burbs a year earlier, where I saw lots of kids with green hair, goth or skater style clothes, and even a few Mohawks - at how these boys are so "average Joe."

"Are we going to do any architecture in here?" Jimmy asks. I've heard stories that he's a really bad kid. "Well, yes, I have some perspective lessons coming up later on in which we get to draw buildings," I tell him. He looks satisfied. His satisfaction won't last for long, but for the moment I naively think that I will be one of those "star" teachers who gets through to this tough kid. But how can I think this, considering what I've just gone through? Denial is a powerful emotion.

After seeing this seventh grade class a few more times, another "iron triangle" of defiance and mayhem has emerged. It's formed by three boys from the Iron Island: Jimmy – the ring leader, Kyle and Joe – the henchmen. Kyle is the tallest, thinnest and blondest of the three, with a long neck and "Roman" nose. Joe is the fattest. All three sport short-neat 1950's style haircuts.

The defiant trio will sometimes ally against me with a girl from the black Fruit Belt, Lillian. At other times the ingrained animosity between Fruit Belters and Iron Islanders causes Lillian and the boys to war with each other. Either way, it spells trouble for me. Lillian is nearly my height, often dresses in dirty clothes, has a semi-afro, or at least flyaway hair, and is even more of a sociopath than Jimmy.

At home I spent hours creating a lesson on "graphic design." Now it's time to teach it. I'm standing at the back of the room, with my desk and a display to my left, a table full of handouts and magazines and art supplies to my right, and all the rows of tables in front of me. "Turn your chairs around and face the teacher." This has been a problem all year with these tables.

As soon as I start to speak, Kyle, who is seated nearly next to me on my right, starts to paper pop. That's this thing they do where they fold paper in a certain way, and then whip it down in the air, somehow causing a loud "pop" noise.

"Stop that." He stops for a moment then continues.

Joe, seated near me and on my left, and next to one of only two Arabic kids in the school, joins in the paper popping. He's grinning and making direct eye contact with me. "Joe!" "Joooooe," he says back, imitating me and giving it a mentally challenged sounding ring. After a few more warnings I command, "Joe go to timeout!" He gets up making a little Egyptian style dance out of it, eliciting laughter from his peers.

I plow a little further through the directions. Jimmy shouts out, "You've wasted ten minutes of our time already!"

104

"That's one warning Jimmy."

"Oooh, I'm scared" he says and wrings his hands.

A smaller kid says, "Shut up Jimmy." Jimmy often harasses his fellow students, and is brazenly defiant. I'm happy to know that under it all a lot of these kids really do want to learn and would prefer their teacher's instructions over Jimmy's antics.

"Thank you, but I need you to stay out of this," I say to the kid who came to my aid, so that things won't get worse.

"Next you will borrow one of these magazines," I continue. As I look down to point to the magazine, out of the corner of my eye I can see Jimmy throw something across the aisle at the kid who told him to shut up.

"There is absolutely no throwing things. Now go to timeout!" I say; then I continue with the directions, "Flip through the magazine, until you find an ad you can use for ideas."

Still not having gone to timeout Jimmy begins singing "I need sexual healing!" tilting his head back like a howling coyote.

"Jimmy. You still need to go to timeout." My mouth is beginning to feel very dry, my teeth hurt from clenching my jaw, and my stomach is queasy.

"No!" Jimmy shouts back.

"OK then, I'm going to need to call your home," I say, beginning to betray real anger. I can feel my blood pressure rising, and I'm getting light-headed. I continue the instructions, "When you find an ad you like…" Jimmy again interrupts.

"Woo! Who farted?!"

Kyle is back to paper popping, while simultaneously growling. The showdown is escalating and I'm getting worried that something bad could happen. I don't want to "lose it" right now, or others will join in.

"No is not an option. Either get to timeout, or I mean it, I will call your home!" I say feeling wronged, embarrassed and angry. Emotions only backfire in discipline. Actually these kids could use a robot teacher, programmed with mechanical if x then y responses, all cool and automatic and never having emotional hooks that the students can play on.

"Shut up! I hate you. You bald headed freak," Jimmy says.

"Oooh, he curred you!" This tall boy from the Fruit Belt joins in, laughing and slamming both hands on the table. Curred, as in making cur a verb, is a popular slang this year. They use it when someone insults someone and the insulted is left with no good comeback.

I feel a little self-conscious. What comeback can I possibly have? *I* know that shaved heads are in, but these kids don't know it yet. In Rust Belt, in late 2000, shaved heads are a rarity. (It will take another year or two until all the white kids, and their dads, in the urban white ghetto start shaving their heads.) So today, in the eyes of the youth at Grand Plans Middle, I'm still a "bald headed freak!"

"Get over there!" I snarl, walking towards his seat and pointing to the timeout.

"You just spit on me!" A girl at his table shouts at me in anger.

Jimmy loudly slams his books down adding, "Shuuuut uuuup!" sounding like a young Archie Bunker. He saunters over to the timeout near the window. I take a deep breath and continue.

"Draw your advertisement with pencil, include illustrations. After that's done you can paint it."

I call the helpers off my list: "Raquan, Johnny, Sherita…" I've started drafting my helper lists the night before. I try to plan every detail prior to class, so no matter how drastic the onslaught of defiance, they can't throw me off track.

"That's not fair. Why does Sherita get to help!" Lillian shouts.

"Raise your hand Lillian." She does and repeats her question. "I chose these helpers the night before," I reply.

As Sherita delivers the handouts Lillian kicks her adding: "I don't want this smelly piece of shit coming near me." Sherita is a chubby, quiet, usually well-mannered black girl, who doesn't bother anybody. But her clothes do smell. She's a near perfect target for a bully: socially isolated and low on friends.

"What the fuck is you doin!?" Sherita shouts at her, giving Lillian some fight. I'm happy to see her not taking it lying down, but Lillian would clearly win any brawl. Lillian kicks at her again.

"Just move on Sherita. I'll handle it," I say. The only justice I can give Sherita is sentencing Lillian to timeout, from which Lillian makes a quick escape. I just sunk to an even lower level of purgatory with these seventh graders than I was in with the eighth grade. After the class is dismissed I'm left with some completed artwork, and a lot of torn and defaced handouts, broken pencils, formerly neat rows of tables titled at odd angles, and chairs strewn around helter-skelter.

Cafeteria duty, Mr. Beanbag and Fred's Shirt.

There's nothing like unwinding after a stressful class with cafeteria duty. Nothing like a lunchroom filled with noisy kids, kids ready to get in fights and throw food at each other, to calm you down. Yes I am being sarcastic, but I can tell you one thing, and I'm not the only one who said this: it's a lot easier than teaching them.

I stand at the entranceway monitoring the room and the kids coming and going. The kids sit at round tables laughing and arguing. Like an alternating pattern, some kid stands with indignant rage aimed at someone else, and then sits down again, disappearing back into the ocean of heads bobbing up and down, alternating between stuffing their faces and shouting.

I survey the room, leave my post and patrol the cafeteria like a guard, with hands behind my back. Kids lift their heads and look at me with crazed smiles and make funny sounds, lips and tongues stained blue from candy. Others look at me with excitement, as they pour the colored sugary contents of pixie sticks down their gaping mouths. It's like cocaine to these little fourth and fifth grade bodies. The sugar addicts stomp their feet as I pass, in joyful anticipation of the extra mayhem they will be able to cause for me with the additional fuel of sugar. Sugar to the rule breaking kid is like a proscribed performance enhancement drug to an Olympic athlete. It offers the rule-breaker strength and endurance in the contest of wills. Better yet, it enhances the participation for their potential audience as well. The more cooperative kids, now high on sugar themselves, find enhanced hilarity in every antic of the rule breaker.

Circling back to my spot at the door I see the fifth grader Fred enter the cafeteria. He's from Mr. Beanbag's class. Mr. Beanbag is a jolly teacher's aide. Fred passes me in a goofy way: waving his arms, looking me in the eyes, wagging his head side to side, and opening and closing his mouth. I notice his T – shirt. "Fred come here," I say. The picture has a chicken egg with a droopy-eyed dreamy looking baby chicken inside, and a thought bubble rising out saying "I just got laid."

I wave over Dr. Iman. "Dr. Iman, I don't know what you think, but take a look at Fred's shirt." He looks at it, and in that serious, low voice that only he can do, says, "Go in the bathroom and turn that shirt inside out."

Jolly Mr. Beanbag walks through the cafeteria doorway, waving and saying hi to kids. "Hey Matt!" The ever-smiling teacher's aide. "Hey Mr. Beanbag." I decide to tell him about the seventh grade class and how Jimmy just called me an "idiot." He offers sympathy and leans in closer before speaking: "I heard something from this other teacher who lives near him and his friends: they're 'white trash.'" I don't know how to take this. He's offering me sympathy and he's getting to say the white equivalent of the N word. "Thanks for the condolences."

So much for new hope. When my next seventh grade class comes to my room, that kid with the birthmark, the one who asked me "if I call parents," takes long leaping strides across tables. He's practically flying. Then he climbs up the large drying rack. A bunch of them start to do this Tarzan speak: "Him say no climb on cabinet. Me say climb on cabinet. Him say he want to teach. Him say me go timeout. Me no go timeout."

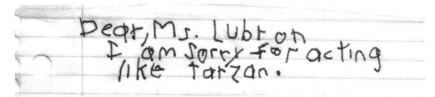

Dear, Mrs. Lubton
I am sorry for acting
like Tarzan.

Illustration of a student apology.

Calling Joe's Parent.

In the lounge sitting in front of the phone I stare blankly at my battle notes. Then I begin to see a pattern in the scrawl. Jimmy, Kyle and Joe, the Iron Island boys, are the most often repeated names. I get answering machines at Jimmy's and Kyle's. At Joe's, his mom answers the phone. She sounds like she's in her late thirties.

"Hi this is Joe's art teacher and…" She listens silently. Finally she breaks silence and says, "To tell you the truth, it's the girl he's sitting next to. She smells bad." This "to tell you the truth" phrase is another black / white cultural difference. White people often use phrases like "to tell you the truth," and "to be honest" when they are going to disagree with you. I've usually only heard black people use the phrase agreeably.

The girl that his Mom claims "smells," is one of the few immigrants in the school. While I think it would be a good chance for Joe to broaden his horizons, I agree to move her son. The move proves fateful. Having won that battle and getting his mom to stick up for him, Joe will become out of control the rest of the year. The next time I will call his mom, she will be cool and unresponsive.

On the drive home from work I stop by a liquor store to pick up something for Lela's housemate's birthday party.

Jenga

I pull into her iced over driveway, and park next to a rusted out 1980's Nissan. A twenty-something Indonesian guy with spikey hair smiles and lets me in. He calls to Lela. She walks down the hall dressed in a traditional looking Indonesian outfit. She dressed up for Debbie's party.

"Hi Matchew, how's work?" She takes my jacket and I follow her into the room.

"It sucks. These kids are so obnoxious. And our vice principal, a really good guy, just had a heart attack."

"That's terrible. I'm so sorry for him. But be patient Matchew, they're only kids." She always seems to speak in this same calm reassuring tone no matter what the circumstances are. Yeah right, "only kids," I think. You have no idea. These aren't kids like you think of kids. But I can't say this. It's important I seem like a good guy at this early stage in our dating. Women are usually turned off by overt bitterness in guys they've only recently met.

I present a six-dollar bottle of wine and add it to the layout on the table. "Hey Debbie. Happy birthday!" I say with exaggerated enthusiasm. The type of enthusiasm you'd show to someone you fear. I am nervous about Debbie. She comes across as mentally unstable, down on her luck, and domineering. We're all sprawled out around the living room eating and drinking, a few puffing on cigarettes, some people on the floor and some on the couch or chairs. Debbie begins talking about TV shows she likes.

I mention "Dark Angel." I'd call it "cyber punk" drama. It's about this sexy brown complexioned Asian looking, or maybe she's half Asian or Hispanic, woman who's supposed to be an android or something. The show is set in a post apocalyptic near-future America. Like most cyber punk, the plot involves the heroes doing computer hacking to thwart a nefarious plot. Sci-fi, like punk rock, and hanging out with Indonesian immigrants, is a good "getaway" from life's troubles.

Debbie announces: "Lela's my brown angel. Isn't that right Lela?"

"Yes Debbie," Lela replies with that same reassuring voice she uses with me. When Debbie isn't getting mad at Bruce, her supposed Indonesian husband, she's saying "my Lela" this or "my Lela" that. She and Lela go shopping together, and she and Lela drive to work together. Lela doesn't have a car, so it's Debbie driving Lela all these places. I'm beginning to wonder if she doesn't have a secret lesbian crush on Lela, manifesting itself in a dominance behavior pattern. The thought isn't especially arousing. If you met Debbie you'd understand why. It's nothing about Debbie being fat; it's about her being her; really, I'm not lying – I am in the silent minority of white guys who appreciate the Rubenesque woman. But even the master-painter Ruben couldn't have stomached Debbie.

Bruce is in the kitchen cooking up some fried shrimp. The kitchen is supplied with large bags of rice, boxes, cans and bottles, all with foreign script and odd English translations written on them, like "Golden Boy Fish Sauce." The label on the bottle of Golden Boy brand has a painting of a baby on it. The baby is sitting on the planet earth, with a radiant blast of light behind him. He's giving the "thumbs up," as he cradles a bottle of fish sauce. The bottle the baby cradles also has the label with a painting of a baby holding a bottle of fish sauce giving the thumbs up. Thus implying an infinite number of babies holding an infinite number of bottles of Golden Boy Fish Sauce.

Bruce works over a pan of boiling oil with depressed resignation. "What did you do in Indonesia?" I ask him.

"I was engineer. Went to college in Indonesia," he tells me, perking up a bit. His degree doesn't translate here. He'd have to take a bunch of classes to get credentialed. He can't work in his field. "Now have to make money. I'm too poor," he laughs, while pulling out deep fried shrimp with chopsticks.

"What are you doing now for work?" I ask.

"Work in factory. Lifting all day," he says.

"Some of those factory jobs pay pretty well. They have strong unions," I say.

"No union," he tells me. Judging by the bleak living conditions in this overcrowded apartment, no one is making much money here.

"That sucks," I offer in consolation. His daily grind for survival keeps him stranded in a go nowhere job with no time to go back to school, and a demanding wife sucking away his money. I try to brainstorm some solutions. I ask if he's a citizen. He's not. I tell him he should apply to become one. I figure this must be the reason he married this lady and must have gotten a green card out of it. If he got his citizenship he could get away from her. I know it sounds cruel, but it's easy to sympathize with him. He doesn't seem in any hurry to apply for citizenship though. I really can't figure out why or what's really going on here, so I decide it's best to not ask any more questions. After not being able to come up with any way I can see him getting out of this, I just help him carry the food in the living room to the awaiting queen Debbie.

After cake, and the sing-along, Debbie gets agitated and starts giving Bruce a hard time. She yells "God damn Bruce why don't you ever…" Lela tries to calm her down, but it's no use. "See what I'm putting up with here?" Debbie looks to me for support. Are you kidding me? She reminds me of that seventh grader, thinking I would side with him over the music sub.

"I don't know," I say letting out a slight laugh, looking down and shrugging. I'm trying to make light of this uncomfortable moment. The whole scene is getting weird. The younger guys leave, and Bruce steps outside in the cold for a minute. Then Debbie disappears into her room and passes out. Bruce comes back in and follows her into the bedroom. I look at him with sympathy as he dejectedly closes the door behind him. As the door closes I get a peak of Debbie's semi-conscious form sprawled out in the dark on her bed with her clothes on.

Finally I've got some time alone with Lela. We sit on the living room floor playing this game Jenga. You make a tower with little sticks and see how high you can get it before it falls. The game offers plenty of chances for our hands to brush into each other, which offers a chance for a late night make out session. She has me leave before things get any more heated. "You'd better go now." She pats me like I'm a large puppy. Despite her short height and quiet voice, she has a way of commanding situations. "Good-bye Matchew. I had a nice time."

Back home, it's about two AM, I settle onto the couch with a beer and an episode of Star Trek Deep Space Nine. As the alcohol kicks in, I let my mind lapse into a pleasant state of disorganization. Deep Space Nine is set on a space station, instead of on the spaceship Enterprise. It's not as entertaining as the regular Star Trek with captain Picard, but it's a lot better than no sci-fi. I feel content. I mentally look over what I have: an OK paying job, a cute girlfriend, Star Trek, and warm beer. Yeah warm beer. Unlike most of us Americans I like it room temperature. It brings out the flavor. I got the idea in England. That's how they do it. Or maybe that's just what I tell people to shut them up.

Quark or Quork or whatever his name is, enters the scene. He's a short, big-eared Roman nosed humanoid creature. He begins haggling over money with someone on the space ship. He's reminding me a lot of a certain ethnic stereotype. A lot of these "alien races" seem based on ethnic stereotypes. I laugh, "Get your money quark!" Then my phone rings. Who's calling at this hour?

"Matchew?" Uh oh, it's Lela. This must be something weird. "Hey Lela," I say, trying to sound happy but feeling worried.

"Why do you like me?" she asks point blank. My mind was just slipping into that dreamy vulnerable state, not an easy state to think on one's feet. I have a lot of doubts about her and us, and I'm not even sure if I don't just consider this a pass-time.

"Well, I...I think you are very kind, and very pretty. I really like your company." She sounds pleased, but she doesn't end her inquiry.

"Matchew, how do you think this relationship is going?" Why now? Why is she doing this now at two thirty in the morning? How many dates have we been on? Not enough to pull this. It's like a form of psychological warfare. An ex-girlfriend from years ago would always wait till late night when I'm tired and at my most vulnerable to start an argument.

"It's going great," I say feeling buzzed from the beer.

"I don't think so," she says. This is really more than I can handle right now.

"What? What do you mean?"

"It's about Reh-ligion. I must marry a Muslim." It's so late, I'm so tired and besides, I've always thought there's truth in all religions, so I'm thinking I could do this. I concede that I *could* become Muslim. Maybe I really said I *will* become Muslim. I can't believe I said this. I try to explain my position like an eclectic-minded liberal would explain it, but she doesn't speak English that well, and unlike Bruce and Marisol, doesn't seem like the intellectual type. So really I'm just throwing a lot of bull-crap at her, words that provide enough of what she wants to hear, so she can ignore the extra verbiage. And I can hang up the phone without having lost anything. If I was hauled into court, I could honestly say that I didn't say anything. I can finish Deep Space Nine, still go to church tomorrow, and still show pictures of my new girlfriend to co-workers on Monday. I've bought time.

12. Soccer Hooligans and the Hidden Garden.

Soccer Hooligans

Before morning hall duty I show a picture of Lela to Mr. Mullet.
"That's cool you're going out with a black woman," he says.
"Actually she's Asian."
"What are you talking about, she's black." I let it be.
Maybe having a new romance will take some of the edge off.
Mellow me out. If I mellow maybe the kids will mellow. After a few periods
of getting mentally beaten on by the kids, my good mood dissolves.

As the seventh graders descend the stairs, Jimmy says angrily,
"Aren't you ever going to be absent?!" I feel a small surge of victorious
feelings. The music teacher is gone, the first Spanish teacher is gone, the art
teacher last year was gone most of the year, and different long-term subs
came and went, but I'm still here. I know it isn't a big victory, but he knows
he's stuck dealing with me and I won't be disappearing. All these rats know
it.

I'm here. I'm still getting my pay and none of you can drive me out.
Not the white kids, not the black kids, not the principal, not the parents, not
the bullies or their cowardly supporters. Not many people can live off a
totally selfish vision, and I'm not one of those few who can. I think about a
picture I found the other day. It's a little illustrated card that shows a kid
lying in the snow looking dreamily up at the sky. When I first found the
picture left in the wreckage of my room, I considered burning it as an effigy.

Then I looked at it again and remembered Amber's Zorro. "This is
the kid I'm here for, the kid who doesn't bother people, the quiet kid who all
the teachers ignore because they are so busy catering to the "high needs
students," as educators call them, and those "at risk." Yeah "at risk" is right,
at risk for being loud mouths and bullies.

So I put the picture of the child dreamily lying in the snow on my
fridge, next to the post-it where I wrote "Tough it out and get your money."

113

In the art room I pick up where we left off. Most of the seventh graders have their advertisements sketched out and are ready to paint them in. I've been teaching a lesson on graphic design. As I survey the student's work I notice some pretty creative ads, like Tanika's ad that reads, "Tanika's Nails. Don't Hate. Celebrate." I like the ads the kids made. It helps them shape their future and it's inspiring to see their dreams on paper.

My happy moment is quickly shattered as I pass Lillian's table. Last class she called the girl passing out the supplies a "smelly piece of shit" and kicked her. She holds up her advertisement and declares, "Look it's the 'Ho-mo-tel!'" She's drawn a decent looking hotel with a big sign, reading: "Homotel." It looks like she really took my earlier lesson on creativity to heart: "Combine two things you are familiar with into something new. Try it!" She sure did.

Kyle, seated at the same table and one of the obnoxious three, starts to shout, "I'm done, yah, yah, yah!" He begins paper popping while continuing his "yah, yah" and rocking his long neck back and forth in a way that reminds me of a giraffe. I try to get him working on something else. He takes the new paper, but quickly folds it up and paper pops it, throwing old papers on the floor.

His popping noises and shouts are like a call of the wild to the other two obnoxious kids from his neighborhood. Joe, who I now realize looks like the Pillsbury Doughboy, begins making chimp noises and scratching his head like an ape. The others at his table are laughing but you can tell they would rather be able to do their work. As soon as I get Joe to a timeout, he starts calling out to Jimmy: "Jimmy smells like fish!"

"Shut up Joe!" Jimmy yells across the room. This is his call to the wild. He quickly leaves his work to start shoving the other kids stuff at his table, and expands beyond that to throw things at kids and hit them. No sooner do I get Jimmy to leave his table and go to timeout, than Joe is at it again making farting noises by blowing into his hands.

Kyle is randomly shouting out "Good old boys!" as he paper pops, rocking that giraffe neck of his back and forth. Then he starts antagonizing other kids in the room by yelling, "Shut up you munger!" I don't know what a munger is, but in this bi-racial room here it sounds oddly like something else that ends in "er."

Joe is now pretending to ride up and down the room like he's on a horse, saying "Yippee" and hitting kids as he gallops along.

"Joe, get back to your seat," I say.

"No," he says.

"Excuse me?"

"Ok you're excused."

I should have known that one was coming. On his way back to his timeout Joe stops by my desk to rhythmically pound on it with a big grin. He reminds me of a character from one of those 1950's beach party movies playing a drum at a Hawaiian style luau.

Jimmy leaves his timeout to wander up and down the room, grabbing kids' books and hitting them on the head with them, then singing some song about "piggy back piggy back." When I approach him to sit down he shouts out, "Shut up and get away from me. I don't care if you do call my mom because she thinks you're a moron!"

Does she think this? I'm pretty lost with this group. I can't call the office or parents for backup.

By the end of the class these guys are looking more and more like a cross between British soccer hooligans and the Dukes of Hazard- the original Dukes from the 1970's TV show.

After Work

It's Monday evening. After I'm finished with school preparations I drop by Lela's for dinner. She's making deep fried food as usual. It's always fried food with her and the others in this house. They don't deep-fry exactly like we do. They tend to deep fry things you'd think of as healthful, like tofu. Still, her dad died from a heart attack. She fills a sauté pan halfway full of oil and drops in tofu and other stuff. Then she pulls it out using chopsticks and lets the oil drain on paper towels.

After dinner we look at pictures from her home country. Her parents are nice looking, and in the photo they're sitting on fancy looking rattan furniture. She goes back to her bedroom and comes out with a large wrapped flat package. She unwraps it. It's a portrait of her with a painted floral backdrop that a young artist friend made for her.

My mind races with a string of questions. Some of them I ask out loud, some in my head. Who was this artist friend? Was she sleeping with him? What was she doing back in Indonesia with artsy friends? Was she a club goer? She majored in political science but doesn't have anything to say about the topic. Are there secrets I should know about?

She unpacks a traditional dress she's saving for a special occasion and shows it to me. It's a gold colored silk with floral designs. Next we move on to pictures from her time in America. There's a nice looking house in the Midwest, with fancy cars in the driveway, and her and her sister standing in front of the cars. I didn't even know she had a sister. It's the home of some sort of "general" they lived with when they first got here. I try to ask her about this general but her answers are confusing and hard to follow. I start imagining all sorts of scenarios, and begin to worry that there was some sex industry thing going on. I never really figure out who this general was and why they were staying with him.

She shows me pictures of her brother who lives in New Hampshire. She says she might move there soon. "What? You might move there soon?" I ask feeling surprised and let down. She can "live anywhere in this country," she tells me with her air of quiet confidence. Her life is pretty crappy here I have to admit: dismal housemate, no close friends, and a squalid neighborhood.

Her dismal housemate is also her sole source of transportation. They work together at an assisted living facility. Worse yet, Lela informs me about this guy at work who likes her, and that Debbie (the dismal housemate) thinks she should "give the guy a chance." Great, now it turns out there is a rival here, who her psycho patron wants Lela to hook up with. I'm sure in Debbie's brain they could be "one big happy assisted living facility staff family," if it weren't for me.

I wonder what it would be like if Debbie had kids, and they were in my class, and I had to call her because her kids behaved badly? She's a hardened, angry lady and would probably react as coolly as Joe's mom.

I figure I'd better spend as much time with Lela as I can either to dissuade her from disappearing, or encourage her to. It's late though and I better get home. I've got to be well rested for these oversized rug rats I have to tame tomorrow. I'm not one of those teachers who can go in half asleep and do his job. These kids test me enough as it is and any mental weakness like sleep deprivation will be sensed.

"So when can we get together again?" I ask, feeling time is of the essence.

She says "I know how busy you are and don't want to bother you during the work week." "It's no bother," I protest putting my hand on her shoulder. But instead of feeling like a handsome seducer I'm feeling like a big, gawky creep. I get a little like panicky. Am I being blown off? I come to my senses and resist the urge to insist we meet again tomorrow. "All right" I say, "we'll wait till the weekend." I give her space and don't call at all during the week, even though I'm anxious about this unseen rival.

While I've got to deal with domineering Debbie in my social world, I've got to deal with the increasingly dangerous student, Lillian, at work.

116

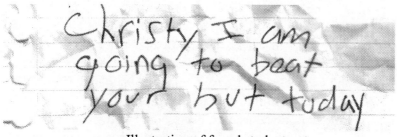

Illustration of found student note.

Prison Style

They say that in prisons, sexual abuse of inmates by other inmates is a way prisoners establish dominance. I've heard that some primates, the bonobo maybe, hump each other to show who's in charge. That's how it seems in this room with these kids today. Last time Jimmy was singing "Sexual Healing" and some tune he made up about "peeing." Today he's calling a kid "faggot." Now he's singing a Village People tune, "Macho, macho man, I want to be a macho man." One of his cohorts starts disrobing himself, like he's doing a strip tease to the tune.

(A couple years from now I'll see two boys wrestling in the hall. The dominant one gets the weaker boy's head pushed between his legs and humps it. They're both bigger than me. When I yell at them, they laugh.)

This is Lillian's day though. The white boy triad is just here to play a supporting role by egging her on. She begins her show by pulling the chair out from under a boy much smaller than she is, the same kid who Jimmy picks on. The boy hits the floor. He laughs the coward's laugh; the laugh that tries to placate the bully; the laugh that tries to save face.

"Lillian," I say, "someone could get really hurt doing that. My grandma told me one of her uncles got paralyzed for life when his own brother pulled out the chair from under him." Lillian seems unmoved. As the lesson progresses she goes mobile from her table, armed with a paintbrush. She dips it in paint at each table and smears the paint on the other students' books. She grabs their artwork and mixes it up. She storms the room shouting at and harassing kids. Like King Kong getting shot at by those little airplanes, she towers over the kids menacing them and knocking their books onto the floor, while Jimmy and his buddies, like the tiny fighter planes strafing King Kong, throw bits of color pencils at her. She turns around looking for someone new to swat. Then a broken color pencil strikes me, coming from Jimmy's direction. Teacher hit. This is getting bad.

117

Lillian is turning dangerous now. She's gotten hold of these hard plastic measuring triangles, and is forcefully throwing them at kids. I walk towards her. "Go to the office Lillian." She won't. She crashes her body into mine as she storms towards the back of the room. I know it makes me look bad sending kids to the office, but this is too serious. Most of the kids were into this lesson, and today like every day, it comes down to one, two, three or four kids out of twenty or thirty who sabotage the class.

When I hear educational leaders, like school board members, principals, professors and superintendents, talk about the issues we face in education, I never hear this fact publicly mentioned, at least not until some years later. The fact that a relatively small percentage of kids, "strategically placed," who get their homes called and get occasional suspensions, just never give up. This small violent faction tests the waters of authority. The test results come back negative. The diagnosis they collectively make is "There isn't much they can do to me," or to put in more street lingo, "These teachers can't do shit." Some of them are hopeless about their futures. Some are going through horrible things at home. Whatever the tragic reasons for the emotionally disturbed youth, other kids watch, learn and have to figure out how to survive with these loose cannons. Sooner or later it comes down to the old cliché, "If you can't beat them join them."

Lillian is frenzied. Her scattered hostility focuses laser-like on mild-mannered Sherita. Whatever it is that is really bothering her, she's decided to take it all out on this one girl. It's typical displaced aggression. Really Jimmy and Joe are more likely bothering her. But even though she towers over them, they are strong boys with lots of friends. Sherita is a quiet loner.

Sherita argues back, "Shut up and leave me alone!" Lillian threatens to kick her ass after school. Sherita defiantly proclaims, "Nobody's afraid of you." I remember that from my school days: someone threatening to kick my ass. It sucks. You're scared to come to school.

Lillian tells her to "Suck my dick bitch!" I can't believe what I just heard. This is seriously prison-style. Next she violently shouts at her: "You African booty licker!" while throwing a triangle across the aisle at her. Not only is it prison style girl on girl sexual harassment, it's even self-hating black. I pick up the phone to call for an escort to take her to the office. I've told her to go several times but she won't leave. "Hello. This is Mr. Lebrun. Please, I need someone to remove Lillian. She's becoming dangerous."

As she lunges at the sitting Sherita, I step in the middle and tell her, "Wait by the sink till they come and get you." She waits, momentarily sulking. Then she begins loudly singing the National Anthem. Our anthem refers to war, and Lillian is having a one-woman war of her own. No one from the office ever comes to get her.

After class, I sit in my ransacked room, and write my conduct reports. I hand some in to Dr. Airington and some to Dr. Iman. No one ever asks me about the write-ups. It seems they are just filed and forgotten.

White Parents

I call Jimmy's house, then Lillian's. Her Dad is going to come in and meet me. He sounds supportive. Considering the volume of parents I call I'm amazed by the good luck I've been having with most of them. While I'm calling both black and white parents about their child's bad behavior, it's the black parents that tend to be more friendly and cooperative with me. Since I'm white, you might think it would be the opposite. There's something going on here, and I'm beginning to figure it out, maybe. I pick up the phone and call about that fat obnoxious Joe. His mom was pretty cold the last time. It feels like I'm calling Lela's housemate Debbie at times.

"Hi, this is Joe's art teacher."

"Yeah," she says suspiciously. She sounds much more stable than Debbie, but just as tough. Now I'm even more nervous talking to her, just like I would feel if I were telemarketing. Maybe it's worse than telemarketing. Granted, as a teacher, if I don't make the sale I won't lose my job, and telemarketers probably don't have a union to get them the benefits I have. But if a telemarketer doesn't make a sale, or gets one irate customer on the phone they can hang up and never deal with that person again. If this kid's mom doesn't buy into my pitch for her to do something about Joe, then Joe's got nothing left to lose acting out in my room, and I'll be stuck suffering with him day after day.

I regain my composure. "Today he was…" and I fill her in. She cuts me off.

"Oh yeah…" Her voice has a blue-collar accent. While the blue-collar accent has a slight drawl, it isn't southern. In my part of the northeast it has a nasal twang. I picture her as blond and chubby like her son. It's the early afternoon. She's home. Does she have a job? I wonder what exactly she was doing when I called. Her voice sounds mean and I'm getting those knots in my stomach again. "Well you know what, I hate to say this, but," she says, and I think "it's never good when someone says 'I hate to say this, but…'" She continues, "to tell you the truth all the kids here are sayin' you can't control the class."

Low-level fear and confusion come over me. I hold the phone to my ear and open my mouth, but my mouth feels dry, my face suddenly feels greasy and my clothes feel like they don't fit right. I'm losing her. I'm not making the sale. She may as well have said, "You're an asshole. I'm sick of you calling, and my kid can swing from the chandeliers when you're teaching for all I care."

Worse, I'm realizing it's not just her I'm losing. I am picturing this gaggle of tough white kids and their tough white parents badmouthing me in the streets of the Iron Island.

Her voice rings with contempt. I fidget in my chair, rocking back and forth, tangling the phone chord. I say, "Yes, well, I've given him plenty of warnings and requested him to go to timeout. If the child doesn't cooperate then, then I am left with no choice but to call. Now it's up to you." She sounds skeptical but says "OK."

I sit shell-shocked for a second after hanging up. I am vividly imagining her and the rest of the parents she's heard say that I "can't control the class" thinking, "This guy thinks he's so smart, but he can't handle these kids." I think there is a class issue here. I can feel it seething through their voices, a resentment at how I speak.

I encountered it when I first moved to a white, blue-collar neighborhood as a kid. My mom, a liberal college professor, decided her second husband would be a mean-spirited factory worker. I don't have anything against anybody for what they do for a living. I might have been happier working in a factory than dealing with these kids, but that wasn't an option for me. Better than just marrying him, she decided we would leave our neighborhood and move to his territory. Our new home was in large housing grid surrounded by busy intersections, bordering an airport, a dumpsite, and populated almost exclusively by white blue-collar families. Parents, their kids, her husband, got off reminding me "You might be book smart but you got no common sense." Actually her husband didn't even credit me with being book smart –just the "no common sense" part.

The tone I get from black parents usually lacks resentment. They seem to be thinking, "Well listen to this 'Frazier Crane' sounding guy calling my house." It's like we were from two different planets, both of us a novelty to the other and neither a reflection on the other's shortcomings. Whereas with many of the whites my voice makes them self-conscious and my difficulties are proof to them that people sounding different than they, are contemptible and easily dismissed as "book smart but no common sense." (It's the same tendency that caused droves of people to reject Al Gore as "an egg head" and choose to vote for a guy who didn't know who

120

the president of a Middle Eastern country was during the debate. I remember him practically laughing off the question with a "who the hell would know that" smirk.) I and some of the white parents, we're just too close to each other yet too different, while I and the black parents, we're far enough apart that few feel challenged or threatened.

AM Call

6:30 AM Friday morning. My eyes are itchy and I'm worried I might have caught pink eye since it's going around the school. The phone rings, there's not enough snow for it to be my Mom calling to tell me "There's a snow day." It's Lela. Her voice sounds sad and teary, "It's been so long since we talked…" That giving her her space tactic worked pretty well.

She has to work late night Friday and Saturday. We set a date for Sunday to go to the Rust Belt Botanical Gardens. They'll be a little tropical oasis in a cold winter.

Meet Lillian's Dad and Getting the hang of teaching.

I've got a moment's peace during prep time. No kids, no parents, no administrators. I'm looking over a series of "how to draw in perspective" illustrations I'm working on. I hope the sketches will fill the void that these art education textbooks have left me with. This past summer when I was studying books to get prepared, I noticed almost none of the ones I sampled offered much in the way of activities or any "how to." Neither do the books I found here in my room. There's a chapter in one book called "Rhythm In Art." The chapter has a few paragraphs on the subject, some vocabulary, and reproductions of paintings illustrating the concept. It concludes with "Now make a painting of your own with lots of rhythm."

It is gradually dawning on me that this method is not working. Not with the kids I'm teaching. But here it is, all these people in art education saying, "Copying is not art." "Cartoons are not art." So I can't even let the kids try to copy my stuff.

Initially I tried using the art education approach, but I'm changing. My normal way is to teach the way these books do and the way I think my supervisor wants me to. I make a painting or drawing, put it up on the board, try to explain the concept, have a handout with instructions, only to find either kids shouting "I can't make that!" or have kids copy what I made. No matter how many times I tell them "This is just for ideas," they rarely seem to hear it. Leave them on their own with a "Now come up with your own idea," and they freeze and get angry.

Since they seem to think they are supposed to copy what I put up, even though I've told students they are not to, the kids will get mad if the picture in the book, or what I made, looks "too hard." I made a lesson that I thought was kid-friendly. I simply told them, "Create a collage using simple shapes to make real things." I spent a couple of hours cutting and pasting shapes into a scene of my neighborhood, complete with cubistic houses and dog on a leash. Then this chubby boy started shouting and angrily stomping his feet: "I don't know how to make a dog!"

A lot of times they get ahold of the drawings I made and eagerly try to copy them. Like the time they took a simple Egyptian scene and secretly started to pass it around the room. I'm surprised at how seldom my artwork is defaced.

When they take my art and try to draw it, I can feel a thirst being quenched. Looking at something and struggling to sketch it seems like an innate human trait. The children relish the challenge. When I was a kid I learned a lot about how to draw by trying to copy drawings. But since "copying is not art" I am afraid to let them do that, afraid my supervisor will catch me in the act.

The voice of the secretary is coming through that PA speaker near the ceiling: "Mr. Lebrun?" They seem to call for me over the PA, using it as an intercom, instead of just calling me on my phone. I don't know why they don't just use the phone. It's weird getting summoned like this, and I feel sort of insulted by it. I decide to ignore the PA and keep working on my "how to" sketches.

So far I've made five. The first shows simply the "horizon line" and the "vanishing point." The next shows what will become a house and some guidelines. It goes on, each step building on the last. I've got more to go, but I think this might work.

"Mr. L" the voice again calls.

"Yes?" I say.

"Lillian's dad is here to see you. He's on his way down." I'm always anxious meeting the parents. What do they really think about me? Am I the only one their kid acts badly for? Are they going to complain about me to the principal?

He peeks his head in the doorway. He's much older than I expected. It's hard to say if he's just had a hard life and is an old looking forty-something, or if he's a sixty-something with a fourteen year old daughter.

Maybe he isn't really her dad. I'm used to these kids having parents around my age or only five or so more years older.

He's got Lillian with him. The two sit down near the sink. Her dad is skinny, and dressed like a homeless guy, and has a homeless guy way about him. His clothes seem dirty and worn out, he's bearded with a graying head of frizzy hair popping out of a dirty brown baseball cap. Lillian sits next to him looking embarrassed and angry, completely mute. Dad and I talk, shake hands and he leaves amicably. Lillian leaves looking bitter and won't look me in the eyes or even crack a smile.

When she's acting out in class again the next time, I say "Your Dad is a nice man Lillian, you should make him proud of you. I don't want to bother him again." She gets an embarrassed look at the mention of her dad. She's angry I've met him. "No he's not. He is not a nice man!" I leave it at that.

Venting

The two new female teachers, Tina and Christine, and Ryan and I, are all in the lounge. Both of the females are buxom. Possibly due to sexual frustration I start talking in Spanish about big breasts with Ryan. Ryan is the Spanish teacher, and I figure the women don't know the language. We're acting like two immature boys, who imagine they are getting away with being naughty. If the women know what we're saying they pretend not to. As I "ham" up my Mexican accent Tina steers the conversation back to our usual topic: bitching about students.

We're all pulling food out of our brown-bagged lunches. Mine is the most minimalist: a whole carrot wrapped in plastic, whole stick of celery, peanut butter on bread and an apple. "These kids don't do anything," Tina says. We all take turns telling different student horror stories and about how these children don't do any work. Then I notice the heating vents, and how loud we are. People's voices travel through those vents and into my room from all over the building. I hear conversations from places I'd never expect.

I stop talking, and before I can advise Ryan to lower his voice, he bellows, "Of course they can't learn, these kids are like monkey's swinging from the trees!"

"Quiet man. Our voices could be traveling anywhere through these heating ducts."

"So what? I didn't say anything!" he says loudly, like he's taking a righteous stand. I expected he'd be grateful I was looking out for him, but I guess he's opted for the new American trend of denial.

"That sounds racist. If someone heard that…"

"Fuck you. You're racist for thinking that!"

"Get out of here man, you're in total denial. Look at that vent."

As I gesture to the vents everyone looks at them as if seeing them for the first time. I think that ended the conversation.

Garden

About a year ago, I decided to start going to Sunday Mass. I'm very groggy and still feeling the effects of drinking the night before as I walk up the church steps. Sleep deprivation seems to heighten the religious experience for me, and I nearly come to tears at various points during the Mass.

After the final round of religious music I drive over to pick up Lela. I followed a friend's advice and offered to take her to the Rust Belt's Botanical Gardens. It's Sunday afternoon and everyone seems in a good mood at Lela's. Debbie's talking happily about what she's going to purchase while grocery shopping. I don't think much of it, but I am relieved she's in a good mood.

Lela gets dressed leaving me alone in the living room with the TV playing. Debbie comes in the room and commiserates with me about how these Indonesians have no concern over the heat bill. They leave doors open, letting in the cold and keep the heat up high all the time. Come to think of it, Lela usually says a prolonged goodbye with the front door wide open while I stand on the front steps freezing. I guess coming from a tropical climate they don't think about things like storm windows and putting up sheets of transparent plastic over windows to conserve heat, like Debbie and I do.

Debbie asks me if I'm "looking forward to going shopping" with them. Going shopping with you? Did I hear this right?

"We're going to the Botanical Gardens. This is the only day Lela has off from work this weekend and I work every week day," I protest, feeling suddenly like I'm a teenager and Debbie's someone's mom.

Debbie becomes visibly angry. She doesn't confront me directly but starts raging around the house about all kinds of things, including how this is "our day to shop!"

Lela comes out. She seems confused. I fill her in. She says, "I'm going to talk to Debbie." I wait anxiously alone watching a morning talk show. A part of me wants to just leave. What am I doing here anyway? Who likes this confrontation? Didn't Lela know this was "their shopping day." Shouldn't she have taken care of this already? But then again, Lela isn't a native English speaker. Maybe she really doesn't understand what's going on. Then I think I should just sheepishly knock on the door and kiss Debbie's ass and say "I'm sorry Debbie; I didn't know. Of course I'd love to spend my Sunday shopping with you."

No, stop thinking like that Matt. Your "running away" and "caving in" days are behind you. This is the era of the new "hang tough" Matt. I suffer every day at the hands of loud-mouthed defiant kids to get my check. I don't quit. I barely even call in sick. I show up and I say to myself, "This is my room and no one can drive me out of it."

If I can suffer there to get what I need, I can suffer at the hands of someone's obsessive, domineering housemate to spend some time with an attractive woman. Lela returns from Debbie's room and I'm expecting her to say "We have to go shopping," instead she says "OK, lets go." I won.

The Gardens are in an out of the way part of the city. We walk up to the large, turn of the twentieth century era building. It has long rectangular glass side wings, and a shimmering dome on top. It's huge glass panels are held in place by white painted steel, wood, and what looks like marble. Snow covers many of the window panes. The effect is like stumbling onto an early 1900's sci-fi set. Cold winds blow in our faces as we approach, yet she keeps her leather jacket open while she shivers. I put my arm around her, but being logical can't help but say, "Why don't you close your jacket." She seems to think it looks cooler open.

Inside the gardens, it's warm and tropical. Fine mists spray down on some of the plants. She recognizes a few of them from back home. It's largely desolate as are most of Rust Belt's cultural icons now. I guess everybody is at the mall.

The solitude allows a long private moment on a bench. We look dreamily into each other's eyes, and I learn how to say "prince and princess" in her language. You can smell the tropical vegetation, and the effect is like being in some Garden of Eden. We kiss and stare some more. I can't remember ever sitting like this, staring into someone's eyes and her starring dreamily back.

But then doubt sets in. My life is more like one of those sad art films than a Hollywood happy ending flic. It can't be this good. Being pessimistic, I begin to think about her life and her living situation. I wonder about her past, that general that she and her sister lived with in the Midwest.

Everything she's told me seems vague. We don't seem to have much in common. I turn away, but keep hold of her hands.

"Look, please don't take this the wrong way. I have to bring it up and I have to get this off my mind. People will think this anyway. How do I know you aren't just interested in me so you can stay in the US?" I'm fearing this question could ruin everything. Her reaction is mild shock. I apologize but persist.

"I am not this kind of person who could do this," she assures me. She tells me "You can pay money to marry an American if that's all you want." She handled my question well, and calmed my fears, but what next? Would she even have the money anyway? It's time to leave this garden and return to the cold and drop her back off at her squalid apartment.

Chalkboard art lesson.

Petition and Race Car

Students have gone home for the day, I'm alone in the room, until the cleaning lady comes and bags the trash. In black and white chalk on a green chalkboard I sketch out a scene of a Mercedes driving up to a moonlit Big City, Canada skyline. The cleaning lady looks at it impressed. The drawing reminds me that there is more to this life than this job. It helps me remember late night drives through the big city, just a few hours away, with sexy and/or disappointing, Internet date ad chicks. While I work on it I fantasize that I'm a hip urban dude living his dreams, that I'm one of those

126

young rich dot-comers. It reminds me there is a huge world out there and I'm not, I hope, eternally damned to eat shit from fifth through eighth graders.

I hope this illustration will inspire kids to work more on their lesson. The fifth and seventh graders and everyone else, sees it the next day. The kids love it. I point to the illustration next to it on "tints and shades" and the refresher diagram I made on perspective, and say, "This is not to copy, it's just to show you how..." I'm interrupted by one of my fifth graders, "I'm drawing that!" he says pointing to my chalkboard mural, and gets to work. I find myself arguing with him, and against what I really believe. "No you can't copy it. This is just for an idea." I can't believe this is happening. If these young guys think my drawing is cool, and want to try to copy it, "go for it" is what I really want to say. This could have been a win-win.

A seventh grade group comes in. This is a group that is always suspicious that I am trying to trick them somehow. A lot of these kids in the "inner city" are suspicious of me, suspicious of each other, and everybody. I imagine them being raised by adults whose only consolation in life is small petty victories, like bullying the bus driver into giving them a free ride with an expired transfer.

Kids are shouting out "*You* didn't make that. Not you. No way! You paid someone." I can't even get credit for something I'm good at from these kids. No matter what, I have to be a loser in their eyes. In the recent past I've heard "You're just an art teacher," or "I don't have to listen to the art teacher" or worse "You're not a real art teacher" and "You can't draw." Now that I've made something they think is cool they won't even believe I did it.

"Come on" I say, "why would I hire someone to come in here and make that? I won't even pay for cable. So I'm sure not going to pay someone to come in here and draw something."

"You don't have cable?" One of the seventh graders asks me in shock. This becomes the new buzz in class. "He doesn't even have cable!" Everyone finds this hilarious.

It's time to get the paints out. Jessica, a slender, pretty African American girl with hair pulled back in a frizzy ponytail, pipes up. Her voice sounds like she's been up all last night smoking cigarettes, "Why you only give us these bunk paints?" As she says it she moves her head slightly from side to side to add emphasis. Others join in. Shaniqua a heavy set girl, with a deep voice and a very elaborate hairdo reminiscent of a pineapple says, "I hear you've got that locked cabinet filled with all the good supplies," shifting her head drastically back and forth, to make her point.

See, this is what I mean how they always think I'm up to something. "Look" I say, "these supplies were brand new when I brought them out of that cabinet. I can't bring out the new until we've used up the old."

"You're tryin to play us! You're keeping the good supplies for some class you like better" a boy shouts. This seventh grade class is bad, but they're not deeply hostile. They're typical tough kids being tough kids. They are an extreme version of the students from the comedy set in a Brooklyn high school, "Welcome Back, Kotter." When they go, Jimmy's group comes.

There is no friendly "ball busting" going on with them –it's just hostility, and me keeping a lid on their growing resentment. One of the kids, the same small white kid who Jimmy likes to pick on, takes a chair and sits at my mural, pretending he's maneuvering a car in one of those video games.

This gets to me; they love the art but hate the art teacher. I don't have it as bad as that professional illustrator Jason Mullet, the band teacher, told me about, but it's close enough. Jason told me about this long-term art sub last year. The guy was a great illustrator and was building a freelance career; but the kids were much more out of control for him than for me. Jason told me that teacher started saying stuff about the kids, really bad stuff. Then he stopped coming in, either by his own choice or someone else's.

Jimmy loudly asks the class "Who wants to have art?!" Others jeer "Not me!" When I threaten calling Jimmy's mom later on that class, he repeats his warning to me: "Go ahead and call my mom. She knows you're an idiot!" After talking with Joe's mom, I think this could be true, Jimmy's mom really may believe I'm an idiot. I feel my control slipping. I can hear kids calling for "a new art teacher!"

A couple of usually relatively well-behaved girls are acting up. One of them is the Arabic girl who Joe's mom insisted "smells badly." After yelling at those two girls, they insist they are "going to the office to get you (meaning me) fired!" Since I always sympathized with the Arabic one, I feel extra stung. "Get back in here!" I say. They cattily waltz out. Dr. Iman catches them in the hall and walks them back in while they angrily list my supposed injustices and offenses.

Next I confiscate a petition circulating the room. It's comical really. It says, "All in favor of getting a new art teacher sign below." One of the signatories' handwriting makes him look like he must be illiterate. Kyle wrote "all the way" next to his name. A girl named Jessica put a little smile face next to her signature. I look at it and laugh. What do these kids want -a return to the chaos of last year? As bad as the mayhem is now, I know it was worse before I arrived.

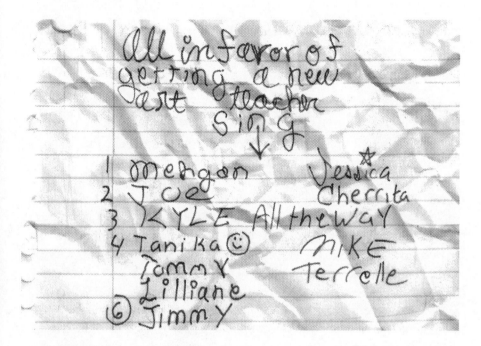

Handwritten note on lined paper:

All in favor of getting a new art teacher Sign ↓

1 Meagan   Jessica ★
2 Joe   Cherrita
3 KYLE   All the way
4 Tanika ☺   MikE
  Tommy   Terrelle
  Lilliane
(6) Jimmy

Lunch Duty

At lunch duty I see Mr. Beanbag again. And again I relate my war stories from that seventh grade, the group with Jimmy and Lillian. He tells me "Jimmy got suspended for peeing in a kid's sneaker in the boys locker room." I tell him "Good, but he never got suspended for anything he did in my room."

13. Mr. Slaughterbutcher and the Secret Santa.

Slaughterbutcher

Not sure if I remembered to brush my teeth, I pull into the Arab owned convenience store to buy toothpaste, before going to work. "Maybe I should be more like Mr. Slaughterbutcher?" I contemplate as I step up to the counter. Sure I've got misgivings about his right wing politics, but my supervisor keeps urging me to "be stricter." Slaughterbutcher is as strict as it gets. Not just strict but unorthodox. I never saw a teacher do things the way he does. His way seems to get results. The clerk accepts my money. Once at school I go to work with the toothpaste.

Slaughterbutcher and I first met during the strike. I remember pulling into the lot alongside a beat-up blue pickup truck. It was the type of pickup that looked like it was used for work and not show. On its bumper it had a "Bush Cheney" sticker. Not unusual on a pickup, but unusual for a teacher. A stubble-faced fat guy, with swept-back hair, climbed out. His weight gave him a slight waddle as he headed over to the picket line.

In line I was surprised to see Fin, someone I knew when I was a teen. We hung out during our "punker" high-school days. He was talking to the pickup driver.

During our teenage years, Fin didn't have a full Mohawk. He had short hair with a dyed (green was it?) tuft of longer hair in the front. He'd sculpt it into a little fin. Today that tuft of green wouldn't seem so unusual on a teenager. But in the late eighties we all suffered a lot of harassment for those haircuts.

"Hey Maaatt!" Fin said with rowdy gusto, like I was still the same person I was at sixteen. After we caught up, he introduced me to the other guy.

"What's up?" the chubby stubble-faced guy said gruffly, with a rapid nod and no smile. We shook hands. "I'm Jack. Jack Slaughterbutcher."

Mr. Slaughterbutcher is a rabid conservative. He reminds me of Rush Limbaugh. Slaughterbutcher owns a bunch of low-income rental properties in a black neighborhood similar to the one our school is in, maybe the same one actually. I'm assuming a lot of the rent money comes from the government. So he's teaching the kids and collecting rent from their parents at the same time. He hates government but gets paid by it at both ends, teacher salary and welfare rent subsidy.

While I haven't met many teachers who are collecting rent from the same parents whose kids they are teaching, this isn't what's so unorthodox about Mr. Slaughterbutcher. What's so unorthodox about him is that he freely and openly insults his students.

Midmorning I see Slaughterbutcher escorting his seventh grade class to my room. A fat black boy, who's taller than the teacher, steps out of line muttering something. Slaughterbutcher shoves him saying, "Get back in line you big moron!"

His voice is harsh. As they arrive at my room and march past me, he says, "You gotta watch out for Lamont, he's a big dummy."

"Shut up!" Lamont says back. While Lamont's words are defiant his actions and pitch are not. He's looking down and smiling submissively.

"Sorry Lamont you're not a dummy, you're a moron."

Ray, a very dark-complexioned African American boy, laughs pointing at Lamont, "He curred you Lamont!" They settle into their seats.

Nowhere did any professor during teacher training ever tell me that the best way to manage a class loaded with "high needs pupils," bullies, and kids who like to get their laughs by putting each other down, was to be the biggest bully and the best at the put-down game. This is what Mr. Slaughterbutcher seems to be doing, and it seems to be working. Over the years, I'll notice other teacher's use this trick successfully. I'm not advising it, but without clear rules, clear consequences and administrative backup, these extra-judicial actions become the de-facto system of discipline. They always have been to a greater or lesser extent, even in the burbs. There the picked on occasionally rise up and go berserk.

I've got Ray, Lamont, and this other kid Eon sitting as far away from each other as I can. Eon is a thin, nicely dressed basketball player. Surprisingly a lot of the worst acting kids dress in new, clean, trendy clothes. Even though they are separated from each other, it doesn't stop them from shouting across the room to one another. They barrage me with loud rude jokes, "Look at the size of his forehead," Ray remarks.

131

"His forehead so big you could fit two of my heads in there!" Lamont shouts, pointing at me. He turns his head from Ray to Eon, seeking approving laughter. The three are laughing and slapping their sides. It's like I'm standing in between three old-time black comedians. Only instead of putting each other down for my enjoyment, they're putting me down for theirs.

I stammer for a comeback, but only come up with "Be quiet!"

"You be quiet! You big headed fake art teacher!" Eon chimes in.

"Ooooh he curred you!" Ray adds, pointing at me and laughing.

"Get over to that timeout!" I say to Eon.

"I outta knock you in that big forehead of yours!" Eon replies.

The humor goes from friendly "ribbing" to violent threats in seconds, and back again. As I look down to get started on a write-up Lamont says "Look he's goin' bald!"

"You need to get some Rogaine!" Ray shouts.

Class is over. I line everybody up to go. Eon is jumping around. I put my hand on his shoulder and say, "Get back in line." He yells, "Don't touch me! I'll get you fired." This is the same kid, who to get my attention, typically jumps up and grabs me by the shoulder. Once I even drove him and his friends to a basketball meet. They were all rough housing with each other, and trying to with me. Now he acts like he's offended.

After they leave, I straighten up the room. Scrawled across Eon's timeout desk is "Fuck Time Out!" I laugh. Old gangsta rap tunes play through my head, like NWA's "Fuck the Po-lice." On the drive home I can still see that desk. If this kid is so "gangsta" I laugh, then why did he even stay in timeout at all?

Hang in til Winter Break

Amber's Zorro, Jaylen's mix tape, and that Polish movie have all helped me to turn on my ignition and pull out of the garage in the morning, instead of turning on my ignition and staying in the garage. As we plow deeper into winter, behavior is getting worse. "Kids always get worse before the break." "Hang in there." "Winter break isn't far off!" People keep consoling me. I hang onto the dream of a holiday.

Before break comes, I've got to think of holiday-oriented lessons. I'm getting mixed signals. On the one hand we have separation of church and state, and many people who are quickly offended. On the other hand ninety percent of fellow teachers, parents and administrators are expecting me to make Christmas stuff. I settle for devising a lesson that meets some art-related goals, like use shading and perspective; and teaches them about all the different holidays going on, or have gone on, around this time. Christmas, Kwanza, Hanukah, Ramadan, Solstice, and Saturnalia. It is not a major success.

Eon's found the lesson so interesting that he's threatened to "jaw" me a few times today. I've finally got him in timeout. Now he and Nicole are shouting at each other. Nicole has long brown hair and is wearing tight blue jeans. She alternates between being helpful and cooperative on the one hand, and bratty disruption like playfully crawling under tables, on the other.

When she's cooperating, she's often painting large hearts and rainbows with her or my name on them, and giving them to me. She gives me a hard time, then gives me hearts.

"Shut up Nicole, you stupid ass-ho!" Eon yells. I can't tell if ass-ho is a mistake or a new form of insult.

A few years later I will see "ass ho" written in marker on another art teacher's table. So I guess it *is* a new insult, combining the concept of ho – as in slut, with ass. Very creative.

Then I have to break up a fight between Nicole and one of the other girls, who apparently has gotten jealous about all the attention Nicole's getting from Eon.

Up in the ladies' lounge I see Laura. Before the others get there we start talking about an escapade she had at a bar with another single female friend of hers. This leads me to bringing up the idea of threesomes. The others come. Laura signals we shouldn't talk about this. But then says something openly flirtatious to me in front of them. "Why don't you come over and help me trim my tree," she says. The ladies all laugh. "He's turning red!" one of them says.

Another buxom older female teacher comes in, the one I met my first day in the building. "Laura did you see what your Secret Santa brought you!" She's accompanied by a male janitor. They're both smiling. A few of us follow Laura to her room, which is now empty of kids. They're at lunch. She opens her gift. Someone says, "It's a vibrator." Everybody laughs again.

Illustration of note handed to me on teacher's stationary.

Teacher's Pet

I don't see Lela often, so Laura's flirtation is still on my mind when Slaughterbutcher's class arrives this morning.

While I'm busy quelling pre-holiday insurrections, Molly comes up bearing a gift of paintbrushes. Molly is always well behaved and I have her sitting with this other sometimes well-behaved boy. She's tall, thin and has blue almond shaped eyes, and freckles. The boy I have her sit with, Isaiah, is chubby, with blond curly hair. I say he's only sometimes well behaved because I've caught him giggling while making penises out of modeling clay.

Molly says, "My aunt bought these for you." I'm surprised by this gesture, and put the brushes in a safe place.

To reward her ever-good behavior I let her be a helper at clean up time. Her reward for being a helper is Ray screaming "Teacher's pet!" Molly comes up to me crying, "Ray threw paint in my eye!" I'm furious, he shoots his loud mouth off at me all period, threatens to "jaw" me, mocks my hair line, and harasses the one kid who tries to be good.

Afterwards I call Ray's mom. Over the next few classes Ray gets it in his head that I'm "just mad because he bothered a white girl" and is "curring" me more than ever.

During this rowdy class, a very small child knocks on the door and enters the room. Kids harass her a little: "Get out of here you little peanut!" She hands me an envelope. "It's from Ms…." (I never called Laura by her last name, so I can't even remember it.) There's a note inside. "I think you're sexy when you blush." It's written on typical teacher stationary. Her handwriting is neat, "teacherly" and very womanly. This could almost be unwelcome harassment, except for the fact that I welcome it.

Meanwhile, Molly, the one who gave me brushes, keeps asking, "Why aren't you using those brushes?" So I start using them. Once Ray realizes these are Molly's brushes, he and his friends start "accidentally" dropping those brushes down the drain. They were small brushes and the pipes were large. "Where's all the brushes I gave you?" She's upset.

"Well…" I explain how sorry I am, "but it just shows how we all really need to follow the rules." Thus I confess the brushes are gone. Now she's pissed at me too.

Flood.

A few classes after they threw out Molly's brushes, and phone calls home and timeouts haven't worked I try a new tactic. I try to "incorporate" Ray and his friends. It's the age old naive "what if I just trust" tactic. I make Ray a helper.

He, and Lamont take advantage of this opportunity by stuffing the drain of the sink full of paper towels, and turning the water on while pretending to help clean up. They step away bent over laughing, as I watch water flood the sink and gently cascade over the sides and all over the floor.

I look at Lamont. He's back at his table. I look at the mess he's made, not just at the sink, but all around and his table and the floor. He hasn't done anything all period, except argue with every girl in the class.

Lamont turns his head from side to side so the whole room can see that he's wedged quarters in his eye sockets. I bark with real anger, "Get over to timeout!" When he refuses and says "Shut up! I'll jaw you man!" I become livid and start to pick on him, like I've seen Slaughterbutcher do.

"You're a slob Lamont!" Am I so angry that I'm drooling? He lugs his big fat self to timeout making weak attempts at defiance. I follow behind him pointing and barking: "That's what you are, a slob!" As I say these things with true fury in my voice, I flash back to my Mom's husband shouting the exact same thing at me, in the exact same tone. I remember that husband following behind me with menace, repeating, "You're a slob Matt! That's what you are!" Shit, I'm guilty of displaced anger. It's like kicking the dog, although this dog is human and bites.

After class, shaking off the frustration I leave to get some coffee. I bump into Mr. Fin, the younger Gym teacher. "I hear you and Laura might get together!" he says excitedly. Next, Fin tells me an X rated story about her. "She will do anything. With anybody," he says, making it sound like I could have a lot of fun. "And tell everybody," he adds as warning.
"Maybe I better pass on this one," I say.

I make it home in time to do a little early holiday shopping. Walking under the fluorescent glow of the giant cube that is Big Mart, I spot Laura. Before I can duck down an aisle she spots me. I'm used to seeing her sitting. Standing I get a full head to toe view of her in one breathtaking glance. She's taller than me and looks pretty appealing. She lets me know her son "hasn't come home for college break yet." Then looks down at me, and into my eyes and asks: "So, are you going to come over and see my tree?" I get nervous and go back to shopping.

Cretins

Back at work, I'm able to reach everyone's parents from Slaughterbutcher's by phone except one girl, Veronica. It's another one of those "no one knows her real number" or doesn't have a phone, situations.
So I head to Mr. Slaughterbutcher's second floor room, to see if he has her number. I'm about to get another example of his unorthodox teaching methods. There are a couple of stenciled buffalo's hanging on the wall outside his room. I let him borrow one of my stencils. Why not? My supervisor won't let me use them anymore. His students put things related to America inside of them. On the table next to his door are a bunch of tiny covered wagons he taught his students how to make.
He's seated at his desk staring down the class. A stir passes among his students when I enter. There's an excited undercurrent, like someone is about to shout something rude at me. Before they can, Mr. Slaughterbutcher says to me, but looking at these seventh graders so they can hear: "Look at these Cretins. Have you ever seen such a bunch of Cretins?"

I'm not sure how to react. A different stir passes among the group. It's a sulky beat dog mood. One of them, seeming hurt asks, "Are you insulting us?"

"No. No. Of course not," Slaughterbutcher chuckles gruffly, with enough obvious sarcasm that they aren't sure.

"What does Cretin mean?" another kid asks defensively.

"It means a really studious intelligent person," he turns his head to me: "right Mr. Lebrun?"

Go along with it, I decide: "Oh yeah."

Before I can ask him my question, Lamont stops working on the computer to look at us. He's at the back of the room, and grinning, he opens his mouth about to speak. Before Lamont can make his remark, Slaughterbutcher makes his own: "Look at the size of Lamont 's head." He pauses looking from Lamont to me, then back to Lamont. "Have you ever seen a melon that big?" I remember being that age and some of the "cool" boys making fun of kids with "big heads." I wondered why would anybody want a small head anyway? Lamont turns back to the screen. He's cowed. He's been curred. Slaughterbutcher has them all cowed. If cut downs were like Wild West gun slinging, then Slaughterbutcher is the fastest gun in the room.

He asks why I'm here.

"It's about a student. But what about Ray sitting here? He could hear us." Ray is silently sitting in a cubicle made of cardboard. His cardboard cubicle is adjacent to Slaughterbutcher's desk. He hasn't even tried to say anything the whole time.

Slaughterbutcher says, "He isn't mature enough for human contact. Are you Ray?"

We walk to the doorway. "I tried calling Veronica's home, but her phone number's disconnected. "

"Stop by her house," he says loudly enough so his students can hear. "Really?"

"That's what I do. I go right over to their home, and put my feet up on their coffee table."

"You do?"

"I do exactly what their kid was doing in my classroom. I just do it in their living room."

He points at her, curls his finger towards himself and calls out, "Veronica. Ca mere." Then quietly just so I can hear says, "Watch this." Veronica joins us, holding onto her left wrist with her right hand. "If I get one more bad report, you're not going on the field trip to Fun World." She returns dejectedly to her desk. "Ms. Henderson won't let me stop her from going. Veronica doesn't know that. You gotta bluff 'em a little."

Before I leave, he gestures towards the covered wagons. "These aren't hard to make. The kids love em. You could do this."

The next time I see his class they're all wild as usual. But Veronica is well behaved.

Slaughterbutcher breaks all the teaching rules. They say, "Don't make threats you can't keep." He just did it and it worked. This guy has an instinct for carrot and stick. For humiliation and reward. He's like an abusive spouse and his students are like victims craving the abuser's approval. Not only are they compliant, they seem to be learning. Just the other day, Ms. Henderson announced over the loudspeaker, "Congratulations to Mr. Slaughterbutcher and his students." They won at some multi-school scholastic competition. He's clearly the Sheriff in his town.

Cretins Lunch

During lunch duty I approach Dr. Iman intending to talk to him about Mr. Slaughterbutcher. I imagine that Slaughterbutcher's methods may be controversial, so I open the discussion with school discipline in general. Iman tells me, "The problem is you have some kids who want to be alpha males, and alpha females. If you could remove them right away, it would send a message. So the others wouldn't follow. But they closed the alternative schools a while back."

They used to have special schools where you could send the habitually disruptive. A friend of mine used to go to one. That friend was pretty crazy. So that's it? There's nowhere to send them. Those kids have free reign.

"Maybe I should be more like Slaughterbutcher. Kids are well behaved for him and he insults them on a regular basis," I propose to Dr. Iman.

"No. No. Don't do that. We get angry calls from parents all the time, saying 'He called my kid a retard.' That's the last thing you want to do."

Kids seem to respect Dr. Iman too. His "wise man" approach seems less stressful and more "me" than playing a 1950's drill sergeant. I'm not a hundred percent convinced though.

You've got this backwards, kid –Starlet.

After lunch duty I face another seventh grade. Slaughterbutcher is one of their teachers.

As I start to instruct, this girl Starlet starts to sing. It's a rhythm and blues tune. She raises her voice to drown out mine. Starlet must practice a lot, maybe at a church choir. She could be a professional. I still ask her to stop, "Could you practice later? I'm trying to teach."

She interrupts her singing to make a speech. How dare I ask her to be quiet? With sincere sounding derision she says, "You'll see. When I'm famous you'll still be down here. Down in this room, in this basement! Doing the same thing you're doing now, teaching the same stuff. But I'll be somebody. And you'll still be a nobody!"

She's pretty good and a lot of rappers really are from the hood –so with a lot of luck Starlet will make it. One day she can come back to Grand Plans middle and say "I made it despite you Mr. L!"

She casually, but forcefully, resumes her singing.

"What the fuck," I think. Like I'm some loser teacher who is holding her back. As if I said "she couldn't make it?" I never said that. When she finally finds stardom, she wants to rub my nose in it? How she succeeded "in spite of this teacher." I mean, she thinks I'm in her way? She's the one giving me shit. But somehow I am in her way. What kind of joke is this?

Did she get the idea from a movie? I think I saw a movie like that. A movie where a teen "had a dream" and the grown ups said, "You could never be a rock star (or substitute any other goal). Face reality. Get a real job kid!" Shit, I feel like that kid was me.

I decide to tell her, "I hope you make your dreams come true. Maybe I still will be here, but that doesn't mean you have to make me feel bad about it." Actually I'm thinking I won't be here, but not because I landed on some star, just because I'll probably end up teaching at a different school.

Field trip and Track Meet.

On my drive in this morning I was looking forward to the field trip. Now I'm not. Not as much anyway. I'm assigned to help chaperone Starlet's group. The school buses arrive at the gleaming head office of Rust Belt Daily News. A crusty gray-haired employee gives us a guided tour.

We take the elevator down to the basement printing press. My nose fills with the smell of ink, and my body vibrates with the whir of machines. Machinery towers to the ceiling, rhythmically pounding, lifting and rolling. Conveyors dump papers into giant bins, and forklifts carry the bins away. The guide tells us how the machines operate, "It's a three color separation process. But we are changing that soon." He gives us all a free newspaper, and stops speaking, to let us freely watch the machines and workers in action.

There's an embattled English teacher next to me. He's balding, tall and slender. We both have newspapers folded under our arms. Isaiah, a student, asks, "Why do grownups always carry newspapers under their arms like that?" Then he wanders ahead. Next, Starlet walks past us. She turns her head slightly in our direction and venomously hisses "faaag." The English teacher and I look at each other. Does she mean me, or him?

We re-enter the elevator. The old timer explains, "In America we have a free press." Free for the ones who own it, I think. Surrounded by hostile students, another embattled teacher, and an old timer, I keep my dissenting comment to myself.

Now we're in a large open sunny area. It's so different than being in that basement at school. One section is filled with graphic designers and illustrators. They use computers, sketchpads, and scanners. It looks like a nice job and a nice place to work. These people get to make art all day and don't have to deal with screaming kids. As the group leaves, I linger behind to get a business card from one of the artists. We both wear white button down shirts, but unlike me, he has a calm look in his eyes. Maybe I can be one of them instead of me, and get out of that basement before Starlet is famous.

It's a couple of days after the field trip. Time to see Starlet again. While I'm walking the hallway I bump into Fin, and confide, "I dread seeing that girl next period. Starlet's a total loose cannon."

"No, you don't have to see her today. She's suspended."

"Why?"

"At an indoor track meet yesterday a girl was passing her in the relay race. Starlet said 'Fuck you, you white bitch!' and hit the girl with her baton."

14. Festival of Lights

X-Mas Party

As winter break draws closer, the staff gets in a better and more hopeful mood, while the kids get rowdier. On a table in my room, I find an anonymous holiday greeting. It's written in a sixth graders scrawl: "Mr. Labrununun is a Bitch and a Fag. Merry Fucking Christmas!"

My main hope is that winter break will afford me a chance to figure out how I'm going to get out of this job. I've got friends who teach English overseas; maybe I'll do that.

Mr. Mullet offers consolation: "It's not just art. Last year the kids drove out a few math teachers. Ms. Henderson even had an assembly where she explained how important Math was and how they needed to cooperate. They didn't listen. By this time last year they were whipping pencils at that math teacher."

"I'm havin a party," he adds. There's an official school Christmas party but it's like thirty bucks. Forget that. Mullet lives in the burbs now. Way out, almost in the country, even though we have a residency requirement. Rust Belt teachers, other than math and science, are required to live within Rust Belt city limits. Some teachers manage to find creative ways around the rule, like listing a relative's house as their own address.

Back in the ladies lounge, Laura says she isn't going, so Pookie asks me for a ride. For some reason, Pookie doesn't feel safe driving out there by herself. I politely decline. Am I freaked out by her flirting? Unlike Laura, who seems serious, I think Pookie is just joking when she flirts. Am I just being selfish? Fin, the young gym teacher, treats me like a bit of an asshole for not giving her a ride. "I thought you were her friend?" he says accusingly.

Slaughterbutcher's at the party with his wife. I was wondering who would marry a loud, domineering right-winger - a thin, reclusive, blond British lady, that's who. He likes foreign culture too. We have that in common. Speaking of liking foreign culture, Ryan isn't here nor the other two new teachers. I go to all these socials, unless it costs. They don't go to any. I will teach again next year. Ryan and Tina won't.

Winter break arrives. I don't quit work, although I've been giving that serious thought. I'm not going overseas. Lela is here. I can't leave Lela. Instead of leaving, I post a doodle on my fridge of a talking dog saying, "how are you going to get us out of this?" It wasn't so long ago I watched Spike Lee's "Summer of Sam," which featured a crazy guy who thought he saw a talking dog.

I pick up my brother from the airport. He lives in Big City, USA and is visiting us in Rust Belt. When he sees the talking dog doodle he laughs, and offers some career ideas. We scour the mall doing last minute Christmas shopping, having a good time, until I spot one of my students walking with a grownup. She looks so small and like a *real* child. And nothing like the way she normally appears to be: a towering, threatening, unpredictable monster.

"You're an imposter! You just want the gifts. Show your true colors now!" I keep all these thoughts in my head and duck into a store before she notices me. In another store two teenage students who know me from subbing see me. They laugh: "What are you doing here?!" as if I couldn't exist outside of a classroom and having paper balls flung at me.

Festival of Lights

My brother and I leave the mall and go to Mom's. I leave him there and head to Lela's.

After the aggravation with Debbie we start to spend more time away from her apartment. I take her to Rust Belt's low budget "Festival of Lights." The city has a large circular road that surrounds an urban golf course. The road's used for biking, jogging, and – while it seems anti-pedestrian - you can also drive your car around it. In the winter, they put up lighted displays of dancing reindeer and so on. I'm expecting it to be free since it sucks.

Instead of free, I'm greeted by a guy in a bulky winter jacket blocking the road's entrance. "Nine dollars," he says. Nine dollars for this meager show? I know not to carp out loud in front of Lela, even though it's my nature to complain. Despite my initial aggravation we have a pretty nice time. On our next date I will pick her up from work. She doesn't get out until late so I make plans to go to Alex's pre-holiday party first.

Alex's Party

This friend of mine, Alex, lives in a large downtown loft. He got the place before downtown started making its comeback. I bought a "top shelf," bottle of Brandy to donate to his party tonight. OK it's not top shelf, but it's a lot more than that five-ninety five bottle of vino I brought over to Debbie's party. They'd know the difference here. (I won't be able to stay late though, since I seem to be displacing Debbie as Lela's source of transportation.) Alex is one of those "knows everybody" types. So it's no surprise that an old friend of his is a young successful NYC illustrator. She's single, and he's trying to set her up with this guy we both know from years back named Seth, and not me, since by now I've foolishly told everybody "I have a girlfriend."

The party's crowded and looks like a scene from a "Lava Life" date ad on late night television, with lots of twenty to not-that-old yet, hip-looking folks standing around with drinks in hand. I spot Seth and walk across the room to him. "Holy crap, Seth!" I say when I see him. "Do you remember me?" I ask.

"Yeah. Matt? Right? How's it goin'?" He's wearing glasses, hair combed to the side, a sort of hip geek look; and has a nasal snuffling way of talking.

I ask him if he remembers the time I "crashed" at his place in California, back in 89? He does. I tell him: "I remember I was "partying" pretty hard, and in the morning when I was "coming down" I was in the middle of a long shower, when that one housemate of yours started screaming about me crashing there for so long. She was pissed she couldn't get in the bathroom. Through the water I heard her say 'we're not running some goddamn halfway house! When is this guy leaving?'" Seth and I laugh.

"Yeah she was pretty neurotic. She moved out right after you left actually," Seth tells me.

A small group of partiers take over the dining table centered in the middle of the main room. Seth, and the illustrator are both there, but it's me who's monopolizing the conversation with her. The illustrator is a slender blond woman in her early thirties. She's mapping out her life story for me, and I'm comparing where our paths diverged, she on to illustrator, and me on to a lot of different things; where mine went wrong and might still go right someday. "Wow that's really awesome. How long ago did you get your first illustration gig?" I ask her.

Seth interrupts the two of us, "I don't mean to cut you off, but shouldn't you get going to pick up your girlfriend?" It is getting late so he has a point, but still, he doesn't even know this "girlfriend." What's he so concerned for? I think he's just cock blocking me. I leave the table with a similar feeling that a kid has at having to go to bed before the show he's watching is over. I have to leave this glimpse of what might have been my own life path, in a just slightly alternate universe; the life of a career artist living it up in New York, instead of getting mentally gang raped by kids all day.

I descend the steep staircase through bleak halls down to the empty street below, and begin the half hour drive along slick snowy night highways to the deep suburban location of Lela's employer, the assisted living facility "Elder Weeping Acres."

I arrive early and have to wait for Lela's shift to end – thanks Seth!

Lela and I make it back to the city line. It's late night on the drive back. The downtown streets are largely desolate. The tower block buildings are mostly dark. As we get closer to her neighborhood they're mostly boarded up.

I'm rambling on about politics, the state of education and other topics that must seem arcane to her. I glance over at Lela and she's staring at me with a slight smile, nodding appreciatively. The look in her eyes is the look of someone in love. On the one hand I'm happy to see that look, but on the other it makes me apprehensive. What is she in love with? Obviously not what I'm saying. We don't seem to relate that well in that way. I can talk politics for hours. She has no interest in it. So what is it? If I can be said to be "in love with her" I think it's mainly for superficial things. A red light. I stop talking and reach over to touch her cheek. Don't look a gift horse in the mouth they say. So I kiss her on the lips. Back at her place with everyone asleep, she tells me she "loves me."

I stumble over the words as I force them out in reply, "I...love...you too."

"That's OK. Maybe you don't love me yet, but you will," she says in response to my obvious choking.

New Year's 2001.

My brother went back to Big City for New Years to watch the ball drop. I would have been smart to have gone with him.

There was a New Year's in the mid-nineties I spent home alone organizing my files. All my friends went to various parties. I made the mistake of half planning with everybody and saying "I'll call you." By the time I made the calls no one was home. Out of desperation I walked over to my college friend Josh's apartment. Knocked. Pounded. Nothing. Dark. I looked at my watch. "Fuck! It's midnight." As I turned back to make the lonely walk home, an old man across the street shouted out to me "Are you OK?"

"Yeah. I'm fine. Thanks."

"Happy New Year."

"Happy New Year." Back at home I opened up my files and began sorting.

This New Year's Eve, some six years later, I'm about to make a similar error. Lela has to work, and I think: "Just focus on your relationship and stay home." I do. But staying in alone leads to drinking alone. Drinking alone leads to thinking about why I'm in alone New Year's and what I'm missing out on. I grow indignant about what I see as her lack of open mindedness, especially about "reh-ligion." I have a universal view on religion, and I'm hoping she can share it. I don't know if I'm really up for a Muslim wedding, and actually becoming Muslim like she insists. Marisol recently introduced me to a bi-religious couple, who participate in two faiths, celebrating Ramadan and Christmas, going to mosque and church. It seems like a good arrangement to me. But I realize this wouldn't make sense to most people, and it will turn out it doesn't make sense to her either.

Midnight comes and goes. Wow, what a great evening: home alone, drunk and having an imaginary argument. Maybe I should plunge deeper into alienation and just call a phone sex line next?

Instead, I realize Lela should be home from work by now. I call and confront her, gently at first. But then I get aggravated with what I've been coming to see as her close-minded attitude, and I'm aggravated over this lame New Year's I've just had. I'm frustrated with this job and my decision to stick with it. All of my nature to complain, confront and badger, that I've been wisely quelling when I'm with her, starts to come out over the phone, in an inebriated frustrated flurry. I bring up that bi-religious couple. "They're stupid," she tells me. "*They're* stupid?" I say accusingly. I can feel her turn cold. I should have seen this coming. Someone who could fall in love so easily could just as easily fall out of love. Her conclusion: "It's over. Mat-chew it's not about you. It's about reh-ligion," she says in that same calm determined plodding voice she uses no matter what the conditions are. Only this time she sounds a million miles away and I have no way to charm her back.

After I hang up the phone, I realized that, big life issues aside, it was still way too early in the relationship to argue with her. You can't get aggravated around or with your special someone, until they're already hooked. Sure, maybe it's for the best letting this relationship go, I mean it seemed pretty superficial, but I still just lost something I had, and loss is always painful. It's like how quitting teaching would be, maybe for the best, but a loss.

When I set foot in church again, I look around at the graying heads. The few age appropriate females who go there just scurry out as quickly as they can after Mass. Even though I've seen some of them at clubs and bars before, here they have this Catholic guilt thing, so you can't say anything to them.

Some people think it's wrong to want to meet a mate at church, they think it's seedy. But it seems like an ideal spot to me; wouldn't meeting someone here increase the odds of a commitment?

Now I look around the church this time with the thought that, "This is a dead end for me. I need to meet my mate, and this religion just cost me a potential one." I'm not having a full-blown crisis of faith; but I'm having enough of a crisis that I do resolve to stay out later on Saturdays.

146

15. Blue and the First Accusation

The N Word.

Winter break is a memory. What was until recently holiday white snow, piled on the sides of the school parking lot, is now stained black from auto exhaust. Stepping out of my car, I tramp through puddles of half frozen oily water. I pause and look at the building. Lela was part of my emotional buffer against student attacks. With her gone, I can feel that buffer wear thin. The sympathetic vice principal still hasn't recovered from his heart attack, and no one's told me anything more about my fallen comrade in misery, the music teacher, Mr. Cantwell. His student led ouster, followed by a convenient injury, began when a kid said, "He hit me!" Now I'm about to get my first accusation.

Mr. Tussle's students march towards my room. Mr. Tussle is shorter than me, in his fifties, with reddish hair and a beard. His voice is low and a little scratchy, but not as drill sergeant like as Slaughterbutcher's. While he doesn't exactly look the part, he gives off an "ex-hippie" vibe.

As Tussle's students settle into their seats, some of the boys are intermittently picking on this girl Kara, and then are intermittently quelled by his stern gaze. Kara is average height for her age, with brown hair and blue eyes. She's not especially pretty or plain, and seems like an unlikely target for bullies. Mr. Tussle gives his final quelling gaze and exits the room. I begin the lesson on "shadows and shading." While I'm standing in front of the group, as I start to speak, Baxter, seated in front of me, does this thing where he starts falling out of his chair. He's been doing this for a while now. It never fails to get the laughs. Lately he will turn his chair in the opposite direction, straddle it with his legs spread, and then when asked to turn his chair around, gyrate his hips like he's humping the air in front of it.

Baxter is a short, stocky, very dark complexioned kid who began to test me during my first day teaching.

I try to seat the most volatile far apart. It's similar to having tropical fish and needing to know which ones will attack each other. When I was

147

seven, I had tropical fish that habitually fought. To stop these blood feuds I added loads of plants so each fish had her own hiding space. It worked. Only problem is the kids, unlike the fish, are all in the same wide-open tank. With these giant tables, instead of individual desks, they don't have any privacy or hiding spaces.

By the middle of class I've got plenty in my battle notes:

Jordan –took my masking tape...

Jordan's a curly haired, as opposed to nappy, medium complexioned kid, who likes to wear a "do rag" when he can get away with it. His unusually gravelly voice makes him seem like a tiny man, instead of a fifth grader; a man who just finished playing poker, smoking blunts, and drinking forties with his crew. His disruptions are relentless, and he's entirely immune to phone calls home.

He and Fantasia get their hands on my masking tape. They've taped their mouths shut, to look like kidnapping victims, and are making "mmmm…mmmm" sounds.

Jordan –out of classroom, kicking kids

Lorenzo –running out of the room

Jordan –shouting "ho's"

Kaitlyn – putting hand in my face

Madison – shouting hiding.

Earl –hiding.

Earl isn't nearly as crazed as Baxter and Jordan. He's thin, energetic, with a flat top, and glasses. His routine is to shout at me when he thinks I'm being unfair.

When I subbed at Fantasy Careers High, the kids often lied convincingly and emotively to cover for themselves and their friends. At Fantasy Careers it was popular among students to skip their classes and sneak into a room where there was a sub like me. The goal was to cause mayhem and avoid reality. They would lie about their names, and other students would leap to their defense. They wouldn't just lie, they would shout with indignation and outrage, "What is you stupid? He is *supposed* to be in this class!" When I came up with checking ID's, their lies crumbled. I was shocked at how *sincerely* pissed at me they sounded. But it was all a lie. Now I don't know what to believe is real.

Jordan -shouting.

Madison -loudly singing "Wa wa wa wa"

Madison's acting out is interesting and disturbing because she is fairly good at art. She's a pretty little blond girl with piercing blue eyes. What typically happens with her, is most of the kids are not anywhere near

148

done with their artwork, but she's already finished and done a good job. I think up enrichment activities for her, but the lure of acting out with those avoiding work in the first place has apparently proved too strong.

Madison –paper popping

Jordan –making bizarre loud yelling…

Mario –running around

Adam –faking injury

Here Adam is doing a fairly common trick, rolling on the floor acting like he just got injured. I give people the benefit of the doubt. "Are you OK?" Uproarious laughter erupts throughout the room.

Earl –climbing up on top of table.

Madison –jumping stomping.

In future years I will take less and less notes because looking down to write creates an opportunity for a child to do something worth writing down.

Kara, the picked-on kid, is getting pelted with various flying objects throughout all this. Especially popular is breaking the oil pastels in half and throwing them at her.

While shouting at kids to get back to their assigned seats, I'm greeted with "What about Kara! What about Kara! You're just letting her do what she wants because she's white!" The angry cries come from different kids at different parts of the room, especially Earl.

Under stress, and knowing I shouldn't be, I am still fooled by this fairness argument. "Kara back to your assigned seat." As I turn my head to chastise her, part of the room drops out of my view. Something else flies at her coming from my blind spot.

Now I realize why she looked so confused when I told her to go back to her seat. She's left her assigned spot trying to find somewhere safe, and moved to an empty table adjacent to my desk. She's alone there, with books propped up around her to provide a shelter. Instinctively she thinks being near me will protect her. I let Kara be.

The other kids don't let up on me. Earl is shouting about my unfairness. So I say, "Why are you talkin all ignorant like that?!" trying to sound sort of "street." Logically I know it's better *not* to try to win sixth graders over by attempting to sound "cool," but that tactic got me through subbing at Fantasy Career's High, so I use it now.

Earl looks at me shocked and seems genuinely angry, like the word "ignorant" really stung him. Not until a little later will I figure out why.

Mr. Tussle comes to reclaim them. As I clean up, I find a student's drawing crumpled on the floor. It shows talent and employs some of the shading I taught. It depicts a scene of domestic violence: a twenty something year old guy with a thick chain and big clock around his neck, grabbing and pulling a twenty something, thick-lipped lady by the front of her shirt.

There's a knock on the door. Dr Airington, the new vice principal, walks in. She acts and talks in that slow white Anglo Saxon Protestant way, although actually she isn't Protestant. She informs me, "Some of the students from Mr. Tussle's room came to me this afternoon." She stops to watch my reaction, then continues, "These children said that you were calling them the 'N' word."

"What? Who said that?" I'm genuinely shocked. Lies. But I'm still scared about what this could mean to me. I feel betrayed. I have some affection for a lot them, and can't believe they would stoop this low.

"It doesn't matter who said it right now, but I have to investigate," she says. "Investigate" is her exact word, very matter of fact. It's fitting with my image of her as moderately arrogant and emotionally neutral.

Yesterday, at the end of the day, I lamented to Airington about Vice Principal Mr. First's tragedy. She said something like, "If doctors were warning him about his heart, you think he would have taken some time off." I didn't know what to say. I switched topics. It was getting late. I'd already been at school an extra forty-five minutes after the official day ended. That "I need to get out of here" feeling came on strong. I asked her, "Are you going to the office?" Could you drop my keys off?" She exhaled a short laugh, and said, "I don't think that would be appropriate."

As part of the investigation I follow her to her office, and tell her what I believe. She listens but doesn't let on as to what she thinks. She does tell me that, "Locating the special subject area classes in the basement is part of your problem. You're isolated from the rest of the school."

This seems like a bit of sympathy, and puts me at ease a little. I don't bother to debate her point, but I know that the public schools' discipline troubles are not limited to special subject area classes in the basements. Although we "specials," I'll notice over the years, seem to get the brunt of it. Students often claim: "My mom says art doesn't matter." Even fellow male teachers, in years to come, will laugh and tell me "We used to 'cut up' in art all the time."

Leaving my room on my way to bus duty, I bump into Mr. Fin. "Matt the Tyrant," he says jokingly.

"Oh come on Fin. Just because I make them have assigned seats I'm a tyrant?"

"That's what the kids are saying." He shrugs and smiles.

"Yeah, I don't know. It's just that my supervisor always tells me to 'crack down and make loud startling noises, you know."

Fin loses his smile, lowers his voice and asks, "Did you really call Earl a nigger?"

I get that paranoid feeling, like everyone is conspiring against me.

"Earl said that? No way," I assure him.

"That little liar," he says, squinting into the distance at the memory of a little lying Earl.

I just don't feel real hatred coming from Earl that would cause him to make that up to get me fired. Maybe I'm being too naïve.

A day later, and at the start of my break, I catch Mr. Tussle alone in his sunny room upstairs. "The kids said I called them the N word? What do you think?"

"They're conducting a great experiment. Keep pushing and see what happens," he says with an ironic smile. I smile back. I wait for him to elaborate, but he goes back to his paper work. I suppose he means his students want to see if they can get me fired.

I leave his room. Time to get lunch.

Downstairs Lounge-Yelling at the Vice Principal.

I'm sitting in the basement lounge with Tina and Christine eating my peanut butter sandwich. "Are me and you the only two teachers who get no 'support' here?" I ask Tina. Before she can answer, Ryan crashes through the door. He's red faced and shaking his head. Christine says "Ryan! I can't believe you," with a cute but scolding tone. He's laughing, and looks simultaneously angry and amused.

"Ryan yelled at Dr. Airington," she says, maintaining that flirtatious smile. He shouted at her right in front of a full class.

"What did you say?" I ask with shock and joy.

"I told her, 'You don't do anything!' What does she do? Nothing," he continues, dragging out the "nuh" in nothing, vaguely resembling one of those fat screaming comedians that were popular a few years back. Vents or no vents, he doesn't care who can hear.

"She looks busy," I add in her defense.

"At least Mr. First yelled at kids. He could handle the job by himself. They had to bring that Dr. Iman because she can't!"

"Thank God for Iman," I say.

"He doesn't do anything either!"

"He talks to kids for me."

"Yeah. Talks. That's about it. They're quiet for two minutes, then they're back at it again," Ryan says dismissively.

"This is true. But I still can't believe you yelled at her. Why don't they fire you?"

"Who else are they going to get to come here and teach these kids Spanish?" There's a shortage of Spanish teachers. Ryan isn't even certified to teach. That's how badly Rust Belt Public needs them. Plus the Spanish teachers disappear a lot. Kids are nearly as hostile towards them as they are art and music. "How many Spanish teachers are they going to burn through this year?"

"You yelled at the vice principal. I'm impressed bro," I conclude.

Base and Blue

After Lela dumped me - or maybe more accurately: I pushed her away - I vowed to start going out more. It's Saturday night, and I am not going to worry about getting up for church tomorrow. I head over to Alex's downtown loft. That's the guy who had the party. Pulling in the parking lot I repeatedly honk the horn until I can see him waving from one of the large factory like windows that surround each floor. Once inside I see his housemate Norm sitting on the couch watching a movie. "You goin out with us Norm?" I ask.

"No, I think I'm gonna go to my friend's cabin." Norm never goes out with us. Alex gets me a beer out of the fridge. It's quality. Not the cheapskate kind I keep at home.

The two are kind of opposites, united by their love of carpentry. Norm's a short introverted guy, who dresses like a non-descript everyman. He looks down when he talks and smokes a lot of pot; which probably reinforces his introversion. Alex is tall, with naturally (I think) long black wavy hair and dresses in ragged bohemian sheik. He owns a large woodworking shop, which Norm helps out with sometimes. His shop gets a lot of contracts to design furniture, bars and anything large, expensive, and made out of wood. He and Norm were both architects but opted to design and actually build things, instead of just design them.

"You know Alex you're lucky you're a creative professional."

"I don't know. Being a teacher is a good and noble profession."

He's smiling. It's hard to tell if he's kidding or serious. He heads over to the turntable to play some of his vintage vinyl. "Joy Division," plays in the "dining room" while a movie plays in the "living room." In reality it's just one large room with a wooden floor, white walls and large curtain-less windows. If there were any neighbors, they could see right in. The walls separating the rooms are ones they must have made themselves.

Across from their loft is a vacant parking lot with a boarded up building. That building used to be a club we all went to in the early 90's. On the other side is a 1940's era granite faced tower-block office used by the power company.

Sitting back at the dinning room table I say: "Yeah well today…."(I tell him a teaching horror story). He's still rummaging through his vinyl albums. He laughs ambiguously, and launches in on a story from his teens, and comes back to the table.

I go to his makeshift liquor cabinet and pour us both shots of the "top shelf" brandy I brought to his last party. It's still here. Barely touched. Guess it isn't all that top shelf. "Thanks," Alex says, and continues telling me about his teenage misadventure. "So it's just me and the vice principal alone. His face is totally red, and he says to me 'Take a shot tough guy!' Come on what are you chicken?'" We howl with laughter, and down our shots.

"I hate to say it but I know how that vice principal felt. This whole running a school thing is like the Wizard of Oz. It's smoke and mirrors. If you acted badly and got away with it, you threatened to expose the little man behind the curtain. If enough kids stopped listening to that vice principal he'd lose his job. But honestly Alex, this job would be easier for someone like you, who was a 'bad kid.' You know how they think. You could relate, and get through to them more easily than I can," I say.

"No. I would kill them," he says. Then repeats, "I would kill them."

"Ha" I laugh, and get up to take a look at an antique looking globe. It's sitting by the windows facing the boarded up building. The water is black on the globe, unusual. The countries are out of date. There's the old "UCCP." As I reach for it I notice the window. Large chunks of glass are missing, with spider web fractures around the holes.

"You've got holes in these windows," I tell Alex with concern.

"Some of Norm's friends don't understand honking the horn and throw rocks instead," he tells me nonchalantly. One of Norm's friends used to be an out-of-control partier, and an intimidating character, back in our youth. Maybe that's the friend Alex is talking about?

"What if a pigeon or something flew in here?"

"They won't."

Norm packs a cooler filled with beers to take to the cabin. "Grab another beer and let's head out," Alex suggests.

We take separate cars and meet up at a bar called "Blue." Walking in, I nod to the bouncer. A nod with a flash of my balding head is usually enough proof of age. But this bouncer I know anyway -from my teens. Since I started going out again to bars and clubs I'm running into a lot of the same people I used to run into at bars and clubs a decade ago. I don't know why I stopped going out for a bunch of years. I guess I thought I was getting old. At age twenty-one I started telling everybody "I've got to get serious. I'm not young anymore." Ten years of saying that didn't help me "get a life." It succeeded in me working hard at go-no-where jobs and skipping opportunities for more adventurous careers. At twenty-three a friend invited me to join him in Korea to teach English. "I'm already twenty three man! I can't screw around with that. I've got to be thinking long term," I said, and stayed at my file clerk post, joylessly doing alpha numeric filing eight hours a day without benefits. So when thirty finally rolled around I had a realization: you've been saying, "You're getting old" throughout your twenties. Now you're thirty. So you better go back out there and make up for lost time."

Ethically I know it isn't right to compare myself with others. But we all do, don't we? We get mad over people who are ahead of us in life, and feel consoled seeing those behind us. Having met Alex's illustrator friend at his last party, and seeing Alex happy in his career, I've been feeling like a bit of a loser. Not as bad as I felt when I was paying the bills by substitute teaching, but not great. So seeing this old friend here making a living as a bouncer consoles and depresses me. "How've you been bro?" I ask him. "Good. Real good man," he says.

The lights hanging above the bar are blue and look like big translucent lava lamp drops. It's a cramped space, but filled with nicely dressed twenty-somethings, with tattoos, piercings and shaggy hair. A dreadlocked DJ is organizing his albums. I find Alex at the bar talking to the bartender. She's around his age.

"Don't I know you?" I ask her.

"Yeah I think so," she replies. It's another familiar face from a decade or so ago.

"What are you up to besides working here?" I ask.

"I'm a manager at an environmental non-profit." Great, I think. So much for feeling like I'm "ahead."

"That's fantastic, you're doing something real with your time."

"I think I want to work with children," she tells me.

"That's great," I say. I don't tell her that working with kids is a real pain in the ass.

154

Another even older female friend of Alex's joins us. She's pretty drunk and seems a little hostile. I never met this woman before tonight. Out of nowhere she says, "Nice hair," with ringing sarcasm. "What?" I say caught off guard. It's grown in since the last time I shaved it. The hair on top is more of a thin tuft than actual hair. She starts harassing me about going bald, "You'll probably be getting a 'monkey's ass' next." That's what they call the bald spot in the back.

"No I'm sure the receding hair will catch up to the back before that happens," I say. She steps away. "Who the hell is she Alex? Harassing me about being bald? I don't even know her. That's as low as if I was giving her a hard time about breast size or something."

"I know. I know," he says reassuringly, patting me on the shoulder, laughing and finding it funny. "Don't worry about it," he concludes, before he strikes up a conversation with two other girls standing nearby. By talking to them we shake his lady friend, the one who harassed me about my hairline. She walks up to us, sees we're busy, calls a cab, and leaves.

These girls are younger. The taller one keeps going on about how "young she is." The shorter one smiles and falls into me a lot as she's talking. It's flattering in it's own way, after just getting dissed about going bald. "How old are you?" Alex asks the taller girl.

"Twenty seven."

The dreadlocked DJ starts spinning and it's too loud to talk anymore. The girls leave us. We leave the bar. On the walk to the next bar Alex says "I've got a theory on women who go on about how young they are. Really they're saying how old they feel." A few bars later and it's closing time.

Back at home the loneliness hits me. I grab a newspaper out of the recycling bin. Scan the classifieds: 1-900-think of three letter and a four letter combination. I dial it. "Hi stud." A female voice says and offers ways I can pay. "It's so easy to slip it in," her pre-recorded voice drags out each word, "Your credit card that is." The sexy sounding voice giggles. By the time I connect to a human, she asks so many inane questions that the mood is broken. Finally I say "Look I'm paying for this here, could we please get down to it." She sounds offended. I offended a phone sex operator. How low can I sink? I hang up. What's the bill going to be I wonder? Better off with Star Trek. I turn on the television. There's nothing on but infomercials. Light is coming through the window. It's morning already.

155

16. Clown Shoes and the Scarlet Letter

Clown shoes and Kara.

It's only the beginning of the day and my feet are killing me. By the day's end I conclude that painful feet are compounding my discipline problems. Walking to the back aisle in the rear of a discount men's store, I look for my size shoe. The pair is black with round, nearly square toes and thick treaded soles. Perfect. Then an effeminate clerk advises me: "They may be good for walking around New York, but they're not appropriate for work." I buy them, hoping better quality and hipper foot support will give me the edge I need.

Tussle's group is back but without Kara. I hear she's been missing from school for a couple of weeks now. She's been picked on in every class. Not just mine. Maybe not having to defend her will give me a fresh chance.

I'm using the art books I've found in the room. If we used these when I was a kid I would have learned a lot, instead of just making cutesy things. A lot of art teachers, and even other teachers of other subjects, scoff at using the books. But I'm dedicated.

(Even more shocking was when I'd student taught social studies and I heard social studies teachers brag, "I'm not a text book teacher!" They were such "star teachers" that they just brought in all this "great" material of their own. I could give some examples of their "great material." Trust me, it's better they stick to the books.)

Plus using the books gives kids like Baxter a break from the visual side of this. Baxter, unlike Madison, is the kind of kid who has no skill at art. He acts out to create a diversion so no one has a chance to see what he's drawing. The problem is I'll soon find out Baxter isn't too good at books either.

"Books in art!" Baxter says in a "this class is going to stink" voice.

"No, it's a good thing. There are all kinds of art related careers, like architects, art dealers, critics, and designers, where you will need to read," I counter.

157

"Well then why aren't you doing one of these careers?!" a more articulate kid chimes in.

"I'm working on it," is what I wish I could say.

I've actually got Earl interested in seeing these books. He angrily shouts at the class: "Anybody who talks is gay!" The class is quiet. Does this include me? I begin to teach.

Helpers pass out the books. It seems to work, putting the kids back into the familiar world of answering questions. But maybe Baxter isn't too familiar with answering questions.

While other kids are trying, Baxter slams books. Baxter tosses books. Baxter narrowly misses hitting kids in the head. He's up from his seat and wandering, making fun of anyone doing their work. A moment's peace ruined.

I call him back to his seat. He returns but with holiday memories lingering, sings: "Jingle bells, batman smells, robin laid an egg!"

He flops on top of the table and lies there with his four foot body and pudgy arms spread out. "Baxter!" He gets off the table and heads to the cutting board and begins chopping. "Get away from there. You could get injured!"

He looks me dead in the eyes, with calm macho confidence says: "Shut up. You and your clown shoes."

"Clown shoes?" I think.

I look at the big black boxy shoes I'm wearing. It just turned 2001, so big black boxy shoes are just now coming to my backwater town. (In a year from now this city starts getting pretty hip). I want to say back to Baxter "Look at you man! This 'yo' baggy pants and sneakers, rap style crap is way out. It's played out. It's been played out since 1995. You're the clown here. These shoes are cool. You're just too out of it to know it." I know "he's just a kid" but I can't help but think of the kind of grown up he will make. He looks like he will be pretty big actually. Wisely I don't say any of this.

He caps it off with a threat "I'm going to prank phone call you." I do get some pranks this year.

I repeat, "Get away from that cutting board" and walk his way. He leaves the cutting board, seizes the chalk erasers and pounds them together to create dust. "I am writing this down," I warn as I walk towards him.

Instead of moving away he charges me like a wild boar. And grabs my clipboard trying to wrestle it from my hand. He's getting physical. I'm feeling cornered and want to respond in kind. I can't. Resist. I back away.

He advances. "He's not a large football in need of punting," I remind myself.

He leaves me and heads for my desk. Papers are flying off it, and he's in the drawers. I follow him again. His eyes have the look of an excited cat. Then he runs around the room messing up kids' papers.

Crap, I'm going to run out of time for clean up. Baxter's working the class into a frenzy. Another boy crumbles up the handouts and sticks them under his shirt, like he has breasts. With glee he rocks back and forth cupping them and grinning. He proudly announces, "My daddy is out of town." In other words "Go ahead and call my house!" Someone else's dad is in prison. Another doesn't have a dad.

"This is a madhouse," I mutter. Baxter makes another charge for me and my clipboard. "He's not a football," I remind myself again as he crashes into me.

Finally Tussle comes. Little is cleaned up. But at least it's over for today.

When I go to the main office I find a handwritten note in my mailbox. In very neat penmanship it reads: "This is Baxter's mom. Please contact me and let me know what is going on with my son." She leaves a different number than the one I've left messages on. Maybe that's why I hadn't seen any change in Baxter's behavior. On the one hand I'm nervous about this parental contact. Is she going to blame me and complain to the principal? On the other hand I need something to break this escalating showdown.

Benign Intervention.

When I started getting in scraps in eighth grade I never hurt anybody. I'd shove kids up against the locker until they said "OK. OK." The only time it came to a real fight I lost. The whole punching and breaking skin or bones just wasn't something I could do. So even if I ever snapped I never would have hurt anybody.

I am almost going to snap right now. Mr. Tussle's class is in here again. Baxter, that fat little shit, has been fucking with me for months now. There's another kid in here, a tall speech impediment trouble-making pain in the ass. The messing with me he does always has a bit of a pathetic air to it. He is never going to be cool or a tough guy in the eyes of his peers. I just can't see it happening any time soon, anyway. "Speech impediment kid" and

Baxter start to throw insults at each other. Baxter, while a basic asshole, is the type of asshole I remember when I was a kid. The type we admired.

When they blow off my "Back to your seats" and "To timeout!" they awaken to their freedom. They don't really have to listen to me. They realize that there is nothing stopping the fight from going down right here, right now. They seize the moment. Baxter chases speech-kid to a spot near my desk and is punching away on him, while speech-kid writhes on the floor flailing his arms like an overturned beetle.

I run over and intervene. Something in me forgets all the trouble speech-kid has been giving me. He's a victim, the underdog, the meek. He needs my help. Some type of superhero mode kicks in, in me.

It looks like a scene from the reality TV show, "Cops." As I bound over to protect him, speech impediment kid withers away from his losing fight. While enjoying his new found safety, he jeers at Baxter from the sidelines, as teacher-policeman rescues him. By now Baxter must realize he's no match for a grown man, yet he keeps up his defiant facade, but the bravado is quickly draining from his voice. For once I can feel the fear in his voice while he's saying things like "Fuck you man. Back the fuck up off me. I'll jaw you."

For the first time his defiance rings hollow and I can tell he doesn't know what will happen next. Once I had to prevent a fight at a group home for adults with a variety of conditions like cerebral palsy and mental retardation. I was trained there in how to restrain someone without hurting them, so I know how to, and that's what I'm doing right now: restraining Baxter.

But that didn't stop my booming voice from betraying hostility while I prevented further violence in the class: "Ok tough guy. How tough are you are you now huh! How tough are you now?!" I am bellowing at him. His rebellious words are betrayed by what sounds like a voice about to cry. He must have imagined his classmates would rise up to his aid, by providing more distracting mayhem. Instead the other kids just watch Baxter's defeat. Time is standing still. The kids are silent, watching. Before I can get another "How tough are you now!?" out, an even deeper hush comes over the class. The quiet brings my attention back to the classroom.

I turn my head from the "arrest scene," to see Mr. Tussle standing in the doorway watching me. I snap back to "reality" and look again at him. He can see me restraining Baxter. Did he hear me? His arms are folded and he looks disapproving. I'm not sure of who: me or Baxter? Then I see a small smile on his face being held back by a forced scowl. He shakes his head, and it looks like he might laugh. The smile telepathically says to me: "Now you know how this job really is kid. Welcome to hell!"

When we talk later he makes no reference to the incident. I think his intent is to reassure me. "Don't think you aren't getting through to some of them. A number of kids are real excited about what you've taught them. I see them draw and then shade it in with pride, just like they learned from you."

Tussle intends his words to boost my morale. They're not. Not now anyway. At this moment I'm too cynical. In my cynicism I view his observation as evidence that I am just giving away all the "secrets" of how to draw, to the uninitiated and ungrateful. No art teacher ever taught me the "tricks of the trade." I had to learn them on my own. I had to pay my dues.

"Thanks. That's good to hear. Glad to know I am reaching somebody. It's just that sometimes I think they all hate me."

Cutting Board

Ms. K leaves the ladies faculty lounge. Pookie leans towards me. Her eyes look unusually large, peering through those thick glass lenses at me.

"You know she likes you," Pookie announces. The others say nothing.

"Who?"

"Mrs. K"

"She's married." I launch into a short speech on the sanctity of marriage, while also explaining I'm not a prude. I've never been with a married woman before. I never would, I think at the time.

After bus duty I return to my room. It's dark like I left it. The only difference is Ms. K is in the back of the room using my cutting board. She turns her head to greet me, but continues cutting. Her dress clings to her hips. Is it my imagination or is she intentionally swaying those hips, as she lifts and lowers that big cutting-board handle? It seemed like she was being flirtatious earlier today in the lounge, before the other women came in. Why didn't she turn the lights on? "Oh, I hope you don't mind?" she says smiling. She's married. I get nervous. "That's fine. I've got to go and do something." I hide in the downstairs lounge. Wait a minute, there's a cutting board right here she could have used.

It's Friday. My mind is on women. So maybe it's just my imagination.

Scarlet Letter

Alex and I head to this packed club. It's done up in a tropical motif and is pretty cheesy really. I see an old friend from undergrad college, with another woman I can't place.

The old friend is a new teacher too. "I love it!" she says enthusiastically. I have a hard time believing the enthusiasm. (A year later her husband will tell me she quit. "I thought she loved it?" I'll ask. "She loved it so much she's not going back," he'll say sarcastically.)

"What are you doing here?" I ask her happily as Alex wanders the bar. She smiles nervously. "Where's Chris?" I ask.

She admits: "We're going to get divorced."

"You're what?"

"He was cheating on me."

"I'm sorry." I go to hug her but decide I'd better not.

"What about the kids?"

"I know; it's terrible."

"I had to grow up with divorced parents and then a step dad. I didn't like it at all. If you two can make it work, I think you should. After my parents divorced they both just married partners even less compatible. My mom did an immediate rebound and my dad just dated here and there for

162

sixteen years until he met his second wife." I get jostled as people file past me to get to the bar, or stumble into me from the dance floor.

"I know. That's what I'm telling him," she says. Now I'm confused. So she doesn't want to get divorced? The music here is a typical Rustbelt hodgepodge of popular songs, from oldies to rap. I find it hard to get into a groove.

"So you're just looking to even the score?" She nods her head in time to the music. Better she evens the score with someone safe, I think, considering myself a candidate. Then I think, no don't even get in the middle of this one. (They never do get divorced).

Alex and I leave and go back into the crowded street. It's filled with drunken young revelers. I stop to talk to some party girls and they invite me to follow. Alex pulls me away, "We can't go there! Not that bar. They tore down a historic façade to put up that huge stupid looking new entrance."

"Come on man, those girls are cute."

"No way, we are not going there." Then he goes on about names of architects and local business people I know nothing about. Now I've lost sight of those girls.

Instead we walk over to The Regal. It's the same goth-punk bar I met Brandy at last summer.

My eyes scan the dance floor. Maybe I can make up with her. Goth girls and boys move their bodies in time to the slow rhythms of a depressing sounding dance tune. The dance is like a cross between tai chi and acting like a ghost. The "spooky dance" I called it when Brandy and I were dating. I see other voluptuous chicks, with push-up black corsets tied tight at the waist and showing ample cleavage, but no Brandy. No familiar faces. It hasn't been that long since Lela, and I'm still feeling lonely and isolated. My human contact seems bleak at the moment. All I get is harassed by kids all week, then the weekend nights are spent losing my hearing trying to meet women, accompanied by a fair weather party friend. I don't really even know Alex, this guy I'm out hitting the town with. Alex comes up to me laughing, drawing my attention away from these Goth chicks with their long dyed hair and sensuous dance moves.

"How come he gets to have a big beer and we just get these little ones?"

"Huh?"

"Look at him," he says.

I look. He's pointing to a guy in his late thirties or forties leaning against the DJ booth holding a large can of Fosters. We're all a little too old for this place.

"What are you talking about, man?" I say, getting self-conscious, since the guy can probably see us looking and pointing, and Alex laughing at him. The guy has a classic eighties mullet and is standing by himself.

"Maybe we should buy him some Rush tickets! I love that mullet," Alex says. He doesn't care if the guy sees us pointing and laughing or not. I walk away before a fight breaks out.

It's two AM. Helena, the woman I saw earlier who said she is getting divorced spots me. She's with her friend. She introduces us. The friend just got divorced and tells me "Hey, you were at my New Year's party a couple of years back. I remember you." At first I feel good, but then she tells me, "I thought you were the biggest asshole…" she says laughing. She doesn't mean any harm and is actually acting flirtatious.

She's around my height with short brown hair and glasses, not bad looking, with a shapely, Rubenesque figure. I probably could have had some fun, but instead I decide it's time to even the score for rejections I've had. So I act outraged over her "having thought I was the biggest asshole." Helena tries to mend it, but I'm getting carried away. "Forget it. I don't talk to people like that," and I walk away from them in feigned disgust. Not only did I prove her right about me, but I just shot myself in the foot as well. My prospects are getting dismal.

It's three-thirty AM and Alex's gone. I left Helena's friend bristling. Now those two are nowhere to be seen. I should have left too. I have no business being here, just a few drunks left stumbling around, and I don't know any of them. I'm ready to call it a night, when I spot another familiar face. She's dressed in black, but looks like a weekender Goth. Her hair is eighties secretary blond and feathered. She's the type who some of my "friends" in the old days would have tossed an occasional ice cube at while she danced, and called her a "poser." "Didn't I go to high school with you?" I ask her. "Oh it's you!" She responds, happily, and gives me a big hug. We dance together and "accidentally" bump into each other a few times. She's married, and here alone. Bumping into her isn't an accident I should be letting happen. She smiles warmly and acceptingly.

It's nearly four AM. "I've got to go home," she says.

"You're going to walk by yourself to your car?"

"Yeah. I'll be OK."

"Oh I can walk you," I volunteer. I'm doing something noble. It's so nice just to be accepted as a good guy. No questions asked, nothing to prove. I haven't had the real thing in a while. No I'm just being a good guy here.

"That would be great," she says.

She's married don't do anything, I tell myself. It's already past four in the morning. Instead of just dropping her off and leaving, I get into the passenger seat. She drives a hatchback. Here I am on a desolate street, with just her and me in this car, in the dark. It's getting harder to see out the windows. Afterwards she reaches in back and takes a towel out of a box. Was she planning this? That towel was awful handy. Now it's going on five, and the morning light is shining through her car window. I didn't have any business staying here this late.

17. N Word Resolved and the Artist's Party

Meet Baxter's Mom: The N word accusation resurfaces.

Monday I'm back in my classroom. The phone rings. "Baxter's mom is here to meet you." The call surprises me. I'm anxious, but I've given this meeting a lot of thought. I've gone over what I'll say, and what my possible defenses will be.

A sub covers my class. We meet in a vacant room on the second floor. Like her son, she is stout and strong looking. We shake hands. "Nice to meet you," I say warmly through my fear. It's too soon to tell which way she will go. Her face seems very serious, possibly accusatory.

She seems responsible and trustworthy though. I think she's a home care aide. The apple seems like it fell *far* from the tree. Hoping for the best I tell her a litany of things: "Whenever I try to instruct, Baxter engages in antics like falling out of his chair."

"He what?"

"Yeah, he's been doing that one for a while. He keeps falling out of his chair." I go on "he was making fun of my shoes calling them 'clown shoes.'"

An angry look crosses her face. She says, "Is there some way I could come into that class?" I get nervous. This is my first year and I am not confident about anything, about my lessons, any of it. "Is there anywhere I could hide, so when he is popping off like that I could catch him." Relief. She's on my side. My muscles loosen up. The tension drains for a minute. I feel like a normal person for a moment.

"Just one thing" she says. Oh no. Her face becomes inquisitorial again. "I feel pretty uncomfortable brining this up but I need to get this out of the way." She pauses.

"Go ahead and ask, if it helps us work together."

"Some of the kids say you call them 'the N word.'" This is unexpected. That was a while ago and it wasn't true. I figured it died.

I am more impressed by how she's handling this, than I am shocked at the question. Here she thinks a teacher might actually call kids that, but she's still going to discipline her son. And is taking it up with me directly instead of going to that paranoid principal of ours.

For better or worse I know that memory is imperfect and anything is possible, and I really don't like lying, so I answer her according to my philosophy. "Well, really I doubt that. First off I can't say I never put a kid down. But I am a believer in what Martin Luther King said 'don't hate the evil doer, just the evil they do.' So even if I'm real stressed and being extremely tested, I always aim to frame it like: you are acting like a 'fill in the blank,' at worst. But not you are a 'fill in the blank.' Secondly I wasn't raised with that N word. In undergrad I hung out with some black guys who used it in the hip hop friendly sense of it spelled with an 'a;' but my Mom, Dad and Grandma never said that, and I didn't either. I heard my Mom's husband use it on occasion, but I never really cared for him too much. My point is that even under a moment of extreme stress when it's plausible I could slip into some less mature behavior, it's extremely unlikely that I would revert to that word, since I never used it growing up."

She looks satisfied: "Thanks I just had to clear that up."

I add more, and thus incriminate her son again. "Actually I was pretty sympathetic to the African American kids who got picked on where I went to middle and high school, and was always nice to them. I think I was operating on that 'blessed are the meek' philosophy Jesus is quoted as saying. So I tend to stick up for people that are outnumbered or getting picked on. And in that class there is this one white girl they all pick on. Baxter takes a big part in it. For instance, one time they all started throwing crayons at her. When I stick up for her some of them say "You're just taking her side because she's white!' It's possible that's where they got this idea that I am prejudice from."

She looks angry again "He's been harassing some girl?"

"Yeah, actually she hasn't been to school for long time, I don't know if she dropped out or what."

N Word Resolved, and the Persecuted Return.

After Baxter's mom and I met face-to-face things change, a little. Baxter behaves for a while and Kara, the kid everyone picked on, comes back. She enters with the other students, as if she were never gone. But something about her seems different. She holds her head high, exuding both confidence and a weird nervous energy, like she's a little bit psycho. She starts calling me "Mr. Wiggles." Hello "Mr. Wiggles," her blue eyes flashing maniacally at me, and getting some laughs from her classmates. I don't know what "Mr. Wiggles" means. The new Kara decides that to survive she needs to attack the teacher, so as not to get attacked by her peers.

She flippantly gives me that "talk to the hand" gesture when I ask her to return to her seat, putting her hand only inches from my face as she casually struts around the room. Finally returning to her seat she informs me, "This class is stupid." Me, her failed protector, now becomes an object of her ridicule. Kara still gets picked on, but she seems to feel better about herself now, and isn't singled out so severely for persecution like before. Even though her survival is partially at my expense, it's good to see that Kara didn't become like those kids I remember when I was a student. The kids who got picked on so mercilessly that they never returned.

I'm sitting on the counter near the front door. It's a position that elevates my height, offers a good vantage point from which to watch everything. Sitting there quiets the class down a little, and cuts down on the number of runaways from my room.

Earl, the one who accused me of using the N word, is acting out again. Again I say, like I did a few classes prior when he first accused me, in that feigned street accent: "Man why are you actin all ignorant?" Earl gets a hurt, angry, unjustly defeated look. He whines: "See he just said *it* again, he just called me a nigger again." The whine implies that I happily sit around this basement, safe from watching eyes, getting away with calling kids that horrible word.

It's the sort of look you'd expect from a child in a Grimm's fairy tale. One who reluctantly goes on a picnic with what everyone but him is convinced is the good fairy godmother, but he knows is the wicked witch in disguise. When all the kids are deep in the forest, far away from where any hero could rescue them, the fairy godmother turns into the wicked witch. That one child might have been right all along, but now it's too late. The wicked witch laughs and prepares herself a child stew. This is exactly the look Earl has on his face, a look that says: "See I told you all he was calling us niggers, but no one believed me!"

Later on in my career when I get a cell phone and call kids' homes immediately when they act out, I will get a similar, "He's lying but he sounds convincing to grown ups" look from students; as they sit mouth open with contained but impotent rage, while I chattily explain what their kid was just doing.

"Look at that! Did you hear him!?" Earl says with an urging plea to Madison, his tablemate, and anyone else in earshot. He's sitting totally erect and looking around the room for support.

"I didn't say *that,* Earl. I said i-g-n-o-r-a-n-t," I reply.

"Yeah, he said ignorant!" others shout back at Earl in my defense.

Earl looks momentarily confused, like a lawyer in a courtroom who prepared the wrong case.

Assembly

On Friday I get out of teaching a couple of classes. Most of the school is in the assembly room for an African American pride celebration. Copies of something called the Black National Anthem are distributed. Black National Anthem? I never heard of this. Everyone, whites and blacks are singing along. They are all acting like this is a normal everyday thing. I know the kind of neighborhood most of the white kids here come from: all white, low income, and tough. What would their parents think? It all seems odd and I think if this song and this rally were known about in right wing radio circles they would have a field day. I understand the rationale: oppressed group needs to form an identity. But if you don't run it through that filter, it seems like it's inviting a backlash.

Then I see that big bully Huey from Ms. Rosebloom's, carrying the American flag down the aisle. He looks like some kind of young soldier. What message, does rewarding him like this with a position of near authority, send kids? For that matter, what message does it send to the teachers?

I know that whoever orchestrated this probably thinks, "We need to engage him and involve him in the school, because he is high needs." Or had some other well-intentioned idea. But to me they are rewarding bullying behavior. Typical. Make the loud violent one the flag bearer, a soldier. The squeaky wheel gets greased. The quiet one is left to rust.

Dr. Iman gets on the stage. He's talking about the Egyptian pyramids. "If you could design and build the pyramids, you have the ability to do well at math. Don't think you can't do it." His use of the word "you" is curious. "You" built the pyramids, and "you" can do your math.

Mr. Tussle is standing next to me surveying the kids. That's what we do during these assemblies: stand to the side, watching like cops. Do I look racist doing this? Do I seem "anti-child"? Should I be smiling? The other teachers are all poised like cops. Guess I should be to. "Look at Huey up there holding the flag," I carp.

Mr. Tussle can see I'm frustrated, "Hey man, it's pay day and a three day weekend."

"Good point," I conclude.

New Home Ec. Teacher

Before I go to pick up my check I make a stop by the Home and Career's room. Normally I would have shared my thoughts about this assembly with her. When I walk into her room, there is another lady in it. The old teacher's gone? Yep. Retired. She went without fanfare. She gave the kids no warning. No last chance to say goodbye. No last chance to act out either.

The new teacher also has sandy blond hair, but it's longer, and she is a good ten years younger. She's wearing her white apron and working at the sink. Will she fill the same niche in my life: counselor and listener? We introduce ourselves.

"How did you end up here?" I ask.

"I told my supervisor I had to get out of my other school: 'High Tech Hell Middle.'"

She told me everything was brand new there. A gleaming new building. Beautiful sunny well lit rooms. Lots of new shining computers. Every two rooms had a shared bathroom. That last improvement turned out to be a mistake.

Despite this new state of the art facility, the middle school kids were out of control. (The most commonly repeated horror story from that school was that a girl was caught giving a boy a blowjob in one of those shared bathrooms. Word had it, that the kids didn't even get suspended. If that's true, the principal might have hoped to keep the incident quiet.) She blamed the mess entirely on the principal.

"So it gets worse than here?"

"Oh yeah."

The conversation quickly goes flat and dies. The lady doesn't take the same motherly interest in me, and my thoughts, like the old one did. After today we never really talk much again. She holes up in her room, like a lobster in a lobster trap. She snaps at hostile students and avoids faculty – at least me anyway.

After wasting my time talking to this disappointment, I pick up my check from the office. After work I whip down the freeway to my suburban bank.

"Do you know about automatic deposit?" the teller asks.

"Yeah, but I like the feeling of having a real check."

"Keeps you coming into work huh?"

At home I make a few phone calls. I definitely need to get out tonight.

Artist's Party

The coffee house is dead on Friday at happy hour time. I'm getting my grading done. I decide to put a plus on the back of the drawings to show the kids they received credit. (This will result in kids shouting, "Why is their an x on the back of my art!" Later I switch to drawing a star). The one's that are A's I put an A on. A couple years later I will get pretty precise and fair in the criteria I use to grade art, fairer and more methodical than most art teachers I meet. But right now I'm figuring it out as I go.

"Great art. Did you make it?" a longhaired barista says as he buses the half-eaten muffin and half drunk latte from the table adjacent to mine. He laughs and adds, "Just kidding." He intends the joke to make me feel good, show me he's on my side in dealing with these students, I know this because he's made the joke before. But really I feel partly at fault for the results. I page through frenetic scribbled artwork, after frenetic scribbled artwork, in the now almost solitary cafe. A lone street-crazy mutters to herself from across the room. These rushed scribbles, with occasional expletives written on them, are the sad results of a revved up class, and hours preparing their lesson. They chewed through it like wolves thrown raw meat. Leaving me with torn and shredded paper and rushed sketches that took only one minute to make. Then they used their remaining forty-four minutes growling that they finished the lesson and were hungry for fresh kill. Not happy with what I threw them for "extra credit work," in the way of "flick through a magazine for an idea," they descended into mayhem.

    If I could maintain better order, this wouldn't be happening. The ones who already had some talent could sit unmolested by their fellow students and get something done. Next I could begin to show the other's some "tricks of the trade." A lot of people say that, "either you have talent for art or you don't." I never believed it was this simple, and I think if I did I wouldn't have accepted the job. Even as a young child I was pretty good at drawing. Kelly was sitting next to me back in third grade art. The teacher was unable to show her how to draw a duck in a pond. Kelly was watching the third grade me draw it. "Can you show me how?" she asked. "OK," I said. I taught her how I sketched things out, and I saw her getting the hang of it. Her duck looked pretty good to both of us. I knew then it could be done, drawing could be taught. People can be taught the things others say, "either you're born with or you aren't."

    I put the art my students made, that while it may not literally say "FU teacher!" may as well, back into its folders and close my grade book. I open the latest copy of Rust Belt Voice, a free paper that lists the goings on about town. "New York City artist to show…" the listing reads. "Bla bla bla" I say to myself. How many of these art openings am I going to go to, wandering around like a loser, with a glass of wine in my hand.

    Instead I go home and settle in on the couch to watch an episode of the "Simpsons." The principal of Bart's school is boasting about the money the school spent on a "state of the art detention facility." Later, a group of children protest in front of the school. Chief Wiggums calls for backup: bring out the timeout gas, boys. Gas is launched into the crowd. The kids disperse. I laugh, but it's me they're making fun of. Just earlier today I was telling somebody "When I was in school I threw one French fry and I got a detention. Here a kid says whatever he wants and walks out of your room and all he gets is a talking to. What we need is some of this discipline taken off our backs. What we need are definite consequences for defined actions. We need good in-school detention rooms with cubicles and people manning them that make sure it isn't fun time for them in there." The show is funny and I laugh at it, and at myself. I better get out of the house, I decide. I dial Alex. He usually has something going on.

"Alex what are you up to?"

"We're having a party for that New York Artist. Come on down." Should have gone to the opening I guess. After honking my horn in the parking lot, Alex's latest girlfriend Rebecca lets me in. She's a tall, thin, very pretty wannabe photographer, with dark brown hair gelled back into a ponytail. She disappears back into the crowd leaving me on my own. Most of the faces are unfamiliar, so I head over to the wall length bar Alex must have built himself, filled with gourmet looking dips and snacks. Not wanting to look like a guy just stuffing his face, I head over to another table centered between the living and dining room. The table holds an assortment of wines. He really must have spent a lot on this thing. Crap, if I don't talk to somebody soon, I'll go from being the guy just standing around stuffing his face to the guy standing around stuffing his face and guzzling free drinks.

Alex walks over to the wine bar with the artist and introduces me. The artist is shorter than me, around my age, and tells me he lives in a renovated loft in a trendy part of Brooklyn. He makes a living entirely from his art, drawing, painting and sculpture. He admits to having some advantages, like being born into an "arts family."

"So what do you do?" he asks me.

"I'm teaching art."

"College?" I'm flattered he assumes college, but then am somewhat embarrassed I'm not.

"No. Middle school in the city."

"You like it?"

"Hard to say. Maybe I will after doing it for a few years and getting a better handle on the discipline, but right now I'm dealing with a lot of defiance." I expect him to say "Hang in there it will get better."

Instead he says: "A friend of mine taught art in Brooklyn. He lasted one month - the kids were so bad. He quit. He couldn't take it. I know a lot of people like that." I feel somewhat consoled. I've lasted longer than one month.

"Then what did he do?"

"He took some digital video editing classes and that was it. He got a job making enough money that he could support his wife and their baby. He was miserable teaching those kids." The whole dot com thing is still in full gear, and it seems anybody with some computer skills can find work. I take out a pen and frantically jot down the software programs he mentions. If teaching doesn't turn around, maybe I can develop another escape plan:

digital artist. I feel some hope again. I need something to hang onto. I'm going to this job now but really I'm fooling them all. I'm not this loser teacher they can kick around, I'm a creative talent just biding his time. I imagine being paged at school, "Mr. Lebrun, you're needed in the office," but this time it's not because I'm in trouble. "You have a call from New York. They need to fly you out immediately to…"

A part of me believes this is a joke. I won't have time or focus. Since I'm not quitting my job, I'm spending all my free time trying to create carrots and sticks to win these kids over. I try to make better lessons, on the carrot end, and call kid's parents on the stick end. When that's done I crack open a beer and cook dinner. When that's done I put in a video and unwind. Then I go to bed early so I'm well rested to deal with tomorrow's mutinies. Wake up, go back to work, and suppress the new days' rebellions as best I can. And repeat the process, so I can survive to fight another day. When I'm not doing that I'm quelling my anxiety by letting off steam at the gym or the bars. If it weren't for exercise and alcohol I think I'd have a heart attack. I'm in the middle of our American rat race, and I don't even have kids of my own to worry about.

Even if I am kidding myself, I need something to keep my head up. I reread the names of the software he told me about, and walk over to an empty seat at the dining table.

It's a big heavy wooden table, with two candles burning on it, more dip, and half drunk glasses of liquor and wine. I bum a smoke from Alex's girlfriend, I guess chain smoking is one of the ways she stays so thin. Bumming a smoke is a way, a deadly way, for me to make conversation. Smoking seems safe now, because I see these young healthy looking people doing it. But wouldn't someone think something similar who was sharing needles with their friends? She introduces me to a middle-aged lady, with jewelry and tastefully dyed hair. Her style seems out of place among ski cap wearing hipsters. "I don't mean to sound 'New York' or anything, but I'm just curious, what do you do?" I ask her.

"I'm a high school English teacher." She says. At first she tells me how much she "loves the job, and helping the kids." Then I tell her some of my horror stories. Her mood changes. She gets a vulnerable look. She admits to having students like I do: chaotic ones.

"I'm that teacher who was in the newspaper," she says in a lower voice than before.

"For what?" I ask, half expecting she got some excellence in education award. "I'm the teacher who had a kid put poison in her coffee when she wasn't looking." She looks scared recalling the incident.

174

"That rat. What kind of poison?" I ask. (It was something you could buy anywhere. I can't remember anymore if they caught the kid or not, or what exactly the poison was.) I offer consolation, "Poisoning your teacher. How sweet. I found paint in my coffee once, if that makes you feel any better," I tell her. After that, I stopped keeping my cup out in the open. Leaving my cup out was a way to say, "I trust you guys." It was a bit of a blow to that trust finding a glob of blue tempera paint floating in my mug.

She laughs a little. We talk about discipline, and I tell her how I call parents all the time.

She tells me, "My son's art teacher called me once, because my son was standing on the table shouting and waving his arms. A lot of kids don't take art too seriously. But you're lucky you're not under pressure to have kids pass exams like I am. I spend all my free time doing grades and trying to prevent them from failing." She's a single mom and has problems with her own child, as well as her kids at school, kids coming from homes in a lot worse shape than hers. It must be rough being really tied to this job, I think to myself.

18. A More Serious Accusation

Should Have Known

By Spring I should have known. How many times this year, have kids shouted, "Don't touch me! Don't touch me!" when I'm not even within a two foot radius of them. A few of them, like Levi, like to expand it to: "Don't touch me. I don't know where your hands have been."

The warnings signs were posted after the first month of school. The ingredients were already there. I was walking towards this malcontent eighth grade girl. I was nowhere near her, yet she was shouting louder and louder, "Don't touch me! Don't touch me!" Some old lady came poking her nose in my room. The woman is some sort of volunteer from the community. Over the years I will see a lot of these elderly volunteers at schools. Later that day that same old lady came up to me again. "I know how mad they can make you, and you just want to shake 'em up. But they know their rights," she advised. Part of me was mad at this old lady because I didn't touch the kid. Who is this volunteer anyway? Who asked her to be here? I didn't. These kids don't need volunteers to give them extra attention. They need volunteers to discipline them, I thought in one of my more cynical moments. Another part of me was grateful for the warning. I didn't heed it well enough, until today. By now it's too late.

Mr. Beanbag – first accusation

The trouble starts with Mr. Beanbag's class. Today, I'm especially on edge. Part of my problem is I'm a little sleep deprived. Sure, I always try to go to bed early. It's one of the ways I've lasted this far. When you're half asleep anything can happen with these kids. This time of year, the birds have begun their return to Rust Belt. Normally their singing is a joyous sound, but not under your window at five AM.

Mr. Beanbag is the aide I talked to at lunch duty. The one who told me about Jimmy peeing in another seventh grader's shoe. As Beanbag walks his class of rowdy fifth graders into my room, he tries to be the kids' buddy.

176

He tries too hard. Sometimes he stays with me while I'm "teaching." (Actually it's been more like me yelling at this class than teaching; his group is one of my worst). His presence only makes matters worse for me. Why is he here anyway? To help? No other aides ever come to help me. I wouldn't call what he does help, unless you can call making small talk with students, especially this pretty little red head girl, while I'm trying to instruct, "help." It would be easier to "lay down the law" like my supervisor wants me to, without this friendly clown in my room. Between Mr. Beanbag and this extremely disrespectful and disorderly bunch of kids, this whole group is really getting on my nerves.

Even sweet Amber is having a bad day. Amber is the student who gave me the Zorro picture at the beginning of year. This kid Malik is bothering her. I can't figure out what he's doing, but Amber looks pissed. Malik is a boy, but he must be lacking male role models. He acts and talks just like an angry inner city woman, complete with rocking his head side to side for added emphasis. As I approach their table, Malik calls Amber a "white bitch." Ironically Amber is half black and no lighter complexioned than Malik, who looks half white himself. I separate the two of them, but the class still rapidly disintegrates. As I scan the room, it appears that a maximum of three kids are working.

It's nearly time to go. I've got to get these kids cleaned up before my next class arrives. No one responds to my calls to clean up. No one. The class is getting more and more out of control. The room is a mess. "Clean up!" They all ignore me. My supervisor's orders to crack down and lay down the law play in my head. What if he were to walk in here right now? Out of sheer frustration I single out a normally well-behaved kid, Brittany, a tiny girl with sandy brown hair. After all, I don't want to only pick on the "bad" ones. "Clean up!" I command the room again, but this time I'm looking at Brittany. She's laughing and joking with the rest of them. I place my hand firmly on her shoulder to get her attention. "Stop it!" I say with venom. Her little blond head reels around to face me. She looks startled. Uh oh, I've never seen that look before. Was my hand too firm, my tone too angry?

Later Ms. Henderson and Dr. Iman come knocking at my door. They look like the police looking for an escaped convict. "Come with us." In the office she says, "Mr. Lebrun what is going on? Did you touch that child?" Dr. Iman is pacing around behind me. I look down at my dirty black Timberland boots, and start to feel oafish again. I was going for a "ska" look, but maybe I just look like a thug?

"Which one?" I unwisely respond.

"There was more than one?!" she says, "I was talking about Brittany."

I explain. She looks skeptical. Thinking on my feet I say: "It's a cultural difference." She looks quizzical. "My dad's half Italian. Both my parents were semi hippies. I was raised with a lot of physical contact. Friendly pats are no big deal to me. I'm not used to how it is here. People are real sensitive. One time at an Italian grocery Dad and the clerk laughed. He grabbed her by her chin and gently shook it. They barely knew each other. You couldn't do that at Shop Right Supermarket."

She chuckled and agreed, "No, you sure couldn't."

My "cultural difference" idea really caught her off guard. Who ever thinks of white guys as being "multicultural?"

"I can't believe it was little Brittney, and not some…" She trails off and doesn't finish the sentence. "Good thing this accusation wasn't from someone from *the community,* or there would be an uproar about you," she concludes, giving community the same emphasis she uses when she says "the children." By community she means the black neighborhood. My accuser was white.

When I leave the office I try to keep my hands in my pockets, as if to say, "Look everybody! I'm not touching anyone! No pats on the back here." I don't want to go through that again.

I've got to see what Slaughterbutcher thinks about this. "You put a guiding hand on the student's shoulder to redirect the child," he coaches me.

Get Back in Here!

Before I learned the, "Don't even give them a pat on the back rule," came Andy. Andy's mom is a teacher's aide at Grand Plans. She's a hardened white lady, like the moms from Iron Island. Her daughter goes here too. She is the girl who twirled her finger at me that one time I was muttering to myself about being a cop - the day when even Ed joined in the attacks against me.

The alleged incident with Andy occurred last week, yet I won't get accused of it until later today. Andy is one of Tina's students. He's normally a well-behaved boy who likes art, so when he insisted on leaving the room because he "can't stand all the noise in here!" I took it a little harder than if it were a usually deviant-acting kid. It was another one of those "even the meek are turning against me" moments.

"Get back in this room!" I bellowed in my loudest drill sergeant voice. I saw Young Mr. Nosey and Ms. Guidance Counselor in the hallway.

Earlier that day, when I passed Ms. Guidance's room I noticed the poster she had on her door. It was a realistic painting of a young African American boy holding the world in his hands. He had a look of joyous wonder, and was surrounded by radiant light. It was so positive. Sure it's easy for her to be positive. She just meets kids one on one. There are rarely discipline issues when kids are alone, isolated from their peers. Most people are congenial one on one. Yet, as easy as she has it, Ms. Guidance walks around this school with a smug look on her face. She's one of those "I'm so wonderful with the children" types.

She and Nosey stopped to look at me yelling at Andy. I got a bad feeling about it. Young Nosey came into my room to "see if everything was OK?" I pretended in front of the students he was "here to back me up," but really I knew he wasn't.

"Yeah, thanks Mr. Nosey, I think Andy is behaving now. Aren't you Andy?"

It's only a few classes after I finished explaining to Ms. Henderson about my "cultural differences," when I'm called into the office again. Andy's mom, the teacher's aide, is sitting in the chair opposite mine. She and Ms. Henderson are starring me down. What is the aide doing here? Ms. Henderson says to me, "Staff here, who shall remain unnamed, are worried that you are mistreating the children. The child didn't even say anything to anybody, not even to his own mother. It was other staff members who brought this to my attention." She tells me who the kid unnamed staff are worried about is: Andy.

I sift through my memory: there is a freeze frame of Mr. Nosey and Ms. Guidance looking at me. One of them must have heard I just got accused. The "do-gooder" smells blood, my blood. Nosey or maybe Guidance or maybe both, are joining the feeding frenzy.

"Yeah, I remember shouting at him, but I didn't *grab* him. I *guided* him back in the room." (Thanks Mr. Slaughterbutcher!) The secretary escorts Andy into the office. He looks confused. Ms. Henderson and his mom lovingly question him, while giving me sideways glances. Andy dismisses the whole incident, no big deal. Ms. Henderson lets him leave, leaving me alone with her and this irate teacher's aide. The two of them are ganging up on me. Their heads rock side to side as they take turns making snide remarks. I'm beginning to get the sense they are getting off on this. "My daughter says you're down in that basement muttering swear words!" I don't remember swearing. I mutter a lot. Maybe her daughter thought I swore that time I was muttering about being a cop? As they spit more venom in my face, I get the feeling that something worse than just being yelled at is about to happen to me, I don't know what. I'm feeling closed in, like a trapped animal. I drop my sheepish, apologetic way and fight back.

I raise my voice, "I'm down in that basement every day in a situation where five art teachers were driven out last year! I've maintained order where there was only chaos. I've been teaching those kids. They've been learning. What thanks have I gotten? Never a good word! Never a good word! If you don't want me here, then fire me," I conclude boldly. I mean it, too. I'm seriously thinking that if I'm not meant to be here then don't keep calling me in this office, get rid of me.

The mood changes. They back off. At first the principal is actually appeasing, but she regains some of her strength. "Should we be thanking you for manhandling the children?" she chuckles with a dash of contempt. The crisis moment passed, and I sense it's time to resume my cooperative apologetic way.

"No, no, of course not. Of course not."

"We'll get you through this year. Maybe next year you could try to get into a good school." A good school? Is she admitting this is not?

At bus duty, I breathe a sigh of relief. Green and yellow buds adorn the once barren trees across the street from the school. Kids scream. Birds sing. Life goes on.

Fake Tims

Those last two accusations were a week ago. Maybe I've heard the last of it. The phone rings during class. Another accuser's guardian is coming tomorrow. Man, they're crawling out of the f-ing woodwork. My stomach is in knots. Nicole from Slaughterbutcher's room, the one who gives me rainbow paintings, senses my fear. After I hang up the phone, she gleefully shouts, "Dead man walking! Dead man walking!"

At home I call Dad. "You're up to your neck in alligators. But you usually land on your feet," he advises.

I make rough sketches of what I will say tomorrow, to the parent about his daughter:

> Kid acting bad. Her showing no fear at having her house called. Tearing up my handout. Dancing in front of me grinning, while she throws torn paper around.
> Since prior accusations don't even pat kids on back.

No never did touch this kid.

Did I?

No.

Of course not.

Done.

Sketched out my defense.

Time to stop thinking. Stop thinking. I've got to be like Scarlett O'Hara in "Gone With the Wind." Everything she worked for was ruined but she didn't give up; she knew when it was time to rest before her next battle: "I can't think about that right now. If I do, I'll go crazy. I'll think about that tomorrow." At the very end of the movie Scarlett clutched the scorched soil, from her ruined plantation, the sun set behind her, and she declared: "Tomorrow is another day." If I keep thinking about meeting this accuser's dad, I'll go crazy. It's time to take a break. Tomorrow is another day. So I put in an old movie. And crack open my first of many beers. The black and white credits roll. The Western soundtrack begins. The cowboy stands alone against his enemies.

Six twenty AM. My alarm wakes me from a bad dream. The drive to work is more loathsome than usual. I'm already at the exit. The decrepit cityscape spans before me. Only two short blocks left until I am back. What's the worst that could happen? What can this parent do to me? It's time for my first class of the day. Shaniqua is a big seventh grader. She prances the room joyously declaring, "Look I'm putting my butt on the tables!" She really is too. God I can't stand her right now. I sign the cross. She cackles, "Look! He's calling his God!" When I approach she says, "What are you, drunk?" Am I? I don't feel quiet right. Did I drink too much last night? Is it still in my system? No matter. I can't bow down. I can't feel shame. Keep it together Matt.

A knock on my door. It's Vice Principal Airington with the accuser's dad, and a substitute teacher. "I'm right in middle of the lesson," I protest.

"He'll cover your class," Dr. Airington says.

I see the accuser's parent. Look him in eyes. He looks near my age, maybe a few years older. He's a black guy. Shaved head. Black suit. I smile. "Nice to meet you," I say. We shake hands.

"Don't mind the suit. I work for an undertaker."

181

He smells subtly of alcohol and self-flagellation, a man after my own heart. I feel at ease, and safer suddenly. He knows struggle. He has a drinking problem. He's real. Dr. Airington, however, is not.

"Let me go and get Lanika. Then we can talk." She says. Then we can talk? I think to myself sarcastically. She leaves. Seize the moment.

"Look I'm not into this whole 'child as king' thing, so maybe we can talk adult to adult before she gets here," I say.

"To tell you the truth I'm not into this child as king thing either." He says. For once someone saying, "to tell you the truth" is a good thing. I feel even better. We bonded.

We walk the stairs. "So you're an undertaker? Do you like it? No, huh? Doesn't sound too bad right now." We enter her office and I forget to turn on the lights. The vice principal's chair is empty. We sit in the two guest chairs across from each other in the dark.

"What exactly did she say?" I ask.

"She said they were saying your Timberland boots were fake, and you got mad and shoved her." I'm shocked. I didn't expect something so ludicrous.

"No. I mean, no. I do remember a few kids saying my Tims are fake. That was a little weird" (How could a loser like me actually wear Timberland?) "But man, I'm not that insane that I would actually push a kid for saying my shoes are counterfeits. I would remember shoving somebody. No one's memory is perfect, but that really doesn't sound like me at all."

"So you didn't touch her at all?"

"To tell you the truth…" and I tell him about "cultural differences" and how earlier in the year I would pat kids on the back, or put a guiding hand on them when they were really out of control. "I learned my lesson months ago. After seeing how it is around here and all, I don't even do that anymore. There was a different kid in Lanika's class who I did offer the guiding hand and…."

He cuts me off. "She mentioned that." He says. Does this make me look bad? Then he adds, "That's why I was beginning to think she might just be making this up, so she could get away with stuff."

"I noticed she's been acting fearless lately. Tearing papers up and laughing about it and saying "call my house. I don't care!""

"To tell you the truth, she does lie a lot."

"You're her dad. You would know."

"Actually I'm not her dad. I'm her uncle. I'm just helping out. Her parents have problems with jail and drugs."

The two of us are still alone and in the dark. No Lanika. No Dr. Airington. A moments' silence. "Well, they still haven't gotten here yet. Maybe I should call the office and see where they are?" I offer.

"No, I've heard enough. Don't worry I'm not after your job or anything. I'm gonna have a talk with her when she gets home. Believe me." We rise. Shake hands and leave.

This is how it is. Parents overwhelmed by addiction or despair, have to beg their closest relative or friend, to look after their kids. Kids raised by a volunteer. Volunteers who themselves are struggling to get through life, but they take on the burden anyway. They don't want their own nephews or grand kids to be raised by foster care. A school system lacking in any real discipline tells teachers to "call the homes." Over the years I'll hear many teachers say, "The homes are the problem." "Maybe they are," I say "but we can't do much about that." A few years later, I start to see the evidence of kids getting abused after the school calls home. Burnt with an iron, a hand broken.

Beaten to death.

Troubled lives combined with getting away with defying authority may lead to real crime. The other night I heard on the news that police found a burnt body wrapped in garbage bags in a church parking lot. The lot is just around the corner from the school.

That body they found near the school belonged to one of our former students. He was a "special ed" kid, who had a transvestite boyfriend. It's a little hazy how things went. But they went something like this: the kid's boyfriend hung out with a rough crowd, into crime and drugs. One night the boyfriend came to the kid's apartment with his crew, made up of a few men and one woman. The crew needed a place to party. The kid let them in. Everybody got high and drunk. Then the boyfriend and his friends tied up and murdered the kid in the bathtub. There was no known motive. It appeared like they just did it for fun. Everyone on the news, and at work, said he was a sweet child.

You don't need to live like this.

When I get back to my room, the sub who was covering my class is still there. He's tall and thin and dressed in inexpensive looking professional clothes. "Thanks" I say. He volunteers to take two boys who act out with him, to give me a break. I don't know why he's doing me a favor. When he comes back to my room he tells me he made them write: "I will stay in my assigned seat" over and over. He hands me the evidence. After the twentieth line, the words bleed together. They become new words. "Asia ned sead."

"You shouldn't have to live this way," he says. He's seated at an empty table towards the front of the room. It's where my supervisor normally sits. "Do you have kids?" he asks.

"No."

"Then you really should get out of this. The other art teacher, the one who was here for years, had to support his family."

I'm surprised at what he just said. Other teachers always told me that the old art teacher did a good job. It was just that Ms. Henderson drove him out. That's why art has been a disaster for the past few years. "Everything was fine until he left." Later on a kid will tell me that he yelled a lot, and he's the one who kicked the hole in the desk. Maybe there was no golden age of art at this school, after all.

What about the art teacher last year? That sub isn't here any longer. So I ask a kid. (While they had a string of teachers, they were mostly long-term subs. There was only one "real" teacher. It's just he was gone most of the year, and most of the long term subs were driven out by students). Isaiah fills me in on the main art teacher they had last year. "He was always getting hurt. Then he had this ice pack wedged in between his back and butt. His back hurt. His butt hurt." Isaiah chuckles as he says the word "butt." Another kid adds to the picture, "That teacher was fruity." Others join, "Yeah he was gay." I guess a lot of kids thought that. I get called "fag" sometimes, even though I don't act especially effeminate and I'm straight. It must be even harder for someone who isn't.

Illustration of student apology.

184

Opening

Since I've decided to get more involved in the arts, I aim to arrive at tonight's art opening early to attend the members' meeting. The art opening is billed as an "installation" exhibit, featuring some hip, big city artists. Unlike most of the other galleries around here, this one is supposed to be cutting edge and thus more youthful. It's located in a renovated factory in a dark, out of the way part of town. The large gray structure is home to a few other galleries, artist's studios and some light industry. On my way to the opening, I pass the building once by accident and have to make a u-turn. On the second pass I find it. It looks completely dark from the front. Why don't they have a sign on this thing?

The front door is locked. I press the buzzer. A bored-looking security guard insists I sign in. As a matter of principle, I sign a fake name. Why should "they" know who I am? They still have an elevator operator here. "Which floor?" asks the seventy year old hunched over black man. "Whatever floor 'Edge Gallery' is on." I walk a long gray passageway from the elevator to the gallery.

The members' meeting doesn't really live up to Edge Gallery's reputation for youthfulness. I sit in a cramped space normally used for showing art films. Most of the members at the meeting are older than I am. I don't know what they're talking about, or how I should vote. Clara gets up to say something to the crowd. She's one of the other teachers I met at the new teacher's orientation back in August. She's the one who boasted how she could handle her assignment since "she taught art on the Mexican border."

Since I don't know what's going on anyway, I leave the meeting early and walk out to the part of the gallery where the bar is. The volunteer bartender is a pretty cute art-student-looking girl. Maybe I should volunteer more. I see another familiar face wandering about. He's accompanied by someone I don't recognize. The stranger is a very tall lanky guy, with a long microphone, headset, and camcorder. He wears an afro-centric hat even though he's white. His hat is circular with a flat top, like a cake. The other face, the familiar face, belongs to this guy Craig who is moderately well known around Rust Belt for having his own cable access show. He's a chubby guy with boyish looks and freckles, contrasted by gray hair. It's hard to place his age. He's an unlikely host, with his nerdish social-misfit persona.

"Hey Craig how's it going?"

"All right."

"Who's your friend?"

"William." William and I shake hands. It turns out he has all this equipment because he runs a volunteer cable access studio from his home. He does film and video for a local independent media center, as well as Craig's show. He walks off to film the exhibit and interview guests as they come in.

"So Craig. You making a living from your show yet?"

"No. They don't pay you to be on cable access."

"You still workin' at the library then?"

"Yeah." He gives very short answers for being a TV host.

"That's cool. Are you a librarian now?"

"No, I'm just working there."

"Oh." Gosh this guy must still be poor. He looks poor, but sometimes that can just be a statement of some sort. I know him from my young punk bohemian days. It's not like I have money yet, but at least for now I'm getting more than six bucks an hour. Yet Craig dedicates all his time to a labor of love, and stays with a stable but low paid gig. I was hoping being a teacher would be like what I imagine being a librarian to be: a steady, OK paid gig. Instead, it's very unsteady.

"That's really cool, you have a show. I always wanted to do something like that," I tell him. He gives a muted response, a slight awkward smile and shrug. I never saw his show and don't know much about it. I'm hoping he will ask me to be on it though. He doesn't, so I hint again, "Yeah, I wouldn't mind being on there sometime."

"Fine. Here's my card. How bout next Friday?" He says.

"Sounds OK. What are we going to talk about?"

"Anything." I start to worry. His show probably has profanity and controversial topics.

"You don't swear on there do you? I mean I'm a teacher. I can't be associated with any vulgar language or anything."

"We have a disclaimer at the beginning," he reassures me.

"No. I mean really Craig. There can't be any sex, drugs or rock 'n' roll talk when I'm on. I can't be associated with that because I could lose my job."

"Alright, but I can't promise anything during the other interviews." Being on a local cable access show is better than doing nothing. At least I'm getting more involved, and broadening my horizons somehow.

I've got a camcorder now, and think maybe I'll start to make some art films of my own. Camcorders weren't as common in 2001, as now, so carrying it around people start to assume I'm involved with something, or doing something cool. It's a pre-digital camera, small, lightweight and very simple. It seems the lack of electronic stuff makes it a lot more efficient in some ways. I film as I walk through the installation exhibit.

There are these repeating doorways you walk through, like in a bad dream, and they are surrounded by flesh tone, and pink, foam that form almond like shapes around the open doorways. It's as if you're walking through giant vaginas. I walk through them, filming as I go. A young college age woman asks me, "What are you filming for?" When I tell her "just for the heck of it," she seems disappointed.

Exiting the last vaginal hallway, I enter another room. This wide-open area is filled with large cellular outer space looking things. Spherical shapes that look like giant germs hang from the high ceiling. Long organic looking tubes cling to the walls and seem to grow from the floor. Lights blink off and on within their translucent forms. The two installations together make it feel like you went through multiple births to arrive in a science fiction movie set.

"What do you think of these?" I say to a twenty-something woman with short dark hair. She answers, and her accent sounds European. "Where are you from?" I ask. "Portugal," she says. Thoughts of topless beaches, casual sex, Catholicism, and left wing activism come to mind. I say everything I can think of relating to Portugal and artsy-ness. It turns out she's in Rust Belt studying poetry. I confess to not understanding poetry, but maybe I could if I tried. "Maybe we could get together sometime," I suggest.

"Sure, but I'm a lesbian."

"Hmm. Well. I…" She laughs at my awkwardness.

Back at the bar area I see Clara. We give each other a big hug. "How's your school year going?" I ask. "These kids are unbelievable. I thought I could handle teaching anybody since I taught on the Mexican border, but this is something else." She tells me some of the horror stories she's been going through, of being sworn at, having things destroyed, kids running in and out of the room. (Her school has a reputation for being one of the toughest in the system.) She tells me how she tries to appeal to their sense of sympathy, and maybe showing she's "cool" too, by telling them to give her a break since she's hungover. As she talks she makes unnervingly direct eye contact with me, her eyes squinting and looking like she's straining to keep them open, body swaying slightly, as if she hasn't slept well in days.

I found when I subbed at her school, Fantasy Careers, trying to be "cool" could help a little, but it's a fine line. If you seem too cool, they won't view you as an authority figure any longer. Although at that school, almost nobody is viewed as an authority figure no matter how uptight and stereotypically "teacher" they are. Don't get me wrong, the extent of my trying to be cool was throwing around a little current slang. Believe me, I didn't reference partying. Appealing to the kids' sense of mercy on the other hand is always a losing idea. She looks stressed. "I don't know if I can make it," she admits. Again I find it's me offering someone consolation. It seems ironic, since I'm just hanging in myself.

By the end of the night it's just me and the Portuguese woman with the short hair wandering around. It turns out we know enough people in common from the art scene here, that she trusts me to give her a ride. She wants me to take her to a bar she likes. A gentle rain mists the windshield. Taillights reflect on the night's black pavement. "Come on in. We can play some pool," she says. I don't realize I'm acting hesitant, but she thinks it's funny that I'm not sure if I want to go in. It's a small dark and a fairly crowded bar, with only one or two other guys besides me. The rest are women. I'm not sure how to carry myself. Normally I would try to make eye contact, but I don't want anyone to think I'm spying or something. I'm really pretty bad at pool, never practiced it much growing up. She tries to give me some lessons. "The important thing is to line up your next shot," she advises. Line up my next shot? That's my whole problem in life. I'm not sure what my next shot should be.

The Final Accuser

Just when I think I'm safe from accusations another one will come along. It's a kid in Mr. Beanbag's class. I made a lesson on texture rubbings. It's time to try it out. Mr. Beanbag's group is here. He's with them. They think they've got me over the ropes: "Do whatever you want in art class, then tell your parent 'the teacher hit me!'" I put one boy in timeout. He refuses to go. I raise my voice, and call his home. After that I don't think much of it. The next time I see that class the kids come waltzing in and whip out bags of chips. Jolly Mr. Beanbag tells them not to eat chips during art, but he is impotent. I grab up bags left and right.

That night, rain, wind, and thunder rattle my house. Morning comes and the winds continue. Power lines are knocked down. School is closed.

When school reopens, the father of the boy I put in timeout comes to see me. That afternoon I'm summoned to the office yet again. Principal Henderson sits in front of me at her large wooden desk. The accusing dad sits to my right. He's a big fat guy, wearing a sleeveless shirt. The air is warm and humid. He tells me in a coded way that if I think I'm tough, he's tougher. "My son says you took his chips!" I offer him fifty cents for the chips. He counters: "It's not about the chips. You called me the other day about my son. So I think this was some sort of payback, how you just snatched his chips up like that." I deny it was a payback. Luckily he's making himself look ridiculous, even to Ms. Henderson. Ms. Henderson comes to my defense, "I'm sure he was just taking everybody's chips, and it was nothing personal." He explains about the "stories" he's been hearing about me. Curling his sleeveless arms, and pointing his thumbs at his man-boob chest he says, "I just wanted to show him that if he thinks he's so big, that other people are big too." His veiled threat makes me want to counter him with, "You might be big, but I'm fast." Then I imagine punching him swiftly in the nose. He's not very articulate, though. But after my urge to face him on his own level subsides, I feel sorry for his inability to explain himself. I'm seized with an urge to help him articulate what a bad teacher I am. Luckily, I don't. For once Ms. Henderson is on my side. After the Dad leaves the office she gives me a look that says, "That parent is a real moron."

Since these accusations began, I've noticed others, like Dr. Airington for instance, grabbing a troublemaker by the arm and redirecting the child. I feel like I've been singled out. During lunch duty I bring this up to Iman. He offers some fatherly advice. He puts his hand up to chest level, the height of an imaginary middle schooler. "Are you going to let somebody this tall ruin your career?"

We talk about what he did before teaching. He was a lawyer. Couldn't take the stress. Developed a heart condition. Vice Principal First had a heart attack from running a school. Leaving law and coming to education seems like going from the frying pan into the fire.

Before the day is up, one of my seventh graders shoves me. Not hard. It was less intimidating than the time Baxter crashed into me when he was trying to grab my clipboard. But if I can't even pat these kids on the back anymore, then the office ought to handle this one. I catch Iman in the hall. "Rayshawn shoved me." The next time I have Rayshawn's class, Iman shows up and questions the kid. Rayshawn looks down, says he's sorry. But that's it. There's no other punishment.

Mr. Beanbag

While sitting in the downstairs teachers' lounge, I start thinking about this latest wave of accusations I've fended off. That kid's dad coming here to threaten me because I took his son's chips makes a total of five times I've been summoned by an administrator so far this year; three of which came from kids in the same class: Mr. Beanbag's. The more I think about the merry Beanbag, and his band of rowdy students, the more aggravated I become with Beanbag.

Ryan is sitting in the lounge with me. The great thing about Ryan is that you can vent to him. He enjoys it. He laughs. He joins in and takes your side. The bad thing about him is he's a loose cannon, and doesn't really care about keeping his job.

"Dude, do you know Mr. Beanbag?" I ask Ryan. "He's that jolly aide. Having him in the room with you is worse than having no one in there. I can be right there in front of the whole class, standing there like a jerk, while he lets kids run up to him and acts like their buddy. Good old fun time Mr. Beanbag."

Ryan laughs away, and joins me in mocking Beanbag. "Ha. Mr. Beanbag!" he says derisively. He seems pretty worked up against Mr. Beanbag. Then we go into the hall. Mr. Beanbag is on his way with the children in tow.

Ryan sees the group, grins, raises his fists over his head, pumps his arms up and down while shouting: "Yeahhaaa Mr. Beanbag! It's Mr. Beanbag kids!" He shakes his arms some more looking at the kids. They look blankly back at Ryan. Ryan repeats, as if he were a rowdy host of a children's television show, "Yeahhaaa Mr. Beanbag!" This time the kids join him "Yeahhhhh!!!!!" Now I'm stuck with a flustered, frantically shushing Beanbag, and two lines of hyper squirming children, children who "know their rights." Ryan disappears down the long hall, red faced, laughing and shaking his head.

Half Day

Spring break is already past, winter break is long gone, and it's still a "long hard slog" –to quote Don Rumsfeld -until summer. Ryan reminds me: "Cheer up dude. Tomorrow is a half day."

Don't get me wrong, I am grateful that the kids are going home at noon, instead of three, but I'm not going home early. That's a bit of a let down. As a kid, I figured the teachers got to go home too, since they seemed

190

in such a good mood. No. It turns out we stay the whole day. We're just in a good mood because we don't have to see the kids any longer.

We art teachers are going to spend our half-day at a meeting at another school. It's the same school where my supervisor held the new art teacher orientation. I drive from the east side to the west. After parking and "clubbing" my car, I follow the signs to the meeting place.

When I've had guests in my car, they often mocked me for clubbing it.

"Who'd steal your car?" friends would say sarcastically.

"Someone in a hurry." I'd counter.

"They can cut right through that club."

"Yeah, but it slows them down."

The signs lead to the auditorium. It's just filling up and I don't feel like sitting yet. I scan the room for familiar faces. There's that art teacher with the feathered back hair, the one I met at orientation. She's the other new teacher, besides me, our supervisor warned: "You two have tough situations."

With her feathered hairdo, pocked marked skin and denim outfit, she still looks like one those cool rock-and-roll kids from the eighties, who looked like evolved holdovers from the seventies. The ones into metal music, with feathered roach clips and fuzzy dice hanging from their car mirrors, fake zebra fur on their seats, and giant combs sticking out their back pockets. I walk up to her smiling. "Hey, how's it going?"

"Horrible," she says with rare honesty.

"Tell me about it," I say with a hearty resignation.

"They never shut up, and they destroy everything," she says in a disturbed voice, with no note of gallows humor.

"Yeah, they're pretty bad," I say chuckling. I'm in a good mood having this half-day, so I can laugh it off right now.

"Any supplies I put out, they ruin. Any way I try to organize things, they mess it up." She isn't laughing it off. She looks in her mid or early forties. Her pock mocked face seems to exaggerate the intensity of how emotionally disturbed she is by this. I wonder how many letdowns she's had before landing this teaching job. How has she survived up till this point? What did she leave behind to choose this as her means of support? How much hope did she put into this job? I can feel her wondering what she will do next, as her hopes are crumbling.

If the grown-ups in kids' lives don't have any sense of stability, then how are the kids from unstable homes, being taught by teachers who fear

191

losing their jobs any day, going to feel stable and secure? Without some sense of stability and security, how are they going to focus on learning?

"Join the club," I laugh, still not fully realizing she isn't finding the humor in watching our lives unravel. "I hear you. I'm going through the same thing. They wreck all my stuff too," I tell her in consolation. But her hazel eyes look back at me un-consoled. She has that desperate look. The look I get when I'm in the midst of battle with these students, or when I'm cornered by my supervisor or principal.

On a pleasant afternoon like this I don't have that fear, pleasant because it's just adults now. Non-threatening adults. No one is going to insult, shout at, or physically menace me. No one is going to "act bad," and if for some reason they do, it isn't my job to quiet them down. I can shake that trapped feeling off.

"What I do is just budget time for the destruction," I say, to help change her perspective on it. "They ruin my supplies, break the containers, mix them all together and throw them around. Then at the end of every day, I tape things up, restock containers, and sort it out all over again. It's just a routine, that's all. I try to compartmentalize it." I do too. I picked up that word when our former president Bill Clinton was first accused of some dirty real-estate deals, then of getting a blow job from his chubby twenty-one year old intern. I remember hearing people in the news say that he and his wife were good at "compartmentalizing." I figured if they could compartmentalize legal suits and a sex scandal, while having to run the country and deal with the world, then I could compartmentalize kids acting badly and routinely destroying the order I brought to the room. I could compartmentalize getting falsely accused of using the "N" word, swearing, and using corporal punishment at work.

My words of comfort only elicit an empty faraway stare. I feel like she's thinking, "This is a nightmare." It is, but it's all about knowing when to forget about the nightmare and have a drink. I don't know if she ever was able to put the defiant behavior in perspective. And take breaks from dealing with, and thinking about, the mayhem.

After today, I will never see her around again (this year and all those to come). She won't be the only new art teacher I never see again. Over the next few years it will not be long until I become one of the "senior art teachers."

The meeting starts and we sit in wooden auditorium seats. The backs of the chairs are etched with profanity and nicknames. Our supervisor chastises us for not using the art books. After he's done, a teacher from the audience comments on computers in the schools. "There are computer teachers and tech teachers teaching the kids digital art. We mustn't abdicate this to them. We need to assert that we art teachers should be teaching this." It's a good point I think. I like computers and I imagine that in a different life I'm a digital artist of some sort myself. No one comments on his comment. I don't think many of these people care much about computers, or books for that matter. I'm hoping someone will comment on what the school system's plan is to get discipline under control, but no one does. No one ever does.

We file out, and up the stairs to our assigned classrooms for group meetings. My assigned room is an art room. It's neat, organized clean and sunny. I don't notice any signs of violence or chaos. The teacher displays her kids' projects. There's student art with a toy bug and a magnifying glass and something written about how artists are like scientists. I feel mild jealousy and resentment. "Sure this teacher thinks she's so special, with her perfect room and her perfect kids." I wish Ryan were here so we could make fun of her. That feathered haired lady is too freaked out to mock things. I spot Sabrina and go and sit with her. If I can't let off steam with jokes, at least I can sit next to a pretty woman. She's one of the other new art teachers I met at orientation: very pretty and very punky.

She's got her Doc Marten boots, tight jeans, and a black shirt on. I make some small talk about punk rock bands, "straight edge" music, vegetarianism, and all that. Despite all the common ground, it's a plain looking, mid forties, former insurance agent, who intrigues her.

The art teacher, the one whose room we're in, quiets us down. She insists we look at her lesson plans on diversity and lectures us about working multiculturalism into art. The teacher poses "challenging" questions we can ask our students. We break into groups to brainstorm on the topic.

Afterwards, I try to re-interest Sabrina in conversation, but I'm flailing. "So how about that band, 'Minor Threat?'" A quick smile, then she's back to the other guy. This must be a mistake. As we all walk out to our cars, I linger nearby, hoping I can get a second chance. Just behind me, the two of them laugh, smile, and exchange phone numbers. Momentarily I feel resentment at an older guy hitting on a lady in my age bracket. The moment passes. I decide I should be grateful that older guys have a chance. I mean, I'm not getting younger. Maybe he is just trying to help her out with annuities or something.

19. Tina & Star For A Day

Tina's Class

Poor Tina. She has it just as bad as me, but doesn't seem to be doing the expected things like I try to. She just does her job and goes home. She's used up all her sick days. She's even filed a "grievance." I sure wouldn't file a grievance during my first year on the job. She acts like it's no big deal, just an everyday thing. Yesterday I saw her in the hall with her class. They were bouncing in and out of line. She looked upset as she said to them, "This is no way to live." I felt for her, but I knew she was giving the kids too much power.

The sub is in today for Tina's class. He's a short guy, with a brush cut. He's nervous and moves fast, like me, only more so. One of the Caucasian students interrupts my teaching to announce, "Your brother is here." I think about my actual brother. At this point, both African American and Caucasian kids are giggling.

"What are you talking about?" I indulge them. Later in my career my mantra will be "stick to business" and do not get caught up in their comedies and dramas. But now I'm too emotionally frazzled to robotically remember my own slogan.

"That Nazi guy. He's your brother," a chubby white boy says.

"What do you mean?"

"He's got his head shaved, like you." Like I said earlier, this is early 2001, and shaved heads are getting big, but they aren't big yet. "You're a Nazi too!" another white boy laughs.

"I am not, and I doubt that guy is either." Then one of the white boys gives a Sieg Heil salute. And then a few of them do. "That is not acceptable!" I say. A funny look passes over the African American faces in the room. They aren't laughing this time, more like nervously chuckling. Normally white and black would unite, and laugh uproariously at any defiance. But this disruption is different and their muted laughter sounds hurt, nervous, confused and excluded. While these are young kids, at some level they must believe that these boys' Sieg Heiling amounts to a show of racism.

Later I chastise Anthony, one of Tina's students, for some other infraction. After class I notice a large swastika he drew in one of the art textbooks. When the Soviet Union collapsed, left wing ideals were discredited, so the next wave of rebellions in the former satellite states were right wing and ethnic. So too, with the American left temporarily in retreat, is the right wing replacing it as an outlet for youthful rebellion? (A counter trend will emerge as well. A few years from now, I'll see sixties nostalgia make a comeback).

FIFTH GRADE"

When I phone Anthony's home, a feeble sounding elderly woman answers. She tells me how upset Anthony is because of something like, "His dad's in prison and mom's on drugs." This elderly woman is stuck raising a hyperactive (ADHD these days), angry, hurt, abandoned little boy. She doesn't have the energy to keep up with him.

The next time Tina's class comes, Anthony is acting a little better. So I decide to make this disturbed kid a helper. He puts away supplies but lingers a little too long.

A couple of classes later the younger gym teacher, Mr. Fin, and the principal come knocking on my door.

Since I knew Fin when we were teens, I don't feel as intimidated as I did when Ms. Henderson came to my door with Dr. Iman. But still it feels like they are here to arrest me.

"Why aren't these cabinets locked?" Ms. Henderson demands.

"There aren't any locks on them."

"Why didn't you get them put on?"

"I asked the custodian but he said they didn't have any."

"Someone got paint from your art room and put it all over the boys' bathroom." They leave. Later she calls me to her office. It turns out Anthony was the culprit.

(While Tina's students have been getting worse, Christine's students have turned around, somewhat. Christine is the other new teacher who hangs out in the downstairs lounge with Ryan, Tina and me. Christine came up with a system. "If you get a good report in art then you can have some outside time." It worked. Teamwork is something I will find lacking over the years).

Show

When I called Craig to confirm my being on his show, we discussed what we would talk about. Teaching seemed like the obvious subject, but I said no. I didn't want to lose my job. "Nobody watches cable access anyway," someone recently said, when I was mulling over what to talk about. "I don't know. You never know. Someone might see it," I said back. The next obvious topic seemed like the T-shirts I designed when I was twenty and was trying to sell again at thirty, as part of my second stab at youth. Craig said fine.

"But a lot of the designs are political and disturbing. I can't have some parent freaking out on me, saying 'that nut is teaching my kid!'"

"So we can't talk about that either?"

"Not really, maybe just show one of them. I've been to Hong Kong. We could talk about that."

I look on my Rust Belt map to figure out how to get to the taping. It's at William's. William is Craig's volunteer cameraman, and studio provider. Whenever I've had some date in my car who's not from here, they laugh at me for pulling out a map. "You're from Rust Belt and you need a map?" I can't know every part of this place. I never drove a car until I was twenty-three.

Craig's show is taped in South Side Rust Belt. That's the general area where some of my white students come from. It looks like a cramped suburb, with cheaply made 1950's era houses. I pull the car over and consult my map again. OK. I think I've got it now. A lady with dyed red hair greets me at the door and brings me in. Craig waddles up to me. "Hey Matt. You want a beer?" he offers.

"Thanks," and I take one. "Craig, can I get a copy of this show I'm gonna be on? I mean, I've been in so many little college films and stuff and no one ever gives me a copy."

"It's up to William. We stopped giving copies. Just tape it off the cable," he tells me. I don't have cable.

Even though he's inside his own home William is still wearing that little afro-centric hat, with decorative patterns. Maybe he's bald under that hat? While Craig busies about, William shows me the editing room. This is all in William's small house. He's got a whole room filled with tape decks and VCR's and computers. I ask him a bunch of questions, thinking about what that Brooklyn artist I met at Alex's party told me about video editing and what a good career it could be. I notice a bunch of notes and addresses posted next to the computer. "Is this what you do for a living William? Edit video?"

"No, I run a process serving business from home." All this for a hobby. He gives me some computer magazines. Craig calls us into the other room.

What might once have served as William's small living room, is now filled with studio chairs, cameras and sound equipment. I'm seated in a chair and given a large bulky head set. "Wait. I can't be seen drinking beer on TV." They get me an opaque mug. Another short fat guy sits next to me. Only this guy is much older than me and Craig, maybe in his sixties. I thought the redhead was the co-host, but it's Craig's dad. They gear him and Craig up with the same bulky headsets I'm now wearing. Craig wears opaque silver reflective sunglasses. Between the head sets and the glasses this looks like the Howard Stern television show.

The redhead reads an intro piece, something about spring and a "young boy's fancy." Now we're on. Craig and his dad take turns asking me questions, then shouting at me. Not angrily, but loudly and obnoxiously. Where is all this energy coming from? This guy is always so quiet and awkward. Now he's bellowing. He doesn't seem like the type to do drugs, I don't even know where he'd get the money, but I never saw him like this before. I hold my own. They don't really seem to care if I talk or just sit there sheepishly. "Anything interesting in Hong Kong?" the dad asks. I can't talk about a late night encounter on the beach. I'm feeling the beer and lack of sleep.

"They have these buildings…" I start to say.

"Buildings?!" Craig shouts out.

"Oh, they have buildings?" his dad sarcastically replies.

"Well, I mean…" I start.

"We've got buildings here. So far I don't think I'm missing too much. Do they have anything we don't have here?!" Craig shouts, high fiving his dad.

"They claim they have the world's biggest statue of Buddha."

Craig's dad starts saying "Ohmmm, Ohmmm." Craig asks about Pyramids. I play along, going on about Pyramid power, and just turn the interview into a theater of the absurd.

"Yeah they've got a pyramid on the Buddha's head with a flashing light and siren," I say. They laugh.

Craig stands up and starts making sound effects, with his hands above his head like a pyramid. He sits down. Having expended some energy a moment of calm sets in.

"How did you get to Hong Kong?" his dad asks seriously.

"By horse," I reply. Got them for once. We're nearly at the end of the interview, and Craig remembers to get in a plug for my shirts. I model it for the camera. That's it. The ten minutes flew by in a frenzy of shouting and inane comments.

We de-gear and Craig shows me some of the footage. "You did well Matt. Usually we do all the talking and the guests barely get in anything. You held your own."

"Thanks." I stick around a few minutes to watch the next guest, and sure enough he doesn't get many comments in, while Craig and his dad steamroll him. As I leave, William hands me a tape. "Thanks a lot. That was really nice of you."

TV's Aftermath

"Are you going to stick around and watch the other guests?" William asks. "No. I've got to be someplace." Really I'm just going to meet Alex and hit some bars. Back at Alex's loft I turn to that globe, the one with the black oceans. Looking at North America I say: "So what do you think about Bush beating Gore?"

198

"I think the very wealthy, and by that I don't mean people who think they are very wealthy, like doctors, I mean people with billions, wanted a guaranteed return on investment."

"What do you mean?"

"The US budget deficit provides a guaranteed rate of return. When Clinton had the budget balanced they weren't happy. A large US deficit, provides a definite almost risk free return on their money."

"That's an interesting way of looking at it."

I pour some more cognac. That bottle I bought back at Christmas time is still here. There's a full-length mirror next to the bathroom. I'm in pretty good shape, but this hair. No way will I take Rogain. I'd like to shave it right down again. But wouldn't that look too drastic for a teacher? (It might not seem like it now, but it did a few years back.) Especially after just getting accused of manhandling kids.

"We need to go," Alex says.

We head out. "See ya Norm."

"Have fun guys." We leave Norm, Alex's reclusive housemate, sitting on the couch watching TV. We make our rounds of dimly lit clubs and bars. It's a good time. But still I think maybe it would be easier finding a new girlfriend if this head were shaved.

TV's Aftermath at Work

Another morning at work and the cable access show I was on has already aired. I wonder if anyone saw it? As I stand poised and ready for the kids at the start of hall duty, that all too familiar anxiety begins creeping in. The loudspeaker announces, "The buses are coming. The buses are coming." It's like a warning of some kind.

Leroy the janitor walks near me carrying a broom. With a big smile he puts one hand to the side of his mouth like he's an old time town crier, and holds the broom with the other. He calls out: "The British are coming! The British are coming!"

"That's exactly how it feels!" I laugh.

As the sea of students washes past, Isaiah, a kid from Slaughterbutcher's, says "I saw you on TV!" A couple of others will tell me the same thing that week. Thank God I kept that beer hidden in an insulated mug.

Mr. Mullet won't be the only one to have his style influenced by students. In a few minutes I will join him. One of my eighth graders, Darius,

199

is telling me off. It's business as usual so far. Then he calls me a "fuzzy headed art teacher!"

"Fuzzy headed art teacher?" I repeat, as shocked as when Mullet was called out on his haircut.

His group isn't one of those groups that hate me. They're not like Jimmy's group. I imagine, deluding myself perhaps, that there's fondness behind their harassment.

Darius even gave me a copy of some rap lyrics he wrote. Apparently he's an aspiring rap artist. It wasn't as endearing as Jaylen making me a whole "mix tape," but I still saw it as a good sign. His rapper name was "Soda Pop." The lyrics went: "There's this nigga soda pop. From around the block…" I forgot the rest of it.

Endearing moments aside, his class isn't well behaved. There's a girl in here named Shaniqua, she's the one who was bragging the other day: "Look, I'm putting my butt on the table!" Today she proudly announces, "I don't have to listen to nobody. Not even Dr. Iman can tell me what to do!" Not even Iman? I thought this guy was like an invincible saint around here. I'm relieved to know some of them think he's as much of a joke as they think I am.

Back to Darius: "Why did you call me a fuzzy headed art teacher?" I ask. I'm standing in the middle of the aisle and he's seated at the front table near the door.

"Look at you!" he says with disgust.

"That's because my hair is thinning out. It's natural," I reply indignantly.

"Why don't you shave it down instead of looking like an ah…" He stops short. He was just about to say: "instead of looking like an asshole."

"You think it would look better shaved, huh?" I say with genuine curiosity. Here I was keeping it "fuzzy" so I seem less offensive and less threatening to students, parents and administrators. I haven't shaved it since winter break. When it was safe I wouldn't be seen by anyone school related. It wasn't so long ago I associated white guys with shaved scalps with skinheads.

When Jimmy called me a "Bald headed freak" I figured he's just out of style. And my fuzzy crew cut was more "in" than his David and Goliath hairdo. When Baxter called my shoes "clown shoes" it didn't phase me either. But I agree with this kid who's making fun of me now.

When I call Shaniqua's mom she sounds tough and street, like her daughter. I try to use semi-slang with her to build familiarity. Only I use it wrong this time. "I was *comin up* on your daughter and she turned and said get the F away from me."

She sounds shocked. "You were *comin up* on her!?" While I've heard this phrase before, it suddenly dawns on me that I really don't know what it means. Immediately I drop any "trying to sound black" and say "No. I mean as I was *walking towards* her and she said..."

After hanging up with Shaniqua's mom, I kick the idea of shaving my head around with the women in the ladies lounge. Laura approves, "I think that would be sexy. You should get your ear pierced too." Pookie disapproves: "A teacher with no hair. That wouldn't be appropriate." I decide to compromise and wait until summer.

I stop by Marisol's for dinner. She apologizes that Lela and I didn't work out. She's in her own go no-where thing with some new Internet guy. I try to hook her and Norm up. But she turns down my offer, for now. I decide my own love life is so dismal I may as well take a second look at coworkers.

Lunch Duty – flirting with an aide.

At the end of lunch duty I entertain myself by talking to the teacher's aide standing next to me. She's a single black female, probably ten years older than I am. She has an OK face but an awesome figure. "Maybe we should meet up at the Round Table sometime," I propose. It's a bar in between where the two of us live. She has a few kids. I don't have any. She'd have to find a babysitter. We're at pretty different points in life. That's why I keep the offer non-committal. "Well, maybe I should see what that place is like sometime. Anybody else from work going?"

Leroy the janitor comes along wearing a muscle shirt, and pulling a mop and bucket. Maybe I'm standing too close to her. It's time to put the chairs up. He gets a funny grin on his face. He starts violently slamming chairs up on the table and pushing them into other tables. He was always so nice to me. It seems like he's joking but it's still scary. She laughs and walks away. I do too.

Somebody tells me later, "Leroy likes her." Leroy's a bachelor. He lives alone in his own home. I never do meet up with that aide.

Tenaya

I'm about to head home. As I cut through the cafeteria, it's loaded with kids. I didn't know there is an after school program. Mr. Tussle is one of the adults with them. What's he doing here? It's almost an hour after school let out. He must really be a dedicated teacher. Halfway through the cafeteria he sees me. Darn, I hope he doesn't want me to stay and help him out. "Hey Mr. Tussle." I look down as fast as I can, and keep walking. Crisis avoided.

The next time it's time to go home, I debate passing through the cafeteria. I'm scanning for Mr. Tussle. Hoping he's not there. Before I can spot him, I see a new young and pretty African American woman. Her hair is long and straight. She's around my height, younger than me, but not too young. She's helping out the kids. I sure would like to meet her.

Crossing the cafeteria is worth the risk of getting sucked into doing some volunteer work. If I get a new phone number it wouldn't seem so bad. There's Mr. Tussle. I stop. Greet him and the kids he's with, so I can get a better look at her. Is she another volunteer dedicated to helping the young? Maybe she's a young mom. Who's that tall young man with the dreadlocks? Maybe they're together. I'd better act caring. "Hey kids. Do you need some help?" I offer to one of the boys. This is taking way too long. It's nearly a half hour later. "I gotta run."

After seeing *her* I stop avoiding the cafeteria on my way to the parking lot. Finally our paths cross. She's alone. We exchange names. It turns out she's not a volunteer here at all. She's not a mom. She's getting paid. This is her job. These teachers here, like Mr. Tussle, they're getting paid too. He never said anything. He just let me volunteer.

After a couple more encounters, I ask for her telephone number. She ignores the kids momentarily. Looks around furtively. The guy with the dreads is on the other side of the room. She tears a small piece of paper off a large sheet, and writes her name and number with a pencil, then quickly hands it to me. "Tenaya." After phoning her we set a date.

It's Friday night, around eight PM. Her street is only a couple of miles from mine. But her neighborhood looks more run down and neglected. I walk up the cement patio steps to her, and her Mom's, first floor apartment. The porch is dark. It doesn't seem like they're expecting guests. Ring. No answer. Ring. As I turn my back the front door opens. A lady who looks barely old enough to be her Mom appears. She's got a blond streak bleached into her bangs, and has one of those ornate hairdos that are popular this year among black women. She looks confused at seeing me. It's like she's thinking: "A white guy in a black leather jacket, at night, in a black neighborhood, and on my porch. What's going on?"

She talks to me through the screen door. The storm windows are up. "Can I help you?" This isn't going according to plan. Didn't she tell her mom I was coming to get her?

"Is Tenaya home?" She still seems confused. Maybe she can't hear me through the door. "Tenaya. Is she home?" Then it dawns on her: "He's here for my daughter."

"She's at the mall. Shopping with friends." She must have chickened out. We are from pretty different worlds, and instead of waiting or calling later, I decide to chicken out too.

20. You Want Me Back. Don't You?

You Want Him Back?

I shout sternly and loudly back at Jessica. As I risk launching into a tirade, I see the silhouette of my supervisor cross the doorway. Then perhaps in response to my shouting, cross rapidly back out. I believe he wants to eavesdrop. I switch to a more moderate tone. Jessica stands alongside of me at the cabinet, like a second teacher. Really, I feel affection towards this group so the switch isn't hard.

We've got the paints out and I let them choose an image from the book to look at and base their assignment on. For a while some of them settle on pictures they like and begin working. The kids at Cedric's table choose to paint Aztec masks. Cedric is related to the disappeared music teacher, Mr. Cantwell. I've asked many times "Where is Mr. Cantwell now?" But even Cedric is tight lipped about him. Calm lasts only a few minutes. A kid starts flinging water. Students are waylaid off task. Art is set aside for self-defense.

"Cedric, come up here! No, no, I'm not mad at you Cedric." He comes up. I start to put my arm around his shoulder but then remember not to. "Look around at this room. See how the kids are acting." We look, and I imagine he can see the low level chaos from my point of view. He nods rapidly. "I need you to set a good example Cedric. You're one of my top artists. The kids really look up to you. You're a role model. Now get back there and act like a role model." He nods rapidly again. He goes back to his seat, picks up his brush, dips it, and flicks water on a student.

At the end of the evaluation my supervisor says, "You put your finger in the dyke (exact words). It was getting dangerous in here last year." But he still feels that discipline is lacking. He wants to get someone new in this art room next year, and send me somewhere else. "Next year I'm *probably* going to put you in a better situation."

I say thanks. But I'm skeptical. I subbed the year before at a place that was as bad or worse than here. I've seen and heard horror stories. Are there really better situations? Part of me is still hoping I can win over these kids and come back in the fall.

It's a few days later and Jessica and Cedric's class come again. Standing at Cedric's table I say: "Come on guys. Behave. You want me to be here again next year. Don't you?" The table feels power packed with rowdy boys.

Rakim, who mostly wanders the room making sexual noises, using profanity, and eating sunflower seeds, says, "Shit. This nigga thinks we like him!" They look at each other and laugh.

One of the other boys continues, "Do you want this nigga comin back?"

"I don't want this nigga back."

"All this nigga does is call our parents!" I have called a lot of parents.

I Luuuuuve Teaching

Despite the put down, I feel up about teaching at the moment. My supervisor is going to get me a job next year, just not here. In the lounge, I say to Ryan, "You should try to get your Spanish certificate. You'd probably make tenure fast."

Ryan replies, "I'm not gonna do this again. Who cares about tenure? I hate this. You hate this. Everybody hates this. All teaching is, is kids screaming. All they do is shout. Do you really want to be around screaming kids all day?"

I list some of the benefits, but he just repeats: "Who wants to be around a bunch of screaming kids?"

He's cracking my positive façade. I'm getting cynical and sarcastic again. "But then why is it that almost every time I meet teachers out somewhere, and I ask them: 'How do you like teaching?' They almost all say the exact same thing, with the exact same radiant glow: 'I luuuuuve teaching!'"

Ryan laughs spitefully, his large body leaning back in the small plastic and metal school chair.

At church, I bumped into this one teacher from Fantasy Careers High, Ms. Fergus. I always saw her getting harassed by students. Another teacher told me that Ms. Fergus had to go on a leave of absence because she had a mental breakdown. And when I saw her at church and I asked her how's teaching, what do you think she said? She said "I luuuve teaching."

A few years from now, I'll meet another young teacher who works at a school where the gym teacher got his face split open when a student threw a metal garbage can at his head. I'll see police cars out in front of it all the time. The school will even make the local news for outbreaks of violence. Yet that young teacher will tell me, eyes shining, "It's a great school. I love teaching."

Ryan is impressed by my observation and is getting worked into his big loud fat comedian mode. "Yeah, they all say it like that too, don't they? "I luuuve teaching!'"

"You've got the tone exactly bro!" It's always fun when two or more join in mocking the same target. Continuing I add, "It's like they're a bunch of programmed robots." It's often the new teachers I hear say this, the ones who have it the worst. I'll hear on Public Radio that most new teachers quit within the first five years. That's how much they "luuuuuve" it.

Most people I see teaching are dealing with some level of student defiance. Maybe some people have it better than others. But it's stressful. Maybe a lot of them do love it. But no way is it all of the one's saying they do. Not after what I've seen. Maybe since they're dealing with people's kids, and we all keep hearing how rewarding and joyous teaching is, they feel they have to say they love it. They have to lie. There's no way someone like that teacher whose students caused her to have a nervous breakdown, could "love it." No way. They're lying, because that's how the work world works. People lie to get and keep jobs. People lie to get and keep all kinds of things. People lie to start wars. We lie to ourselves because we don't want to admit we were lied to in the first place. And because confronting unhappiness can be overwhelming.

"They're so full of shit," Ryan concludes.

We eat in silence for a little while. I half don't believe he's going to leave this career. "What are you gonna do then?" I ask.

"I don't know. Maybe go back to Africa once I get my pilot's license."

"Back to Africa? Damn. I remember the Philippines –that was the Peace Corp, but what were you doing in Africa?"

"Workin for a not-for-profit that tried to protect chimpanzee habitat. I don't know about that again though."

"Why not?"

"I get tired of these aristocratic types who are more worried about chimps than people."

"Yeah that's a tough thing. But it's the economic system we have, that pits people against chimps," I say half joking and half seriously. "I mean if wealth were distributed a bit more evenly, people wouldn't have to make choices between poaching and starving. Most of these third world countries have very rich people and foreign corporations hording the wealth. There should be enough for people to have their big vehicles, and leave some wild areas left over."

Ryan hates materialistic people as much as he hates anybody else, so he agrees with me.

"You're really not going to come back?"

"No way. This sucks." He's honest anyway.

21. Survivor

Letting Off Steam

It's nearly summer. This is the last time I will ever see students from this particular seventh grade class, at least during the school year. It's the group with Lillian and those three defiant white boys. Jimmy, their ringleader, is missing. So are Lillian and Joe. That leaves only Kyle. Maybe this won't be such a bad day.

Even without his buddies here, Kyle's giving me shit as usual. He's the blond with the short 50's style hair, long giraffe neck, who loves "paper popping" and shouting "Good ol' boys." Without Jimmy he doesn't seem as intimidating.

I've been taking it from him and his pals half the year now, hearing stuff like "shut up faggot." I'm really sick of it by this point.

He thinks he's got nothing to lose by acting out this last day. I'm becoming incensed. "Can't we just leave on a good note?" I ask.

"Noooooooohhhh!" He says growling and dragging out the "o" in no. He continues his disruptions.

"Get to timeout!"

"No way!" he growls, and continues singing loudly and paper popping. I've gone from incensed to enraged. Kyle, having insulted me many times over the year, is becoming the symbol of all the insults I've endured all year as an art teacher, and last year as a substitute.

"Even on the very last day. Even on the very last day," I repeat the phrase with a growing growl of my own, "you're going to harass me like this?!"

"Yeah that's right!" He stands and starts making a mess on the floor with the paints.

I'm nearly ready to snap. You've held it together all year Matt, don't lose it now. Then it dawns on me, maybe Kyle is right. Maybe there is little to lose on the last day. I do a quick mental calculation. What can I get away with? How much stress could I unload right back on this kid, who's dumping all his pubescent defiance and teen anger on me? The principal

209

knows I won't be back. Why would she want to bother with me? It's the last day. I've survived accusations of using corporal punishment. My supervisor was just here last week. He probably won't walk in the room right now. Kyle's main man, Jimmy, isn't here to back him up. Lillian and Joe aren't here either.

I embrace the rage. I square off with him. I don't even try to be PC or use any education-speak. I'm feeling like the black music teacher must have felt when he allegedly shoved a black student in a brief black on black attack. Mr. Cantwell said, "It's like we were right back in the projects on the street and I'm thinking 'his ass is mine.'" That's how I'm feeling -it's just me and him, and his ass is mine. I'm bellowing right in his face. He shouts at me, but his vocal chords are no match for mine. I drown him out. With each step I take forward, he takes one back. My face must be conveying, "Please take a swing asshole!" His tough guy taunts weaken, as his head bobs side-to-side looking for allies to join him in jeering at me. No kids come to his defense. No one says anything. They just do their work. It's like a western movie, where the town folk shut their windows before the shootout. Secretly they're happy to see this bully get his comeuppance. I continue my advance towards him as if I'm in a fencing match. Finally I can see that look in his eyes. It's the same look I saw in Baxter's eyes when I stopped him from beating a kid up. It's the look of fear one feels when one suddenly isn't sure what will happen next. He backs down and sits in the timeout. It's a small payback, and I was still hoping I could have concluded class with a happy good bye, but I mean come on, enough is enough.

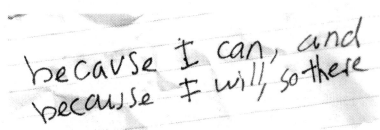

because I can, and because I will, so there

Kyle's reply to my question, "Why are you doing this?!"

After leaving the art room, I'm still red faced from the blowout. A female teacher sees how upset I am, "Hang in there, it's almost summer." I take her advice and do some "get ready for summer" shopping. Buy a backyard canopy, lawn chairs, and a small barbeque grill. Ryan comes over to my house and helps set up the canopy. As we begin the work, he shouts "Partay!" My new middle-aged black neighbors look over the fence at hearing his words. They've done a lot of work on their new home. "Keg-er!"

Ryan cheers, once we get the canopy up. The neighbors' heads jerk over in unison like startled deer, to look again. I've seen white partiers portrayed in black movies; slamming beers, rhythmically shouting, "Chug! Chug!" drunk and overturning cars. The new neighbors must be thinking, "Was moving here a big mistake?" After Ryan pulls out of my driveway in his beat up rusted 1980's subcompact, I walk over to meet the new neighbors and reassure them.

Pre-End

Exams week is over and grades are "closed." (Closed is education-speak for "grades have been handed in to administrators and can't be changed any longer.") However the school year won't officially be over until next Thursday. Ms. Henderson is stressing to the children that, "attendance still counts." She's at cross-purposes with the teachers. We're mostly worried about having a lot of students in the building with nothing to do, and knowing none of it counts for a grade. Kids were overheard boasting about "last day fights" and other mayhem.

In the upstairs lounge teachers swap recipes for warding off students. The ingredients usually consist of draconian last day activities. A fifth grade teacher says, "I tell the children, anyone who comes to school has to scrub the room with a toothbrush." Slaughterbutcher is gonna close all the windows, doors, keep the room dark, and tell the kids no passes. Bear in mind it can be hot in the building this time of year.

Come Monday, the kids who were not scared off are put to hard work. When I walk the halls I see students scrubbing and mopping. I'm on my way to give Slaughterbutcher a "prep." Since I don't have a room full of kids of my own, I go to other rooms and give the teachers breaks.

When I arrive at his room, it's pretty much like he said it would be. The room is dark. Kids look disoriented. No one is going anywhere. After Slaughterbutcher leaves, one of the boys creates a makeshift "sculpture" out of masking tape and plastic bottles. He tapes a note on it: "To fat boy." I don't know what it's supposed to be. "Give me back the tape," I warn him. "This is for Mr. Slaughterbutcher," he says, gazing at his sculpture.

That was Slaughterbutcher's first day tactic. The next day when I go back to relieve him he's lightened up on the kids. I guess he figured he's dissuaded all he could. Ray and Lamont, the two boys who act like old time comedians, are playing violent video games. Apparently this is the only thing they've been doing all day. I make some weak objections, not really sure how to handle it. They are completely revved up and high on a full day

211

of violent gaming. Anything I say is just met with howls of laughter, insults and threats. I let them play their game.

Last Day

It's the last day. No kids. Just adults. While I'm in my room packing, Ms. Henderson announces over the PA system: "It's finally here. The day some of you have been waiting for since September." I laugh, alone in my room. She says "Congratulations Mr. Slaughterbutcher on winning the union election. I was trying to get rid of him. Guess I can't now."

Fin, Slaughterbutcher, Mullet and a couple of others come to my room and get me. We unload tons of new weightlifting equipment for the school. For once I feel like I belong. But I tell them, "I won't be back next year. My supervisor wants to put me someplace new." Slaughterbutcher says, "Tell him you want to come back. You want to prove you are up for the challenge." Then he gives me a short speech about how I should say I don't want to run.

Most of us go to the end of the year picnic. Mullet, myself, and a few others, kick a soccer ball around. Tussle brings his age appropriate daughter –meaning she's age appropriate for me to date. He brought her to school earlier in the week, and I let it out that I thought she was cute. Word must have gotten back to Tussle. I guess he thinks I'm OK. She's here now, on summer break from college, it's a golden opportunity. But instead of trying to talk to her, I just hang out and get drunk. That aide who yelled at me in the principal's office is here with her child, the one I was accused of "grabbing." I'm hoping Ryan will come so I've got someone to be cynical with. I'd be happy to commiserate with Tina. Neither show.

Ryan and I stay in touch a while longer. We go for a hike in a ravine. He tells me about his backpacking and hitchhiking adventures through Afghanistan, way before nine-eleven. Back when we supported the Jihadists. Ryan was up in the Afghan mountains. He got invited to a large gathering. Afghan men came from all over the countryside to watch and play at a horseback polo tournament -Britain's legacy. In a large tent deep in the mountains, they asked Ryan if it's true that American guys perform a certain "thing" for women. When he said, "We do," they reeled with laughter, and waved their hands in front of their noses.

We hike further to the riverbed and stop at a large rock on the bank. We're silent. All I can hear is the buzz of the summer cicada. The barren tree limbs of winter are gone. Green is the dominant color. A slight breeze cuts through the hot air. This is really living, I think to myself.

Ryan says, "I wonder if Christine (one of the other new teachers we always had lunch with) and her husband are swingers?"

"Why do you think that?"

"They keep trying to get me and my wife into their hot tub."

Summer's Wait

Mid July and my supervisor still hasn't told me what school I'll be going to. I'm not too excited by his promise of: "Don't worry. I'm going to put you in a better situation." These Rust Belt schools sound bad all over. I already knew everybody at Grand Plans middle. Despite all the mouthy rebellion I didn't feel hated, overall. I had a room with a sink, stocked full of art supplies that I'd spent all year sorting through and organizing. I had a "setup," and a system. Next year would have been better than the one I'd just been through.

But my supervisor wants to switch me, and he isn't the type who likes being contradicted. So that's that. I don't feel great about it, or especially bad.

I wile away the summer in an allergic haze cleaning and organizing my house. I inherited its mess, like I did the one in that art room last year. Actually it's not my house. It belongs to granddad's estate. The house is in limbo (as is my career) while my dad and his sister fail to communicate. Their stalemate is broken when she calls a lawyer.

August, and still no word on what my new school will be. I phone Ryan to see what he's up to. I get the answering machine. His wife returns my call.

"Ryan went to Africa for sixth months."

"Isn't that hard for you?"

"I'd rather he does that than be here and unhappy."

Should I pay her a visit? Better not.

Finally, the supervisor calls with my new assignment. I'll be at two schools this year, Iron Academy and High Tech Hell. Iron's located in the very same neighborhood where the white kids, like Jimmy, who gave me a hard time come from. Some of the kids from that neighborhood are bused into Grand Plans, the rest stay at Iron. High Tech is the school that the new Home and Careers teacher at Grand Plans Middle couldn't stand, and switched to our school to get away from. This is better?

Dear Mr. L
I'm sorry for acting that way,
I have Adh.d really bad
and I forgot to take my pill.

Illustration of student apology.

Epilogue:
Lessons Learned.

On Your Own

My doubts that my supervisor would be putting me someplace better proved well founded. My next placement was as rocky as the first, rockier in some ways. I was split between two schools, traveling each day to maintain my full time position. Due to budget cuts, staffing cuts, and the nature of being a "specials" teacher, that second year began what has, as of this writing, been a six-year roller coaster ride of changing schools. Each year my supervisor has assigned me to at least one new one. One year I taught at three.

While constant change can be maddening, there is an upside. This bumpy ride has given me a birds-eye view of the problems urban public schools face. Repeatedly I've witnessed teachers driven out of classrooms by students they can't control, bullies given free reign to torment the weak, and chaos that makes learning nearly impossible.

At every school where I've served time, one theme remained constant; at numerous faculty meetings at numerous schools, I'd listen to a principal tell us: "Teachers, you are sending too many kids to the office. You need to deal with discipline yourselves." Heeding this advice, I've rarely sent a student out of my room. However I have written up conduct-reports and sent those to the office. Over six years, and countless write-ups, I can only recall two or three times a student was ever suspended on my account. Sometimes it felt as if principals were handing out medals for acting out.

While I quickly got used to *not* having support from the main office, I was shocked at the times a principal or vice principal actually undermined my discipline. Once, a new vice principal came waltzing into my room and declared "You're good kids. Now get out of those timeouts!"

Even more "helpful" than the principals have been Rust Belt's revolving School Superintendents. Since I started teaching we are on our fourth. Not until last year, after a wave of headline-making student violence, some of it involving teachers being physically attacked, did I hear any of our superintendents directly address the crisis in discipline. Instead they've focused on changes in curriculum, scheduling and infrastructure. One boasted of all the new facility construction and technology upgrades underway. Having worked at one of those new facilities, and seeing no improvement in behavior, I didn't find the promise of "more upgrades" very reassuring. Another superintendent claimed that parents were taking their kids out of the Rust Belt System because, unlike the privileged suburban schools, our city couldn't afford amenities like "theater." The Holy Grail that our present superintendent pines for is the "longer school year;" more time for someone to get injured.

I'm not laying all the blame for the schools' ills entirely on the administrators. I understand that we teachers need to have well-planned lessons, and strategies for engaging students and managing their behavior; but when those plans are not succeeding, why are principals so often hesitant to discipline? At one faculty meeting a principal explained why, saying, "If I keep suspending kids, downtown is going to think I can't control my school."

This is, in a large part, why nothing changes. In order to appear in control, both teachers and administrators often sweep all but the most egregious misbehavior under the rug. By then it's too late.

Neither Left nor Right

Is America doomed to have student defiance and bullying gradually drag down our urban public schools, while charters and private schools cherry pick the most ambitious students? Why do so few in public office address this crisis directly?

The American Liberal/Left and the Conservative/Right wings of the Democratic and Republican parties respectively, are at least partly to blame for this crisis in education. Liberals to their credit, have, for the course of my political memory, been calling for and succeeding in gaining much-needed funds for public education. They have been the ones, historically, to bring us proactive programs like Head Start to help those at the bottom. For all they have done to promote a sound public education, perhaps out of fear of not sounding politically correct, they have failed to make the call for a restoration of discipline in our schools. The left is typically concerned with helping, not punishing those at the bottom. It's the American Conservative/Right the public might have expected to call for a return of "law and order" in the schools. But they haven't. Why not? In my opinion, it's because their priority for many years now has been privatizing much of America's public goods. Rather than calling for "order in the public schools" they call for "school choice," vouchers, and charters. These market-based solutions do not directly address the breakdown of student discipline, and are a shell game with our children's futures.

On another level, a simple human tendency is preventing the problem from getting solved: lack of honesty and the inability to get to the point. First, many people won't admit that there is a crisis of discipline. Second, when they do admit it they make it seem to be something more complicated than it actually is. It has nothing to do with race. It's this simple: kids interrupt adults whenever they want to. Much of the other chaos stems from this habit. Focusing on roundabout solutions, like "charter schools," "better teachers," "testing," and "school uniforms," "junior ROTC," won't directly alter any of this. Kids need consequences for misbehavior; the truly disruptive need special settings; most teachers need more training in child psych and less in high flung educational goals; all schools could use some sort of well supervised detention rooms; and the disruptive kids need a lot more exercise than they are getting. (Exercise has been used as treatment for ADHD and ADD).

The way schools are run now, dominated by the belief that kids won't act out if they are presented with stimulating lessons by qualified teachers, may have some truth in it, but it's naive. When an adult fails to stop at a traffic signal he or she is given a ticket. The law officer doesn't blame himself for failing to fully involve the driver in the benefits of traffic safety. For better or worse we live in a society where people follow rules based in large part on fear of punishment. How can society expect children to be more concerned with the common good than adults are?

Whatever Happened to Everybody?

While I was spinning my wheels thinking about politics over these past six years, the wheels of my social life kept turning. After Lela dumped me, she immediately went to the coworker I heard Debbie wanted to hook her up with. They quickly got married. Since marriage is a sure way to gain legal residence in the US, I guess that solved her visa issues. Last word on Debbie was that she tried to scam Lela and Marisol out of money. Debbie's supposed husband Bruce, got deported after 9-11 for being in the US without a valid visa. I say supposed husband because if they were married then his visa would have been valid. With that group, things always were

217

hazy. I was finally able to introduce Alex's reclusive housemate Norm to Marisol. (Alex is the guy who had the parties). The two of them hit it off so well they decided to get married. Norm was involved in a local arts fest. Because of my introducing him to Marisol, his art fest got to have Indonesian dancers, and I got to see Lela's picture on the cover of the local newspaper dressed in traditional garb, performing at the fest. That certainly was not the thanks I had in mind. My own search for true love abruptly ended when I met a woman at a graduate student party. After a year and a half long relationship we got married. That's a whole other saga.

I don't know if Ryan and his wife ever did get into Christine and her husband's hot tub. I haven't seen him in years. Now I only know Ryan as part of his mass email list, where I receive streams of messages chronicling his world travels. He kept his word and quit. Last time Ryan was in Rust Belt, he told me that Tina, the other new teacher who was struggling worse than me, was not called back to teach in the fall. This came as no surprise to Ryan or me; she did miss tons of work. Oddly enough, it was a surprise to Tina. She was so "delusionally" confident that her supervisor wanted her to keep teaching, that she took a low-wage summer job instead of filing a claim for unemployment. When her supervisor didn't call her back she was stuck as an office temp, making less working than she would have if she filed her claim. Late one Saturday night I saw the injured music teacher, Mr. Cantwell at a sub-shop. He looked at me blankly. Finding it amusing that he couldn't recognize me I just returned Cantwell's blank gaze. A few weeks later, a substitute teacher who knew him from church, confirmed that Mr. Cantwell was still collecting workers comp and defensively explained that, "He probably couldn't recognize you because his back was causing him so much pain." Mr. Nosey stayed in the school system, albeit not in the classroom. He became a school administrator. A gym teacher from that school told me that discipline during Nosey's watch deteriorated. Fin and Slaughterbutcher are still teaching. Mr. Mullet moved on to another school, and never did grow his mullet back. Ms. Henderson, well…, may she rest in peace.

CPSIA information can be obtained
at www.ICGtesting.com
Printed in the USA
LVOW11s0339111017

551989LV00002B/134/P